To Write Paradise: Style and Error in Pound's *Cantos*

To Write Paradise:
Style and Error in Pound's
Cantos

CHRISTINE FROULA

YALE UNIVERSITY PRESS
NEW HAVEN AND LONDON

Designed by Sally Harris
and set in Monticello type.
Printed in the United States of America by
BookCrafters, Inc., Chelsea, Michigan.

Library of Congress Cataloging in Publication Data

Froula, Christine
To write paradise.

Includes bibliographical references and index.
1. Pound, Ezra, 1885–1972. Cantos. I. Title.
PS3531.082C2852 1984   811'.52   84-3649
ISBN 0-300-02512-2 (alk. paper)
The paper in this book meets the guidelines for
permanence and durability of the Committee on
Production Guidelines for Book Longevity
of the Council on Library Resources.

10 9 8 7 6 5 4 3 2 1

For Patricia Swindle

I have tried to write Paradise

Do not move
 Let the wind speak
  that is paradise.

Let the Gods forgive what I
  have made
Let those I love try to forgive
  what I have made.

  "Canto CXX"

Contents

Acknowledgments

It is a pleasure to acknowledge the advice, encouragement, and aid of the friends and colleagues who made this study possible: Jerome J. McGann and Robert von Hallberg, who said "There digge" and supported the project in its beginnings; James Laughlin of New Directions, Louis L. Martz, former director of the Beinecke Library, and Donald Gallup, former curator of the Yale Collection of American Literature, for permission to work on the Pound Archive manuscripts; Mary de Rachewiltz, Peter Dzwonkoski, and, again, Donald Gallup, for their generous assistance with my research; Ronald Bush, Hugh Kenner, Edward Mendelson, Herbert Schneidau, Hugh Witemeyer, and all those named above for helpful comments on an early version of the manuscript; Robert Fitzgerald, Penelope Laurans, Louis L. Martz, and Paul Wallich for criticizing the final version; Barbara C. Eastman, John Espey, Philip Grover, Alice Levine, Omar Pound, Peter du Sautoy, and Guiguo Wang for help with special research problems; Jiajun Jiang of Southwest–China Teachers College for calligraphic transcription of the wind poem's Chinese text and for scholarly advice; Jan Wilson, for typing the manuscript with meticulous care; and Cynthia Chase, Carol de Dobay Rifelj and Nanette Auerhahn for friendship and *hilaritas* during the days when most of this research was done.

I am also grateful to the Ezra Pound Literary Property Trust, New Directions Publishing Corporation, and Faber and Faber, Ltd., for permission to publish new material from Pound's manuscripts and correspondence and to reprint material already published; to Ralph W. Franklin, director of the Beinecke Library, and David Schoonover, curator of the Yale Collection of American Literature, for permission to publish manuscript materials held in the Yale collections and to reproduce photographs of several manuscript pages; to Ellen Graham of the Yale University Press for expert advice and heartening patience; and to Lawrence Kenney, whose skillful editing refined away many errors. I am all too conscious that I, like my subject, have not managed to escape error entirely even with so much excellent counsel, and I can only acknowledge the mistakes that undoubtedly remain as my own. Finally, I would like to acknowledge the generous assistance of the Readers' Service staff at the Beinecke Library; the Library of Congress and the libraries of the American Academy of Arts and Letters, the University of Chicago, Columbia University, Harvard University, and the University of Texas for making unpublished documents available to me; and the Ford Foundation, the American Association of University Women, the University of Alabama Research Council, and the Griswold and Morse Fellowship Funds of Yale University for grants which supported this project.

Abbreviations

The following works are cited by abbreviations within the text. The publisher for the printed works is New Directions. When two dates are given, they are those of the first publication and of the edition I used. For full information concerning the publishing history of Pound's works, see Donald Gallup, *Ezra Pound: A Bibliography* (London: Rupert Hart-Davis, 1969; rev. ed.: Charlottesville, Va.: St. Paul's Bibliographies by University Press of Virginia, 1983).

C   *The Cantos of Ezra Pound* (1975)
GB   *Gaudier-Brzeska: A Memoir* (1916, 1960)
GK   *Guide to Kulchur* (1938, 1970)
LE   *Literary Essays of Ezra Pound*, ed. T. S. Eliot (1954, 1968)
P   *Personae* (1926, 1971)
SL   *The Selected Letters of Ezra Pound, 1907–1941*, ed. D. D. Paige (1950, 1971)
SPr   *Selected Prose, 1909–1975*, ed. William Cookson (1973)
SR   *The Spirit of Romance* (1910, 1968)

MANUSCRIPT COLLECTIONS

L   Letters of Ezra Pound, transcribed by D. D. Paige, Yale Collection of American Literature, Beinecke Rare Book and Manuscript Library, Yale University
PA   Ezra Pound Archive, Yale Collection of American Literature, Beinecke Rare Book and Manuscript Library, Yale University

Introduction

Looking back on the beginnings of this study, I am reminded of a fable Virginia Woolf tells in *A Room of One's Own*. She describes how, walking the paths of "Oxbridge," she remembered an essay by Lamb on one of Milton's manuscripts, in which Lamb wrote "how it shocked him to think it possible that any word in *Lycidas* could have been different from what it is. To think of Milton changing the words in that poem seemed to him a sort of sacrilege."[1] Wondering which word Milton had changed and why, Woolf followed Lamb's footsteps to the library which holds the famous manuscript only to be refused entry as a woman unaccompanied by a "Fellow of the College." This anecdote, in relating historical scholarship to differences in the ways that readers conceive literary authority, captures something of the methods, premises, and interests of this book. For Lamb, Milton's literary authority is timeless and transcendent and the poem a kind of sacred text which cannot be altered without "sacrilege." Woolf, by contrast, is eager to see the changes that prove the historicity of Milton's poetic authority, and for obvious reasons: the authority that closes the library door in her face is not unrelated to the authority that made Milton's work a sacred text for Lamb and a "bogey" for Woolf.[2] The idea that Milton could have changed a word in *Lycidas*, or by extension in *Paradise Lost*, intimates to Woolf the fictiveness of that story of paradise which weighs so heavily upon the history of English poetry. His changing of a word, never mind which word, highlights the fact that both Milton's story and the "divine Muse" he invokes as the authority which brings it to him are products of an imagination which, however powerful, is finally only human.

Pound is not Milton, I am not Woolf, and the library doors have always been open to me; but the institutions of literature and criticism have not changed so greatly since Woolf pondered Milton's changing of a word as to have followed up on the implications of her curiosity, or to have entirely freed us from what we might call literature's bogey, the power that stories such as Milton's wield over their readers. Although the academy to a great extent preserves Lamb's reverence, discoveries in the arts, as in science, far predate their practical applications as critical, analytic, and pedagogic tools; and one way of understanding the literary experiments of modernists such as Woolf

1. Virginia Woolf, *A Room of One's Own* (New York: Harcourt, Brace and World, 1957), p. 7.
2. Ibid., p. [118].

is as an effort to subject "sacred" assumptions about literature and its authority to historical scrutiny, and in doing so to forge a new realism.

At the time Woolf was writing *A Room of One's Own*, Ezra Pound was in
the midst of composing a long poem that he described variously as "a long
imagiste or vorticist poem," an epic or "poem including history," "the tale of
the tribe," "a record of struggle," and—alluding to Dante—"my paradise."
Pound's epic was a poem that might never have been written for reasons not
unrelated to Woolf's sudden interest in Milton's manuscripts. In 1909, having begun to entertain the idea of writing a long poem, Pound had rejected
Isabel Weston Pound's suggestion that he do so:

> Kindly consider what an epic needs for a foundation:
> 1. a beautiful tradition
> 2. a unity in the outline of that tradition. Vid. the Odyssey.
> 3. a Hero, mythical or historical
> 4. a damn long time for the story to lose its garish detail & get
> encrusted with a bunch of beautiful lies.
>
> [L, Autumn 1909]

Pound's definition of epic, while not explicitly referring to *Paradise Lost*,
encompasses Milton's beautiful tradition, the "beautiful lie" of his paradise,
along with Odysseus's story. One important aspect of the "record of struggle"
that became *The Cantos* is implicit in Pound's turning away from this early
idea of epic as a "beautiful story" to his later definition, "a poem including
history." The turn from story to history reflects not only Pound's commitment to what an early manuscript refers to as "the modern world" but a
consequent commitment to the struggle of transforming the traditional model
of epic authority, transcendent and absolute, into a human and historical one.
In 1909, although old stories like Homer's and Milton's were as obsolete as
the fiction of a divine Muse, Pound could not yet conceive of an epic in any
other terms. About 1915, however, he began a poem which, following upon
Robert Browning's *Sordello*, ventured to take history as its muse, leaving
aside beautiful stories to seek modes of representation more true to the dis-
ruptions and unclosed difficulties of modern experience. Sixty years later the
last installment of Pound's long poem was published, concluding the record
of this struggle toward a form and language for modern history. *The Cantos*
cannot be read as we read *The Odyssey* or *Paradise Lost*—as a finished poem,
static and unchanging, serenely overseen by a mode of authority that is consistent from beginning to end. In an important sense, to read *The Cantos* is
to "read" the drama of Pound's struggle to transform the terms of epic to
accommodate the modern world. The "story" of Pound's poem including
history is not one narrated by the poet, as Homer tells Odysseus's or Milton
Adam and Eve's; it is the drama of its writing. Its story, in other words, is its

history. This story is much larger than the local meanings of its words and lines, encompassing the forces that shaped both the possibilities for epic poetry in the modern world and their particular realization in *The Cantos;* but at its core is the history of the poem's composition.

To conceive *The Cantos* in this way is to complicate the concept of intentionality, expanding questions of form and meaning beyond the author's own declarations about the work to the historical forces that determined those intentions. The context within which Pound's "intentions" for the work were formed is essential both to the description of those intentions and to the reading of the poem. If we view expressions of intention not as final explanations but as ideas having their own history, we can begin to understand shaping forces that, although they may not have figured in the author's conscious purpose, worked no less powerfully for that. Indeed, such causes may have far greater explanatory power than the author's expressed intentions; so artists themselves often suggest, picturing themselves not as creators of their work but as mediums of forces that subsume their own intentions. Gertrude Stein in "Composition as Explanation," for example, describes the act of composing as unthinking, untheoretical, guided by instinct; she uses the words *natural* and *naturally* again and again, as: "Naturally one does not know how it happened until it is well over beginning happening."[3] Jean Cocteau speaks of the artist as a "prison from which the works of art escape,"[4] and Yeats, upon receiving the Nobel Prize, said of his poems, "What came so easily at first, and amidst so much drama, and was written so laboriously at the last, cannot be counted among my possessions."[5] Malraux applies a similar idea to Cézanne: "when Paul Cézanne wants to speak, he imposes silence on M. Cézanne, whose fatuous remarks get on his nerves, and he says with his picture what words could only falsify."[6] And for Pound, the commitment of his long poem to history entailed a concept of authority that includes the collaborative and the contingent; as he put it in Canto XCIX, "This is not a work of fiction / nor yet of one man" (C, 708), gesturing toward the diffuse causality intrinsic to his modern epic.

This book presents a small part of the vast background relevant to an understanding of *The Cantos'* history. It began with an opportunity for historical study and an intuition about its possibilities not unlike Woolf's when she set out across the "Oxbridge" lawn in pursuit of an erring Milton. I was not seeking, however, to revise Pound as author of sacred texts into a histor-

---

3. Gertrude Stein, *Selected Writings*, ed. Carl Van Vechten (New York: Random House, 1946), pp. 453–61.

4. Quoted by H. D. by way of Edmund Wilson in *End to Torment: A Memoir of Ezra Pound*, ed. Norman Holmes Pearson and Michael King (New York: New Directions, 1979), p. 56.

5. William Butler Yeats, *The Autobiography* (New York: Collier, 1965), p. 359.

6. André Malraux, *The Voices of Silence*, trans. Stuart Gilbert (Princeton: Princeton University Press, 1978), p. 347.

ical Pound, for the historical Pound was already definitively present in his historical poem. Rather, I wanted to understand the historicity of Pound's epic, the implications of that commitment to lived history which caused it to differ so radically from epics of the past. It was not Pound's stated ideas about history that interested me, nor the specific historical events and authors to which the poem alludes. Rather, it was history conceived as the conditions of the poem's radically innovative form and language.

At the time I undertook this study, I was participating in an informal reading group on *The Cantos* at the University of Chicago, held in the spring of 1974. Most of us seemed to be attracted to the poem by the sheer power of its language, for we had little idea what it was "about." This language seemed alive in unfamiliar ways, and the problem of reading the poem seemed as much one of understanding this strange life as of figuring out what it was saying. The difficulties we encountered had to do not with the local opacities created by allusion but with the more fundamental difficulty of the poem's forms, linguistic and poetic. The broken images, silent juxtapositions, and elliptical, inconclusive fragments of meaning appealed to no familiar muse, no conventional literary authority. Yet even in its near incomprehensibility the poem's form conveyed a sense of momentous import if only its implications could be read and its necessity understood.

What it meant that Pound in *The Cantos* had taken history for his muse was a question too difficult even to articulate at the time; but our collective effort to read the poem opened up the historicity of the text quite concretely. All of us were using whatever texts of *The Cantos* we happened to own, and we frequently noticed textual variants among our several editions. Our struggles with what and how the poem meant were desperate enough not to be affected very seriously by the mere issue of what it said, but with the discovery of the variants, the words on the page lost the aura of graven images and became the track of a human being in time. The sense of the poem's historicity evoked by evidence of errors in the text and of revision after publication was strengthened by a coincident development. That spring, Yale University announced that it had acquired the Pound Archive, including almost all the manuscripts documenting the composition of *The Cantos* as well as a great collection of correspondence. The availability of these papers opened exciting new possibilities for studying *The Cantos*. "The origin of something," Heidegger wrote, "is the source of its nature";[7] and in this case the "nature" of the thing seemed particularly to invite the kind of explanation that a study of its origins as traced in the manuscripts Pound had accumulated in composing it would make possible. In 1975 I began a study of the manuscripts, proposing on the one hand to study the evolution of Pound's modernist style,

---

7. Martin Heidegger, "The Origin of the Work of Art," in *Poetry, Language, Thought* (New York: Harper and Row, 1971), p. 17.

and on the other, to research the history and state of the text as groundwork for an edited text of *The Cantos*.

My first task was to read through all the available manuscript materials for *The Cantos*, at Yale and elsewhere, supplemented by the major relevant collections of correspondence. The quantity of manuscript material for *The Cantos* is very large, and it will be a long time before its record of the poem's evolution has been fully reconstructed and its uses for interpretation and criticism explored. As a comprehensive study of the manuscript material in the archive was not feasible, I worked out a paradigmatic approach centering on Canto IV. Pound worked on this canto during the period between 1915 and 1925 when he was struggling to launch his long poem, moving from the uncertain Browningesque pastiche of "Three Cantos" to the creation of a modern style. Even this relatively brief period involves quantities of manuscript material too large and disparate to be treated thoroughly in a single volume, but Canto IV and the manuscripts relating to it offer an excellent cross section of this important period of *The Cantos'* history. First, the compositional history of the fourth canto extends from the earliest drafts to 1925, when *A Draft of XVI. Cantos* was published. Second, despite its belated numeral, Canto IV was the first to be substantially completed. Pound had an early version by the time of his first recorded mention of his long poem, and it was printed in nearly final form in 1919—more than two years before his important editorial work on Eliot's *Waste Land*—whereas the "Three Cantos" he published in *Poetry* in 1917 were drastically revised in 1923. Third, its compositional history is extremely complex, involving a representative array of the early manuscripts for *The Cantos*, and almost all the documents of this history are available in the Pound Archive. Its background thus presents an extraordinarily rich record of Pound's development into the poet to whom Eliot dedicated *The Waste Land* with the homage *il miglior fabbro*— the better craftsman. Fourth, the history of Canto IV holds much of interest not only for a view of Pound's first formulation of his modernist poetics but for an understanding of the motives that governed the fifty-year progress of *The Cantos*. Finally, the issues that underlie the themes and techniques of Canto IV are not peculiar to Pound but reflect the crisis of representation that was occurring during those years in all the arts. In particular, by virtue of explicit references to the Vorticist painting and sculpture of Henri Gaudier-Brzeska and Wyndham Lewis, the manuscripts for Canto IV link Pound's developing poetics to the emergence of abstract form in the visual arts.

Part I of this study presents an analytic history of the composition of the Fourth Canto and an edited text of the manuscripts which document that history. Although the methodology of these studies is primarily determined by the exigencies of presenting the manuscripts and their history, my analysis conceives Pound's poetics in its epic dimension and takes as its point of departure the problem of writing a poem including history in the twentieth century. Pound's first groping toward a Fourth Canto links the breakdown of the story to the incomprehensible scale of destruction made possible by the technology of modern warfare. The early manuscripts show that Pound began his epic in reaction against the traditions of war and conquest in which the Western epic has its origins, and that his own epic departure defined itself as a search for the cross-cultural humanism, an *abstract* "paradise" which transcends the dogmas of closed cultures. Pound's endeavor to find a form and style to embody this idea of "paradise" can be described as structuralist in nature, from a perspective which links his early poetics with contemporary developments in science, philosophy, and the visual arts. By way of explicating the affinities of Pound's developing style to the more general phenomenon of abstract form in modern art, I bring to bear an essay on poetic technique he wrote in 1913 which prefigures the themes of Canto IV as it illuminates Pound's conception of the "paradise" of poetic style. The history of the Fourth Canto, then, exemplifies in microcosm Pound's struggle in *The Cantos* to bring together modern history and a "paradisal" language.

While the main interest of Part I is on the evolution of a style, Part II is concerned with error. Specifically, it begins with the errors in the text of *The Cantos*—drawing not only on Canto IV but on the Italian, Chinese, and American history cantos, *The Pisan Cantos*, and *Drafts and Fragments* for evidence—and takes up the central problems that Pound's work presents to its editors. Composed and published in four countries over a period of fifty years, Pound's long poem poses one of the most complicated editorial tasks in modern literature. The editorial difficulties have to do not only with the technical problems posed by the poem's highly complex textual history but, more important, with a perhaps unprecedented divergence between the author's intentions regarding his text and those which the policies of his editors have tended to project upon it. Normally, the editor of an author's work aims to realize as faithfully as possible the author's intentions regarding the words on the page. Because of the extraordinary complications of Pound's text, editorial work on it commenced almost as soon as the poem itself did, with editors working more or less in collaboration with the living author on various problems in the text. Surprisingly, however, these editors found that Pound's "intentions" for his text did not always agree with their own, and the case presents a curious little drama in which author and editors at times confront one another from opposite corners.

The crucial point of disagreement centers on the question of how to treat Pound's own substantive errors. In general, the editors pressed for corrections, while Pound, giving various reasons, resisted the changes they proposed often enough to raise questions about the significance of this conflict. The interest of this situation is not merely whether the text at a given point reads "Hsiang" or "So-Gioku," "Ho Kien" or "T'ao Ch'ien," "17 June '83" or "17 May '83." Rather, the divergent views of author and editor on whether or not to correct the errors implicitly arise from antithetical conceptions of the poem. The history of Pound's text dramatizes the fact that editorial policies emerge from critical and interpretive presuppositions which are not always explicit. The study of the text made possible by the availability of the manuscript material leads to questions about the significance of this gap between readers' conceptions of the poem and its author's. The errors in the poem, relatively trivial in themselves, thus challenge some deeply rooted assumptions about correctness, about history, about poetic authority, about the ability even to posit, let alone to "recover," an "authorial intention" or an "ideal text"; and they suggest new directions for exploring the significance of Pound's poem including history. In particular, they point beyond the editorial interest to what is perhaps the largest problem in Pound studies, the question of the poem's form in its dimensions as a modern epic.

Chapter 3, taking the problem of authorial error in the text of *The Cantos* as its point of departure, explores its significance for the conception of *The Cantos* as a modern epic—a poem which, in its final achievement as in its first intentions, casts a critical light upon the heroic values and redemptive forms of the Western epic tradition. The relations between epic wandering, modern history, and error in Pound's poem suggest that the modern epic differs categorically from earlier epics in that the wandering that defines the genre is no longer closed by any such plotted "redemption" as concludes the wanderings of Odysseus, Aeneas, Don Quixote, Redcrosse, Adam and Eve, or Dante. The significance of Pound's epic venture, I argue, is integrally bound up with the way his modern poem including history enacts the constitutive status of error in modern experience. In representing the loss of— or an awakening from—the redemptive ends of error and wandering implicit in the traditional epic story, *The Cantos* has revolutionary implications for the concept of history embodied in the epic form. As chapter 1 analyzes the beginnings of *The Cantos*, chapter 3 analyzes its "ends" in the double sense of purpose and conclusion.

The fourth chapter returns to the question of an editorial project for *The Cantos*. It begins with a theoretical discussion of the problem of defining the authority that directs *The Cantos* and the consequences of that idea of authority for the kind of text the editorial project will aim to produce, drawing upon chapter 3 for a sense of the issues and upon the history of *The Cantos* as a whole for evidence. After discussing two major alternative conceptions of the editorial project, it concludes with an editorial model for the Fourth Canto, documenting its history from 1923, when the setting copy for *A Draft of XVI. Cantos* was completed, to 1970, when the last revisions were made in the text. Again, the Fourth Canto makes a particularly apt model for documenting textual problems in *The Cantos*, the more so as the transcription and collation of the unpublished manuscripts associated with it in chapter 2 permit a full survey of its textual history. This history spans that of the whole poem, since in addition to being the first completed canto it received corrections by Pound's editors as late as 1970. In addition, Canto IV contains representative examples of textual problems that exist throughout *The Cantos*.

Both textual studies, then, the genetic and the editorial, approach the history of Pound's poem with questions about how to understand its idea and intentions, its beginnings and its ends. Perhaps the most useful discovery made available through the methods of historical scholarship is a concrete and detailed awareness of the consequences Pound's decision to take history as his epic muse has for the form of his poem. This discovery raises many more, and much larger, questions than can be resolved in a book of this scope, pointing beyond the facts of the text to new questions about the relation of poetic form and history, epic and modernity. The history the manuscripts record does not always simply reaffirm what we already understand, or think we understand, about the way Pound's epic mirrors the modern world, but rather calls into question many of our assumptions about the relation between poetic form and history. If attending to details perhaps trivial in themselves makes possible a more accurate image of the way in which *The Cantos* includes history—and is *included in* history—this investigation will have served its purpose. I present these studies, then, as the beginnings which they are, an early effort to analyze the very considerable implications of *The Cantos'* textual history for our understanding of the poem. Perhaps they will prove to be, with respect to that wider and deeper exploration, something like what the Fourth Canto is to *The Cantos:* a first completed step, and a provisional but fruitful beginning.

PART I

CHAPTER 1

"To write Paradise":
The Beginnings of *The Cantos*

Je peux commencer une chose nouvelle tous les jours, mais finir . . . ?
Constantin Brancusi

There was a groping for using everything
and there was a groping for a continuous present
and there was an inevitable beginning of beginning
again and again and again.
Gertrude Stein, "Composition as Explanation"

Pound's *Cantos* has many beginnings, and no end. Continually departing from its own past, it is the epic paragon of the modern art Brancusi and Stein describe, beginning and rebeginning again and again and again. Within this epic of new ventures, the Fourth Canto stands as a beginning of beginnings. Its first versions belong to the earliest drafts for the first "Three Cantos," published in *Poetry* in 1917, and its final version predates all the other cantos.[1] Canto IV has the resonance of an invocation: "ANAXIFORMINGES! Aurunculeia! / Hear me." And it is a formal beginning, a modernist landmark, as well, for this poem resembles nothing that existed in 1919; even Eliot's "Love Song of J. Alfred Prufrock," placed beside it, appears a relatively conventional extension of the dramatic monologue. In addition to beginning *The Cantos*, then, Canto IV marks an important threshold of the modernist mode in English poetry.

Canto IV had its own beginnings again and again and again; it is a miniature version of the journey by "periplum, not as land looks on a map / but as sea-bord seen by men sailing" (C, 324) which governs *The Cantos* as a whole. It shares its first point of departure with "Three Cantos," which takes off rather glumly from Browning's *Sordello*: "Hang it all, there can be but one *Sordello*!" By the time Pound began to see the possibilities Browning's

---

1. *Poetry* 10 (June 1917): 113–21; 10 (July 1917): 180–88; 10 (August 1917): 248–54; cited by canto and page numbers in the text. For discussions of "Three Cantos," see Leon Surette, "*A Light from Eleusis*": A Study of Ezra Pound's Cantos (Oxford: Clarendon Press, 1979), pp. 8–15; Ronald Bush, *The Genesis of Ezra Pound's Cantos* (Princeton, N.J.: Princeton University Press, 1976), chap. 3; John L. Foster, "Pound's Revisions of Cantos I–III," *Modern Philology* 63 (February 1966): 236–45; George Dekker, *Sailing after Knowledge* (London: Routledge and Kegan Paul, 1963), pp. 149–54; and Myles Slatin, "A History of Pound's *Cantos* I–XVI, 1915–1924," *American Literature* 35 (May 1963): 183–95. Bush reprints these cantos on pp. 53–73.

poem created for his own work, he had been seriously seeking a conception for a "great forty-year epic" for about a year, speculating in his 1914 essay on Vorticism on whether "a long imagiste or vorticist poem" were possible, trying out Byronic gestures in "L'Homme Moyen Sensuel," dropping mention in a letter of doing "an epic of Anglo-Saxon times," and accumulating many pages of outlines, sketches, and false starts. These early manuscripts show that Pound was seeking a subject in literary and historical sources: the *Anglo-Saxon Chronicle*, the *Mahabharata*, the Fenollosa notebooks, William Roscoe's *Life and Pontificate of Leo X*, and others. The manuscripts mark a trail of fragmentary treatments, each breaking off abruptly as though suddenly found unfit for the kind of poem Pound wanted to write. After many false starts, it was *Sordello* which led Pound to his first conception of his poem, and to a poetics which made meaningful the accumulation of fragments at its origins.

Looking back on his work, Pound later remarked that when he began, "Browning was the one thing to go on from—the only live form."[2] He himself had given some thought to using the troubadour histories as a subject for his long poem; a line in an early manuscript in the archive reads, "No Homer sang them—only Uc St Circ [the troubadour biographer] . . . dare I?" Coming upon *Sordello*, however, he found a more subtle and profound treatment than he himself had been able to imagine. Not only could he not write *Sordello*, as it must have seemed to him he would have done had Browning's not stood in his way; he could not even write *a Sordello*, a poem modeled on Browning's. Though the early manuscripts include notes and sketches based on the troubadour lives, Pound soon saw that a true analogue to Browning's "live form" could only be another live form, not an imitation.

Pound's "live form" begins in the recognition that he had, and could have, no such story as Browning's. The fate of all the subjects with which he experiments is to trail off indecisively, or to be broken off abruptly as another intrudes, or to be reduced to the "luminous detail" rather than painted out fully. The phenomenon of fragmentation in the early manuscripts speaks of something larger than local failure. Whereas Browning's formal innovation involved fragmenting the linear coherence of his story, Pound saw that his own historical position denied him the single story altogether:

> You had one whole man?
> And I have many fragments, less worth? Less worth?
> Ah, had you quite my age, quite such a beastly and cantankerous age?
> You had some basis, had some set belief.   [I, 115]

This dialogue with Browning engages the issue that underlies the phenom-

2. Interview with Myles Slatin, in "'Mesmerism': A Study of Ezra Pound's Use of the Poetry of Robert Browning" (Ph.D. diss., Yale University, 1957), p. 263.

enon of fragmentation in the early manuscripts. Pound understood the coherence and closure of a story like Homer's, Dante's, or Browning's to be
predicated on a basis of "belief"—a common world view endowing the events
of history with shape and meaning. His sense of the impossibility of a modern
epic story reflects his reluctance to impose on history a form which is neither
intrinsic to it nor commonly "believed" to exist. Pound's commitment to
history was also a relinquishing of the story; and it anticipated the more
recent efforts of historians to demonstrate the wish-fulfilling status of all forms
of narrative, which are not "found" in the matter of history but made in the
image of a desire, as Hayden White puts it, "to have real events display the
coherence, integrity, fullness, and closure of an image of life that is and can
only be imaginary."[3]

Pound's sense of the implications for poetic forms attendant on the absence
of a common "belief"—here expressed as envy of Browning's less "beastly"
age—was also, more positively, a means by which Pound could understand
his difference from Browning and so move out of the shadow of *Sordello*. His
"Three Cantos" revolve around the question of the relation between poetic
truth and historical event, inaugurating the preoccupation that would dom-
inate his poem including history for the next fifty years. Pound sees that
Browning's true "story" in *Sordello* is not Sordello's but Browning's own;
history, for Browning, was a set of props for animating his own "intensest
life":

> And half your dates are out, you mix your eras;
> For that great font Sordello sat beside—
> 'Tis an immortal passage, but the font?—
> Is some two centuries outside the picture.
>
> ....
>   You had your business:
> To set out so much thought, so much emotion;
> To paint, more real than any dead Sordello,
> The half or third of your intensest life
> And call that third *Sordello*;   [I, 114]

This being so, Pound finds the liberties Browning takes with historical accuracy perfectly legitimate. In "Troubadours—Their Sorts and Conditions,"
he observes that "Browning with perfect right alters [Sordello's history] to
suit his own purpose." (LE, 97) Pound himself, however, has "loved fact not
fancy, / And sought what is, no[t] so much glorious 'might be's,' as he put it
in a manuscript draft of "Three Cantos." He is impatient with literary "dodges"
that confound or replace truth with graceful lies, molding conventional wis-
dom in conventional forms:

3. Hayden White, "The Value of Narrativity in the Representation of Reality," *Critical Inquiry* 7 (Autumn 1980): 27.

> Magnifico Lorenzo used the dodge,
> Says that he met Ficino
> In some Wordsworthian, false–pastoral manner,
> And that they walked along, stopped at a well-head,
> And heard deep platitudes about contentment
> From some old codger with an endless beard.   [III, 249]

The old stories and histories, although they hand down what has been valued enough to be saved from the past, also mark the boundaries of all that has been lost, excluded, and forgotten:

> What have I of this life,
>   Or even of Guido?
>   Sweet lie!—Was I there truly?
> Did I know Or San Michele?
>   Let's believe it.
> Believe the tomb he leapt was Julia Laeta's?
> ....
> Sweet lie, "I lived!" Sweet lie, "I lived beside him."
> And now it's all but truth and memory,
> Dimmed only by the attritions of long time.
> "But we forget not."
>   No, take it all for lies.   [I, 120]

The problem with the old story-based epic form for Pound was that its coherence was a false coherence, a "sweet lie." He perceived its studied closure as a closing out for the sake of an illusion of completeness, and he sought a poetics which would not pretend to such completion, which would render the texture of history more truly. Accordingly, he moved to transform the unprogrammatic fragmentation at the beginnings of his epic into a viable form, one inspired by his encounter with *Sordello* rather than exemplified by that poem.

Although Pound later discarded "Three Cantos," they remain an important document in his progress toward a form for his poem including history. His use of the fragment in the context of his poetics of history makes it, even at this stage, a highly interpretable form. His "rag-bag" of fragments was close in spirit to the historical forms commended by the Confucian sage in Canto XIII who remembers "A day when the historians left blanks in their writings, / I mean for things they didn't know." (C, 60) Against the myth of comprehensiveness implicit in the closure of poetic or narrative form, Pound's fragments signify a recognition of all that has been left out, lost, or effaced. Against the myth of the immortality of the written word, they symbolize the word's vulnerability to time and weather, as of the lost manuscripts of Joios of Toulouse mentioned in "Three Cantos." Considered in this light, the poetics of the fragment appears not as the expression of nostalgia of which Pound is often accused but rather as an effort to find a poetic form to embody a changing experience of history. To include the past as fragments—a page of the *Odyssey*, a scene from Ovid, a line from Dante, a letter to Sigismondo—is a critical act which at once acknowledges the presence of the past and implies the insufficiency of old coherences for a later time. The fragment obliterates the formal boundaries that separate the story from the world and symbolically writes its words into live relation to other words—open, unfinished, always potentially dialectical. Browning's disrupted but, finally, complete story of Sordello, then, was not a structural model for *The Cantos* but a bridge between the narrative epic tradition and Pound's modern poem including history.

The earliest version of the Fourth Canto, MS Ur1, was composed as Pound worked on "Three Cantos." It documents the effect on narrative form of the changing experience of history in the twentieth century. This is the poem to which Pound most likely alluded in his first mention of the cantos to his father on December 18, 1915: "I don't want to muddle my mind now in the Vth Canto by typing the first three cantos."(L)[4] MS Ur1 is a ninety-eight-line passage in rough blank verse which has little more than ordinal place in common with the final canto. Aspiring to present "the modern world," it consists mainly in an English soldier's account of his experience of World War I, spliced between allusions to Stendhal's *La Chartreuse de Parme* and a cluster of images alluding to several religions. Unfinished and ungainly as it is, this composition is yet a remarkably solid "ideogram." It is not a jumble of images arbitrarily juxtaposed but an eloquent, if rough-hewn, expression of Pound's intent to create a form in which poetry and history coincide.

The opening allusion to Stendhal signals Pound's determination to make poetry a fit medium for presenting the modern world. The novelist's dismissal of poetry as "a damn nuisance" (Pound's paraphrase) recurs in Pound's critical prose, as when he recalls Stendhal's view that "poetry, with its bagwigs and its bobwigs, and its padded calves and its periwigs, its 'fustian à la Louis XIV,' was greatly inferior to prose for conveying a clear idea of the diverse states of our consciousness." (LE, 31) The disheveled language of MS Ur1 reflects not only its "first draft" status but also Pound's interest in developing a poetics to accommodate ordinary experience and ordinary language. Although the soldier's monologue is almost wholly without interest as verse, the very choice of his experience for the poem's subject is remarkable for two reasons. First, it shows that Pound's epic, his poem including history, began with contemporary history even in its earliest stage. Further, the soldier's fragmentary and inconclusive discourse dramatizes what Walter

---

4. Cited in Slatin, "A History of Pound's *Cantos*," p. 185. See the List of Manuscripts and Editions and figure 1.

Benjamin would later identify as a crucial break with the very possibility of storytelling—the sharing of coherent, meaningful experience—marked by the First World War: "Was it not noticeable at the end of the war that men returned from the battlefield grown silent—not richer, but poorer in communicable experience? . . . And there was nothing remarkable about that. For never has experience been contradicted more thoroughly than strategic experience by tactical warfare, economic experience by inflation, bodily experience by mechanical warfare, moral experience by those in power."[5] Pound's "pro-German" English soldier cannot comprehend the war he has fought in. His confused and broken speech portrays the war as an incursion of senseless hostility into a life whose concerns are not defined by national boundaries. His patriotism, or "loyalty," is "hard to explain," an unconsidered emotional reflex rather than a matter of conscience, conviction, or even comprehension—a theme which anticipates Paul Fussell's account of the typical soldier's experience of World War I[6] and foreshadows Pound's furious castigation of war as the manipulation of nations by financial interests in *Mauberley* and *The Cantos*.

The soldier's moral confusion resonates with concluding images of disturbance and change in Eastern and Western religious traditions. As his monologue expresses the absurdity of a world arbitrarily divided into antagonistic nations, so the gathering of images alluding to the world's religions expresses a crisis of "belief" as the authority of the myths underlying different cultures erodes. The Christian, Buddhist, and Hindu myths coexist uneasily in a world already shrunken into what McLuhan would name the global village; none of them can claim any longer the absolute authority on which closed cultures are founded. Pound's poetics of the fragment, abandoning the closure of story, captures the impinging of these myths upon one another to represent a world in which no single myth or "story" can endow the events of history with order and meaning.

Yet if the war theme of MS Ur1 indicates Pound's intent to bring epic poetry back to the real world, to make its means equal to history, its religious images reflect a complicating, but inseparable, desire to make history equal to poetry. Michael André Bernstein has argued that Pound wished to reappropriate history from prose without relinquishing the special powers of poetry.[7] To the "diagnostic" powers of prose, he would add the "curative" powers of poetry:

5. Walter Benjamin, "The Storyteller," in *Illuminations*, ed. Hannah Arendt, trans. Harry Zohn (New York: Schocken, 1969), p. 84.
6. See Paul Fussell, *The Great War and Modern Memory* (London: Oxford University Press, 1975).
7. Michael André Bernstein, *The Tale of the Tribe: Ezra Pound and the Modern Verse Epic* (Princeton: Princeton University Press, 1980), pp. 20–23.

Most good prose arises, perhaps, from an instinct of negation; is the detailed, convincing analysis of something detestable; of something which one wants to eliminate. Poetry is the assertion of a positive, i.e. of desire, and endures for a longer period. . . .

This is a highly untechnical, unimpressionist [sic], in fact almost theological manner of statement; but is perhaps the root difference between the two arts of literature.   [LE, 324]

As Pound's characterization of this distinction as "almost theological" suggests, his desire to make poetry write history did not diminish his desire to "write Paradise." The image of Père Henri Jacques communing with the Japanese spirits—which survives in the final text—already suggests what will emerge as a crucial interest of Canto IV, the "rhyming" of images from different metaphysical traditions to point to their common ground. In the context of the soldier's monologue which begins the draft, this harmonizing of the spirits of East and West appears as a "curative" antithesis to war over national differences. As Pound's next effort toward a fourth canto shows, the poetics of the fragment which he developed in reaction against Browning's fictionalizing of history would prove as crucial to the curative or paradisal motive as it had to the historical motive. As the correlative fragmentation of experience and narrative exhibited in MS Ur1 suggests, the fragment was for Pound the necessary form for expressing a modern paradise which, as he would put it in *The Pisan Cantos*, "n'est pas artificiel / but spezzato [broken] apparently." (C, 438)

The double intention of writing history in writing paradise and vice versa informs the evolution of Pound's long poem throughout. As Pound was preoccupied in "Three Cantos" with reconceiving the relation between poetry and history, so he also desired to find new forms to affirm the spiritual in a modern world from which the old gods had departed. In the *Poetry* cantos, however, he has as yet only the clumsiest means: adopting Browning's trick of pretending "we can be where we will be" (I, 116), he moves from Sordello's world to Catullus's, from Metastasio's to Ficinus's, evoking spirits everywhere: thus, "Gods float in the azure air, / Bright gods, and Tuscan, back before dew was shed" (I, 118); "the place is full of spirits" (I, 116); "Small boats with gods upon them" (I, 119); "When I was there, / There came a centaur, spying the land" (II, 182). Yet Pound, like Keats, confronts fancy's cheating and repeatedly falls back to earth:

> And shall I claim;
> Confuse my own phantastikon,
> Or say the filmy shell that circumscribes me
> Contains the actual sun;
>   confuse the thing I see

> With actual gods behind me?
>   Are they gods behind me?
>   [I, 120]

In "Three Cantos" Pound finds no clear resolution to the problem of reconciling subjective vision with the common world, but a second version of Canto IV which he composed while writing them reaches toward a solution that the final Canto IV would test. In the process of revising "Three Cantos" during 1916–17, Pound composed a fragment which he temporarily intended as the fourth canto: MS Ur2, titled "III" in the first and "IV" in the second typescript draft of "Three Cantos." This poem may be read as an acknowledgment of the inadequacy of the "Three Cantos" mode to Pound's intentions and a groping first step toward the poetics of the final Canto IV. Pound begins in the self-conscious voice of the *Poetry* cantos:

> 'What do I mean by all this clattering rumble?'
> Bewildered reader, what is the poet's business?
> To fill up chaos, populate solitudes, multiply images
> Or streak the barren way to paradise
>   [(Here was the renaissance)]
> To band out fine colours, fill up the void with stars
> And make each star a nest of noble voices.

The bewilderment Pound attributes to his reader is obviously his own; he sees the *Poetry* cantos as "clattering rumble" but has, as yet, no clear idea of what to do instead. The lines fill with ethereal imagery, with stars, voices, groves, and undines borrowed from the Renaissance "poeti latini" and Dante. But the effect fails, as Pound himself is the first to note: "and I am all too plain, / Too full of footnotes, too careful to tell you / The how and why of my meaning."

Pound's concern in this draft with the Latin poets' "paradise" extends beyond imagery to style. In *The Spirit of Romance*, he had observed that it was these poets who had best escaped the "rhetoric, and all the attendant horrors" that the Renaissance had brought in with its "cult of culture". The poets who

> wrote in the mother-Latin have the best of it, since in them alone does the inner spirit conform to the outward manner. They alone do no violence to their medium; their diction is not against the grain of the language which they use. In these men dwelt the enthusiasm which set the fashion; their myths and allusions are not a furniture or a conventional decoration, but an interpretation of nature.   [SR, 223]

Pound's insight here is that the "paradise" of the Latin poets is not purely thematic but also stylistic. It resides not in their myths and imagery alone but in the harmony of the Latin language with their paradisal themes. The "grain" of their language, worn smooth through a lineage of old mythologies, befits a paradise of light, souls, and muses' gardens. But this paradise does not translate so easily into modern English. As MS Ur2 attests, it went "against the grain" of the experimental, post-Browningesque style of "Three Cantos." In MS Ur2, Pound recognizes this untranslatability and begins to seek a modern analogue to the Latin poets' paradisal language—a verbal medium to match the visual languages which his fellow artists Henri Gaudier-Brzeska and Wyndham Lewis had developed. Contrasting his own work with Gaudier's and Lewis's, Pound locates his dissatisfaction in the explanatory flourishes of his own poetic discourse, quoting a line he had written a moment earlier as an example:

> [Say that the prose is life, scooped out of time,]
> [A bristling node . . . and I am all too plain,]
> Too full of footnotes, too careful to tell you
> The how and why of my meaning "here was the renaissance,

Then, as though in answer to his own complaint, Pound completes the passage with a single image: "'And Ka-hu churned in the sea, / Churning the ocean, using the [sun] moon for a churn-stick."

This image, which Pound later used in Canto II ("And So-shu churned in the sea, So-shu, also, / using the long moon for a churn-stick" [C, 9]), has eluded scholarly source-hunting. While it was obviously inspired by Pound's study of the Fenollosa notebooks, no attempt to tie it to a specific source has been successful.[8] What is interesting about coming upon it here in the early manuscripts is precisely that here too it has no illuminating thematic context. It is as though Pound conjured it out of the air. In its very gratuitousness, its lack of a particular thematic meaning in the context of passage in which it occurs, the Ka-hu image bespeaks an impulse toward a change of poetic method rather than the introduction of a new subject: it is an image of the Image. Its meaning has to do not with reference to any specific moment in oriental poetry but with the "paradisal" language which Pound is seeking and which this image, in contrast to the Browningesque bombast that precedes it, embodies. If this interpretation seems farfetched, we may recall that Pound's Imagist poetics, which underwent considerable development as he

---

8. Akiko Miyake, "A Note on So-shu," *Paideuma* 6 (1977): 325–28, records So-shu's origin as Ka-hu and concludes, "Whatever the reason Pound evoked So-shu together with the sea and the moon, we have to seek it in some interpretations other than Pound's sources." (p. 328) Eva Hesse, in "'So-shu' in Canto II/6, 9: An Identification," *Paideuma* 7 (1978): 179–80, tries ingeniously to reestablish the dependence of the image on particular sources. Despite her energetic argument, I find her effort to account for the image in this way unconvincing. The premise that everything in Pound's poem must be referred to a source, with respect to which it is either an accurate rendering or a mistake, allows no room for the creative and interpretive play in which the poem, even in the act of citation, is always engaged.

was working on the early cantos, can itself be understood as an attempt to create a modern analogue to the Latin poets' paradisal language.[9] This intention readily appears in its rhetoric, which, like Pound's distinction between prose and poetry, is "almost theological." Imagism, indeed, may be understood as a quasi-theological effort to distill the very essence of poetry, conceived as an organic perfection of language, an "absolute" and "perfect" coincidence of language and poetic idea. Thus Pound writes in a 1912 "Credo," "I believe in an 'absolute rhythm.' . . . I believe that the proper and perfect symbol is the natural object. . . . I believe in technique as the test of a man's sincerity" (LE, 9); and in "Affirmations: As for Imagisme," "one believes that emotion is an organizer of form." (SPr, 375) The religious rhetoric here—"credo," "I believe," "absolute"—underlines the import of Pound's remarks on the Latin poets: that the "paradise" of poetry is its language and nothing else.

The link between Imagist theory and the abstract art of Lewis and Gaudier appears in the abstractness of its linguistic "paradise." Whereas the Latin poets had a mythological tradition already "engrained" in their language, the modern world, as MS Ur1 shows, offers no comparable thematic paradise. The paradise of the Image is instead an abstract one, conceived not in terms of literal themes but as the perfect correspondence between the poetic idea and its expression. The Ka-hu image, appearing from nowhere and referring, apparently, mainly to its own Imagist form, reinvokes this literary analogue to the abstract art of Gaudier and Lewis. As MS Ur2 suggests, Pound was deeply involved in the Vorticist movement at the time he composed it. In the Imagist/Vorticist theory he evolved in *Gaudier-Brzeska*, the "paradise" of poetic language becomes the idea of correspondence itself rather than the Latin poets' gardens, groves, and stars; and the abstract perfection of the Image is described by comparison with the formulae of analytic geometry:

> . . . the equation $(x - a)^2 + (y - b)^2 = r^2$ governs the circle. It is the circle. It is not a particular circle, it is any circle and all circles. It is nothing that is not a circle. It is the circle free of space and time limits. It is the universal, existing in perfection, in freedom from space and time. . . . The statements of "analytics" are "lords" over fact. They are the thrones and dominations that rule over form and recurrence.
>
> [GB, 91–92]

The correspondence between the words of the poem and its idea or emotion is likened to that between the formula and the circle. Again, it is less the

9. Pound composed his *Gaudier-Brzeska: A Memoir*, in which he parlays Imagist into Vorticist poetics, during 1915–16. Herbert N. Schneidau discusses the religious rhetoric of Pound's Imagist theory in the context of American Puritanism, viewing it as "founded on the idea of a discipline, an *askesis* necessary to poetic purity," in *Ezra Pound: The Image and the Real* (Baton Rouge: Louisiana State University Press, 1969), pp. 173–87.

signification of the words than their material (aural and onomatopoeic) qualities that operate in this perfect correspondence. Thus Pound writes, "I believe that every emotion and every phase of emotion has some toneless phrase, some rhythm-phrase to express it." (GB, 84) The later revision of the Ka-hu image emphasizes the role of sound in this correspondence. In Canto II it becomes an onomatopoeic expression of the sea-sound that is the poem's thematic and prosodic undercurrent: "And So-shu churned in the sea, So-shu also, / using the long moon for a churn-stick." The material sound of the words, their onomatopoeic mimesis and their rhythms, express not a literal fact but the *idea* of—or the desire for—a seamless fit between the poetic apprehension of nature and the words that express it. In the Ka-hu image, the words animate the shaft of light extending into the "churning" waves; in the So-shu image, aural correspondences intensify the poetic effect. The transformation of the invented "Ka-hu" into the fortuitous "So-shu" underlines the fact that the image is not intended to be understood literally or traced to historical sources. Here, rather, the Image stands a mute test of whether, and how, and how far, language possesses the paradisal power to imply a necessary correspondence between words and the world, form and idea. Pound's abstract poetics, like the Latin poets', is an "interpretation of nature," a mimetic formalism which celebrates not the particulars of the correspondence but the implication of enduring patterns.

Pound defined the Image as "that which presents an intellectual and emotional complex in an instant of time." (LE, 4) The most famous Imagist poems—H. D.'s austere word sculptures, Pound's "In a Station of the Metro"— are as brief as this definition suggests they must be, and the Ka-hu image was no exception. If it brought Pound to the threshold of a "paradisal" style for his long poem, it did not give him to understand how he was to sustain it. In "Three Cantos," he had proposed to "Give up th'intaglio method" (I, 113), to abandon the carved brevity of the Image in order to write a long poem. With MS Ur2, however, he found himself back where he had started, dissatisfied with his own rhetorical bombast. His problem was now to extend the inherently brief Image into the desired long poem, to maintain the virtues of an "intensive" art in an extensive one. In a note appended to his "Vorticism" essay in *Gaudier-Brzeska*, Pound speculated about the possibility of a long poem based on Imagist tenets:

> I am often asked whether there can be a long imagiste or vorticist poem. The Japanese, who evolved the hokku, evolved also the Noh plays. In the best "Noh" the whole play may consist of one image. I mean it is gathered about one image. Its unity consists in one image, enforced by movement and music. I see nothing against a long vorticist poem.
>
>   [GB, 94*n*]

The feat of a long Imagist poem would be to reconcile in a single work the apparently antithetical qualities of extension and intensity. This paradoxical effect had been achieved before, according to Pound, by Dante in his *Paradiso*: "the most wonderful *image*" ever achieved (GB, 86); but the modern world offered no successor to the Christian cosmology that gave Dante's "image" extension. Pound's problem, then, was how to write a modern paradise, an abstract linguistic analogue to Dante's mythic spheres. In fact, though Pound's poetics of the fragment had committed him to doing without a story, his idea of a work "gathered about one image" would indeed prove fruitful for the Fourth Canto. But it was only in 1918, more than a year after he finished MS Ur2, that a workable structural principle crystallized: this was, as Pound variously called it, the "repeat in history," "subject-rhyme," or "superposition."[10]

The subject rhyme makes its initial appearance in the first holograph sketch of the final Canto IV, MS AA. This rough sketch, composed in haste on random scraps of paper with little care for niceties of style, has small verbal distinction. But crude as it is, it was the seed from which the final version of Canto IV grew. Its eighty-seven lines parallel events of classical myth and troubadour legend: Itys and Cabestan; the Trojan War and de Tierci's war against the Dauphin of Auvergnat and Peire de Maensac, for whom de Tierci's wife left him; Catullus 58, an urbanely bitter poem about Lesbia's many lovers, and the story of Gaubertz de Poicebot, who left his wife to go to Spain and returned to find her a prostitute. The "rhyme" of Troy and Auvergne was an old idea which Pound had been playing with for some time. In "Troubadours—Their Sorts and Conditions" (1912), his paraphrase of Piere's *vida* runs: "And he took her to the castle of the Dalfin of Auvergne, and the husband, in the manner of the golden Menelaus, demanded her much." (LE, 97) In "Provincia Deserta" (1915), he wrote, "I have thought of the second Troy, / Some little prized place in Auvergnat," (P, 122) and, as noted earlier, an early manuscript experiment for *The Cantos* ends, "No Homer sang them— only Uc St Circ . . . dare I?" Manuscript AA, then, takes up the same theme and elaborates it by drawing further parallels between the literatures of Provence and the ancient world.

In MS Ur1, history dominates the paradisal; in MS Ur2, the idea of a paradisal style begins to reemerge. In MS AA, what Pound called the "repeat in history" appears as an attempt to find a poetic form which would bring them together, realizing in history the "almost theological" aesthetic of Imagism. In the subject rhyme, it is not inventions like Ka-hu and So-shu which are the terms of the correspondence but historical particulars in whose congruence Pound sought the "rule" of recurrent forms. The particulars of

10. Pound used these terms in outlines for the early Cantos. "Repeat in history" and "subject-rhyme" occur in a letter to Homer Pound of April 11, 1927 (SL, 210); and "super-position" in GB, 89.

MS A, however, come from *literary* history. They recall a speculative geneal-
ogy of a certain kind of poetic impulse which Pound had presented in a 1912
essay titled, "Psychology and Troubadours: A divagation from questions of
technique," reprinted in *The Spirit of Romance*. In retrospect, this essay appears a discursive prototype for both the themes and the poetics—or the
"psychology" and the "technique"—of Canto IV. In it, Pound theorizes about
the psychological motives of the intricate and deliberately difficult forms of
the *trobar clus*, and his discussion may be understood as an allegorical explanation of his own poetic experiment in Canto IV. He begins by suggesting
that chivalric love was "an art, that is to say, a religion"—not unlike his own
Imagist poetics. (SR, 87) He finds the clues which link the troubadours'
psychology to their technique, he says, "not so much in the words—which
anyone may read—but in the subtle joints of the craft, in the crannies perceptible only to the craftsman" (SR, 88)—for example, in a kind of canzone
which, he ways, "must be conceived and approached as ritual," having purposes and effects "different from those of simple song. . . . They make their
revelations to those who are already expert." (SR, 89) As evidence, he cites
a poem of Arnaut Daniel—Dante's *miglior fabbro*—in which love is a secret
"dream-castle," and the lady extends over the lover "her fair mantle of indigo,
so that the slanderers might not see this." (SR, 89)[11] Pound goes on to develop the idea that troubadour love poetry has its roots in a pagan "cult of
Amor" extending from the "half memories of Hellenistic mysteries" through
classical myth and on to Guinicelli, Cavalcanti, and Dante. (SR, 95) "If pa-
ganism survived anywhere," Pound speculates,

> it would have been, unofficially, in the Langue d'Oc. That the spirit was,
> in Provence, Hellenic is seen readily enough by anyone who will com-
> pare the *Greek Anthology* with the work of the troubadours. They have,
> in some way, lost the names of the gods and remembered the names of
> lovers. Ovid and *The Eclogues* of Virgil would seem to have been their
> chief documents. [SR, 90][12]

What is important to recognize here is that Pound is seriously entertaining
the idea that classical myth and troubadour poetics were two versions of the
same art/religion. He regarded the classical myths as "explanations of mood,"
universal embodiments of intense emotions which could find expression in
no other way: "I believe that Greek myth arose when someone having passed
through delightful psychic experience tried to communicate it to others and

11. Pound's translation of this poem, "Doutz brais e critz," is found in his *Translations* (New
York: New Directions, 1963), pp. 173–75.

12. Leon Surette, in "'A Light from Eleusis': Some Thoughts on Pound's *Nekuia*," *Paideuma*
3 (Fall 1974): 191–216, shows that Pound developed this idea from Josephin Péladan's *Le Secret
des Troubadours* (which he reviewed in 1906) and discusses its thematic ramifications in *The
Cantos*.

found it necessary to screen himself from persecution." (SR, 92) The "inner significance" of the chivalric love code, then, was its carrying on of the "aristocracy of emotion" embodied in classical myth: "Did this 'close ring,' this artistocracy of emotion, evolve, out of its half memories of Hellenistic mysteries . . . a cult for the purgation of the soul by a refinement of, and lordship over, the senses?" (SR, 90) Pound stresses the speculative nature of his discussion, and in fact the essay moves by the same poetic intuition that inspired the subject rhyme, not by historical evidence and argument. What he says, however, parallels his remark that the Latin poets' style implies an "interpretation of nature." As classical myth interpreted nature by tracing mystical lines of force between human beings and natural phenomena, so, Pound theorizes, chivalric love may have provided a way to mystical experience, an alternative to the ascetic path:

> The problem, in so far as it concerns Provence, is simply this: Did this "chivalric love," this exotic, take on mediumistic properties? Stimulated by the color or quality of emotion, did that "color" take on forms interpretive of the divine order? Did it lead to an "exteriorization of the sensibility," and interpretation of the cosmos by feeling?   [SR, 94]

As historical questions, these are unanswerable, but as a "divagation from questions of technique," they suggest that the "theological" cast of Pound's poetics is no metaphor. Pound's tentative argument implicates in this pagan "cult of Amor" many of the poets who would later enter Canto IV—Ovid, Horace, Daniel, Vidal, Catullus, and Cavalcanti—and when he came, some years later, upon the subject rhyme, it was as the poetic form of his speculation, by which he placed himself in the line of succession. The speculations he had judged inconclusive as historical argument became the seed of a style or technique that carried conviction born not of fact but of "belief" and "sincerity": "I believe in technique as the test of . . . sincerity." (LE, 9) Rewriting "Psychology and Troubadours" as Canto IV, Pound invented a style to embody his belief that the "repeat in history" testified to "a permanent basis in humanity"; to the "recurrent moods," the "eternal states of mind" (SPr, 47), for which, he elsewhere writes, the metaphor of "the gods" stands: "No apter metaphor having been found for certain emotional colours, I assert that the Gods exist. . . . I assert that a great treasure of verity exists . . . in Ovid . . . and that only in this form could it be registered." (GK, 299) The subject rhyme, then, originated as a modern continuation of the spirit of myth and the *trobar clus*. This abstract and "intensive" form expressed Pound's desire to affirm a "basis" in "belief" without affirming any *particular* fiction as an image of "reality." What Stevens said of his supreme fiction is also true of Pound's gods, his paradise: "It must be abstract."

To see how the subject rhyme inspired Pound to "write Paradise" as the themes and techniques of "Three Cantos" had not, we may follow through the manuscripts the emergence of lines 13–31 of Canto IV, the Itys/Cabestan vignette. The first version of these lines occurs in MS AA and their final version six drafts later. In this case, it is useful to review Pound's sources. Itys's story is told by several classical writers, including Ovid and Horace. Although Pound's version alludes to Horace ("et ter flebiliter"), he would have known this story too well to have depended upon any particular source when he wrote the poem. In brief summary, Procne of Athens married King Tereus of Thrace, and they had a son named Itys. After five years, Procne grew lonely for her sister Philomela, and Tereus went to Athens to fetch her for a visit. He fell in love with Philomela on sight, told her Procne had died, and pretended to "marry" her. After raping her, he cut out her tongue and left her hidden in a guarded place, returning to Procne with the tale that Philomela had died. Philomela, however, wove her story into a tapestry and sent it to Procne as a gift. The outraged Procne sought revenge by murdering Itys, cooking his limbs, and serving them to Tereus. Learning what he had feasted upon, Tereus drew his sword to murder Procne and Philomela, but they were metamorphosed into a nightingale and a swallow and escaped.

The "rhyme" of this myth with the troubadour biography of Guillem de Cabestan, who, like Itys, was murdered in revenge for betrayed love by the husband of his lover Soremonda, is readily seen. Pound uses only the ending of the story:

> And when the lady had eaten, Raimon de Castel-Roussillon said to her: "Do you know what it is you have eaten?" She answered, "No, save that it had a good and savory taste." And he told her that what she had eaten was the heart of Guillem de Cabestan; and that she might believe him, he had the head brought before her. When the lady saw and heard this, she fainted. Returning to herself, she said, "My lord, you have given me such fine fare that I shall never have any other." When he heard these words, he ran at her with his sword and would have struck at her head; but she ran to a balcony, let herself fall, and thus she died.[13]

Manuscript AA contains two short sketches for the Itys/Cabestan vignette. One merely outlines the Cabestan story, omitting Soremonda altogether: "The Lord of Polhonac / killed Cabestang in the hunt— / cooked up his vitales— / served the stuff / in a pie." Its most interesting feature is its confusion of the Viscount of Polignac with Soremonda's husband, Raimon de Castel-Roussillon, which indicates that Pound was composing from memory, not

---

13. I translate only the last sentences of Cabestan's *vida* from the modern French in Jean Boutière and A. H. Schutz, *Biographies des Troubadours* (Paris: A. G. Nizet, 1964), p. 534. Pound knew the troubadours from several sources, and, as the "Polhonac" error shows, was not using any particular text in composing Canto IV.

consulting a source. This error also shows that the word "Polhonac" in line 113 of the final text was intended not to introduce a new subject but to recall the Cabestan story in the recapitulation of themes at the end of the canto. The second sketch rhymes the stories, but in an unexpected way. To the rhyme of Itys and Polhonac, Pound adds two more details which create a double rhyme:

> Stumbling, stumbling along
>   muttering, muttering Ovid—
> Ity & Polignat et ter flebiliter—
>   flebiliter. Ityn—
> and she went to the window
>   & cast her down—

Pound takes "Ityn" and "flebiliter" from Horace's Ode 4.12.2: "nidum ponit, Ityn flebiliter gemens, / infelix avis . . . " (The unfortunate bird builds its nest, mournfully wailing, 'Itys').[14] The words thus allude not only to Itys's disastrous fate, but also to the metamorphoses of Procne and Philomela. Eliding the Itys/Cabestan : Tereus/Raimon ("Polignat") relationship, Pound then selects from the Cabestan story the single detail of Soremonda's leap. Weaving these together, he creates an internal subject rhyme, as it were, within the initial rhyme of the like fates of Itys and Cabestan. Like Procne and Philomela, Soremonda takes to the air at the moment of revelation, and this implicit metamorphosis expresses the deeper correspondence which Pound construed in the stories' structural similarity.

Even in this first sketch, we can see the essentially abstract character of Pound's poetics. The rhyme of the two texts subordinates both to the structural pattern which their juxtaposition reveals. The stories, indeed, are all but erased as the true subject becomes the pattern itself, and that not for its own sake but as an indication of that "permanent basis in humanity" which Pound sought as the substrate of separate creeds in "the modern world." The receding of the object in abstract art moves formal pattern into the foreground: as abstract painting purports to exploit the directly expressive powers of form and color,[15] so Pound's allusive mode blurs and partly erases the individual narrative lines of the stories, giving the expressive powers of sound and rhythm precedence over the representation of the object.[16] While we

14. For an illuminating discussion of Pound's "impressionistic verbal reminiscence" of Horace in Canto IV, see Alan J. Peacock, "Pound, Horace and Canto IV," *ELN* 17 (1980): 288–92.

15. See Wassily Kandinsky, *Concerning the Spiritual in Art*, which Pound cites as an analogue to his Imagist theory in *Gaudier-Brzeska*, pp. 86–87.

16. For an extensive prosodic analysis, see Walter Baumann's "The Structure of Canto IV" in *Ezra Pound: The London Years: 1908–1920*, ed. Philip Grover (New York: AMS Press, 1978), pp. 117–37.

must know the stories to understand the poem, it is not given over to retell-
ing them. The mimetic source texts make legible Pound's abstract form, yet
his form is given by an "inner significance" to be read not in the signifying
words but in the "subtle joints of the craft" that fuses the stories in the passage.[17]

In the third version, fragment a (plate 1), Pound rewrites the opening lines
intertwining Soremonda with the swallows, and the closing lines about her
leap from the window, and adds the narrative of the story's climax:

> And she said: The swallows are
> crying *Ityn*.
> Procne. Procne.
> And he said—[How is the dish?—]
> How do you like [the flavour]
> the meat I have set before you
> And she said—it pleases me—
> [and she]
> and he said—Cabesteyn's
> heart might taste so—
> & looked up
> it was true

17. The abstract character of the Image suggests a different view of an apparent contradiction
between the absolutist and subjectivist aspects of Imagist theory and practice which David Simpson
discusses in his excellent article, "Pound's Wordsworth, or Growth of a Poet's Mind," *ELH* 45
(1978): 660–86. Simpson argues for "a prominent objectivist fantasy within Imagist theory,"
yet acknowledges that Pound's poetic practice (which Simpson exemplifies by the Itys/Cabestan
vignette) does not support his thesis that "the main thrust of Imagist theory is . . . toward the
provision of an absolute denotative language; one which is outside time, and one which stands
in an authoritarian relation to its readers." (pp. 680, 668) If the effect of the Image conceived as
an abstract form resides not in the denotations of its words but in the patterns formed by the
thematic and prosodic elements comprising its "complex," however, its claims to absoluteness
and perfection apply not to signification or reference as such. Rather, they assert the power of
this poetic form to express and communicate a (structuralist) sense of what Foucault calls "the
same within the different": "modern thought . . . moves no longer towards the never-completed
formation of Difference, but towards the ever-to-be-accomplished unveiling of the Same" (*The
Order of Things: An Archaeology of the Human Sciences* [New York: Random House, 1970)], p.
340). As such patterns remain open in the sense of being both infinitely repeatable and insub-
stantial, this view would reconcile Imagist theory with the nontotalizing "endless sentence" of
the Pound/Fenollosa poetics. It would also reformulate the relation of this poetics to its readers
as a stance antithetical to that which Simpson sees as intending the authoritarian imposition of
a "meaning." The Image as a "word beyond formulated language" (GB, 88) appeals, as does
Kandinsky's aesthetic, to a sense of form conceived as finding virtually physiological recognition
in the perceiver. It thus aims, in theory, to dissolve the inherent contingency of signifying language through subordinating signification to a mode of communication that crosses, if only
symbolically, the linguistic boundaries of phonetic language. There is, then, no stronger theoretical affinity between Pound's Imagist poetics and authoritarian politics than there is between
that politics and the structuralist project in general.

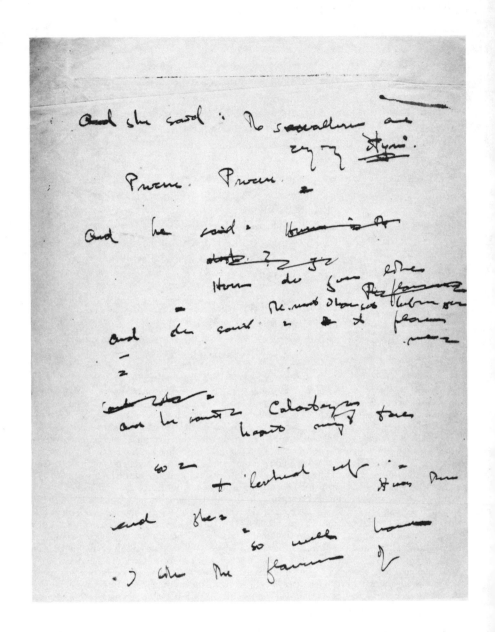

Plate 1. First leaf of fragment a, reduced from 20 cm × 26 cm. Courtesy of the Collection of American Literature, Beinecke Rare Book and Manuscript Library, Yale University.

> and she—
>   so well have
> I liked the flavour of
> this food that I will
> not spoil it with other;
> and walked by him to
>   the high tower window
> & cast her down.[18]

By adding the dialogue in fragment a, Pound has made the vignette fuller
and clearer, but this expansion has obscured the parallel of Soremonda and
the swallows. In MS A, he recovers this internal rhyme by adding the line
from the end of the passage, "And she went toward the window, and cast her
down," to the opening lines and repeating the detail of the swallows' cry at
the end:

> [Itys and Polhonac:]
>   [*Flebiliter,*] *Ityn et ter flebiliter* [*Ityn*] [*Ityn*],
> "And she went toward the window, and cast her down."
> "And she went toward the window . . . the swallows crying . . .
> "How like you the dish" he said,
> And she "None better."   dish."
> & He said: "It [was] is Cabestan's heart [you have] in the [flavour]
> & said "So well, it suits my taste, that I will taste of none other"
>   [Will spoil that taste with none other,"]
> [Walked past him and cast her] down.
> & walked to the high arched window & cast her down.
>   [Actaeon, Vidal.]
>   [Ityn, et ter flebiliter, Ityn,]
>   the swallows
>   crying on high

By repeating the "rhyme" at the beginning and end, Pound frames the dramatic dialogue in a stylized symmetry. Narrative becomes scene and temporal
movement becomes spatial design as the climactic moment is caught in a still
image like the fleeing "Dafne with her thighs in bark." Abstracting and tran-
scending temporal movement, this spatial design is a formal expression of the
appeal to a "permanent basis in humanity" bound up with the subject rhyme

---

18. Quotations from the manuscripts employ a simplified form of the conventions of transcription outlined in chapter 2 (see "Presentation of the Text"), using one font for both holograph
and typescript; enclosing words and lines which Pound crossed out in square brackets; and
silently correcting obvious typographical errors.

and the motives of abstract art more generally.[19] A small detail of MS A records the approach of Pound's literary art to the visual: this is the little arch sketched at the end of the Soremonda passage (see plate 2). To call it even a sketch aggrandizes it; it is just a flick of the pencil, the double arch of the window or the curve of the swallow's wings. In theme as well as medium it departs from the source; more than the balcony could do, the window contrasts the close, limiting walls of signifying language with the open air of the abstract pattern into which Pound's Soremonda leaps. Pound's transformation of her fate is a preeminently formal event. The little hieroglyph is an opening into light, a preverbal sign of the desire to transform the deaths that close the history into the metamorphic continuities by which myths interpret nature, and to read human history not in terms of death, separation, and closure but in terms of pattern, continuity, and unending change.

In MS B, Pound redraws the window in words, tightening the opening lines and elaborating the ending:

> "Ityn, et ter flebiliter, Ityn, Ityn,"
> And she went toward the window,
> —— the swallows crying ——
> "It is Cabestan's heart in the dish."
> "I thought as much."
> and she went toward the window in Polhonac,
> And held to the [central] slim white stone-bar
> Breaking the window arch,
> And the wind out of the hills by Rhodez
> caught the turn of her sleeve,
> —— the swallows crying ——
> Ityn! Actaeon:

He omits in MS B the first half of the dialogue and simplifies the second half, its first line keeping the final form attained in MS A and the second degenerating temporarily into bathetic cliché, Pound's mind apparently being at the moment on the new details of MS B, the stone bar of the arched window and Soremonda's sleeve billowing in the wind. And indeed, these last details bring fully into words the significance inherent in the original linking of Soremonda and the swallows in MS AA. The uncanny leisureliness of "And the wind out of the hills by Rhodez / caught the turn of her sleeve" creates an effect of arrested motion: the wind catching her sleeve as it might buoy the swallow's wing, Soremonda seems rather to float than fall, and the swal-

---

19. The key theoretical statement of the will to permanence as the prime motive of abstract form is Wilhelm Worringer, *Abstraktion und Einfühlung (Abstraction and Emphathy)* 1908/10.

IV

Rise , O thou smoky palace ,
            " Troy but a heap of smouldering boundary stones"
Rise , O thou smoky palace !
    Silver mirrours catch the bright stones and flame ,
    Dawn to our waking , drifts in the green cool light ,
    Light foot with the goat-foot alternate ,
            Dew haze blurrs
    the grass , pale ankles moving .
    A black cock crows in the sea-foam

            ....

    Itys and Polhonac :
            Flebiliter et ter flebiliter ,
    "And she went toward the window , and cast her down . "
    " And she went toward the window ... the swallows crying ...
    " How like you the dish " he said ,
    And she " None better " ,
        " It is Cabestan's heart in the ".
    So well my taste , that I will taste of none other "
        Will spoil that taste with none other "
    Walked past him and cast her down .

                    .
    Ityn , et ter flebiliter , Ityn ,

lows surrounding her heighten the implication of her metamorphosis. With these words, Pound completes the transformation of the Itys/Cabestan vignette into the Procne/Soremonda rhyme.

In the next draft, MS C, the vignette arrives at its final form. Pound adds the old man and the image of Soremonda's hands on the stone and emphasizes the symmetry of design in the ritualized repetition and half-rhyme of the dialogue:

> By the curved carved foot of the couch
>   claw-foot and lion head, an old man seated
> speaking in the low drone:
>   "Ityn,
> Et ter flebiliter, Ityn, Ityn,
> "And she went toward the window and cast her down,
>   "all the while, the while, swallows crying:
> "Ityn,"
>   "It is Cabestan's heart in the dish."
> "It is Cabestan's heart in the dish?
>   no other taste shall change this."
> "And she went toward the window,
>   "the slim white stone bar
> "Making a double arch,
> [The] firm even fingers held to the firm pale stone,
> Swung for a moment,
>   and the wind out of Rhodez
> Caught the full of her sleeve.
>   ......the swallows crying.
> Ityn! Ityn.

"Psychology and Troubadours" also prefigures the emergence in MS C of the old man, the indeterminate speaker of the composite tale. Quoting Horace's claim that "that which is greatest in me will escape dissolution," Pound writes that the "*accurate* artist seems to leave not only his greater self, but beside it, upon the films of his art, some living print of the circumvolving man." (SR, 88) Pound bases his thesis of the continuity between the mythologists and troubadours on an elaborate image of "the body as pure mechanism"—"a few buckets of water, tied up in a complicated sort of fig-leaf"—possessed, in poets, of a "germinal" consciousness: "Their thoughts are in them as the thought of the tree is in the seed." (SR, 92) Ultimately, the link he posits between the classical and troubadour poets rests on this theorized bodily basis in nature, which, he suggests, is the origin of mystical and ecstatic experience. The indeterminate figure "speaking in the low drone" is

an image of the poem's authority, a voice paradoxically abstracted and embodied at once: the Greek mythmaker translating the wordless language of
nature, spelling its sounds into tales; Horace, translating received myth into
new Latin; and Pound, who hears in Horace's Latin "Ityn" an impossible
pun (eaten) that parodies his own desire for a poetic language that is a second
nature.

Teller, tale, and language—which repeats sounds, words, phrases, even an
entire line—all participate in the romance of repetition established by the
subject rhyme. The manuscripts tracing the development of the Procne/
Soremonda passage show that the subject rhyme brought with it an impulse
toward style which aimed at a "paradisal" language of patterned continuities
in which poetic idea and the words, sounds, and rhythms that embody it
reflect each other. That Pound drew his hypothesis of the motives of poetic
style from "the subtle joints of the craft" (SR, 88) of such poets as Horace,
Arnaut Daniel, and Catullus proves, if not the motives of their art, the motives of the style he himself was evolving in Canto IV. The simultaneous
appearance of this densely repetitive style with the subject rhyme in MS AA
illustrates Pound's Imagist doctrine of "absolute" or "interpretive" rhythm:
as he wrote in 1918, the year of MS AA, "I believe in an 'absolute rhythm,'
a rhythm . . . which corresponds exactly to the emotion or shade of emotion
to be expressed." (LE, 9) Pound's translation of "Psychology and Troubadours" into Canto IV inspired a language to exemplify the stylistic "paradise"
that the essay could only speculate upon—one that sought to express "the
ineffable, *trashumanar non si potria per verba*" (MS Ur2) not by signifying
words but through their subtle joinings, the "crannies perceptible only to the
craftsman." (SR, 88)

These two forms of Pound's reading of poetic history from the Latin poets
to the troubadours, "Psychology and Troubadours" and Canto IV, both
dramatize the problematic nature of his attempt to create a language in which
poetry and history coincide. In the former, Pound explicitly limits the claims
of his argument, stating that he has "no particular conclusion to impose upon
the reader" and that he "can only suggest the evidence and lines of inquiry."
(SR, 95) The imagist medium cannot easily accommodate direct disclaimers,
but even so, Pound indirectly limits the terms on which he offers the "repeat
in history" in the opening lines of the canto, already in rough form in MS A:

[Rise, O thou smoky palace,]
    ["Troy's but a heap of smouldering boundry stones"]
[Rise, O thou smoky palace!]
    Silver mirrours catch the bright stones and flame,
Dawn to our waking, [in the] cloud palace drifts in the green cool light,
Light foot [with] the goat-foot alternate,

[And there] The [Dew haze] Dew haze blurrs [round the ankles]
                              [round, their ankles in the grass,]
                                          sunk in the maze of dew
[in] the grass, pale ankles moving.
A black cock crows in the sea-foam. [Cytherean!]

Pound's rhetoric here is unmistakably invocational. But there is a dissonance
in these invocational tones in which the complexities of a twentieth-century
epic embarkation resound. Pound abandons the fiction of the muse to invoke
the historical origins of epic art in the image of burning Troy flashing in
Homer's "silver mirrors." But, if epic art is the crossing of poetry and history,
the imagery of this invocation insists that it is poetry that dominates history
in the epic genre rather than the other way around: Calliope's "truth" is
informed by desire, not fact. The dance of nymphs and satyrs and the black
cock parodying the birth of Venus image the desire which is at the root of
history-writing and epic no less than of myth and the *trobar clus*. The ironic
overtones here recreate between the lines Pound's disclaimer of a particular,
objective "conclusion" to impose upon the reader in "Psychology and Troubadours," a limitation of authority as necessary to his poetics as to the essay.
Pound brings history and poetry to terms in this innovation not by carrying
history's supposed objectivity over into epic but conversely, by calling into
question the very possibility of historical objectivity. At issue here is what
Hayden White has called the "metahistorical" content of all history-writing,
that "deep structural content which is generally poetic, and specifically linguistic, in nature."[20] Not simple truth to "fact" but a complex reading of fact
by obscure desire moves Clio's projects as well as Calliope's, and this desire
is discernible less in signification than in style. The problem of style in Canto
IV, then, is not only a technical one. Rather, the poem is in some sense "about"
style as history—about the "crannies" of wordcraft which are the mute re-
pository of its own and every text's desire. As we shall observe in returning
to Pound's work on the invocation in MS D, style conceived as constitutive
of history brings into play values which are at once ethical and aesthetic and
which inform Pound's program for "How to Read" as they inform his own
poetics.
    In Canto LXXXV, Pound advocates a "process" of knowing that moves
between "techne" and "seauton," technique and "thyself." In line with the
Greek concept of techne, the technique he identifies with "sincerity" has the
sense not of practical knowledge but of power to give perceptible form to
what is present to the inner eye. As we have seen in the evolution of the
Procne/Soremonda lines, the distinguishing stylistic feature, repetition, ap-

---

20. Hayden White, *Metahistory: The Historical Imagination in Nineteenth-Century Europe*
(Baltimore: Johns Hopkins University Press, 1973), p. ix.

peared simultaneously with the poetic idea and was not consciously con-
trived. The distinction between technique conceived as sincerity and technique conceived as practical competence is brought out by a comparison of
the Soremonda passage with some of the failed rhymes which Pound discarded as he worked over the drafts, unable by mere skill to bring them into
verbal form. Though the Procne/Soremonda vignette developed surely and
rapidly, the structure of Canto IV as a whole required a good deal of experi-
mentation before it reached final form. Manuscripts A and B, both very different from the final text, document the early stages of the poem's structural
development, which approached completion in MS C. Except for the first
three sections of the poem (invocation, Procne/Soremonda, Actaeon/Vidal),
these drafts were composed independently. They diverge after the image of
the three Ovidian pools (ll. 66–68 in the final text) to follow separate courses,
MS A working out the classical/Provençal parallels sketched in MS AA, and
MS B assembling images from earlier manuscripts. In both, Pound pro-
gresses toward a structure which can be conceived as the Image writ large,
composed not of words but of smaller "super-positions" (GB, 89), as he
attempts to solve the problem of writing "a long imagiste or vorticist poem."

Returning to the body of MS A, we see that Pound conceived it as an
elaboration of the four classical/Provençal parallels of MS AA. He works the
Procne/Soremonda and Actaeon/Vidal material to a fairly advanced state, and
then proceeds with the Catullus/Poicebot and Paris/Peire de Maensac rhymes.
Neither catches his imagination as the earlier two did, however, and he casts
about in MS A for more material to fill out the poem's shape. As he does so,
the metamorphic theme which informs his classical/Provençal parallels emerges
in less specific forms. For example, recopying the Gaubertz material, Pound
leaves it after only three lines to work on the "rhyme" of the three Ovidian
pools—Salmacis's pool, the scene of Hermaphroditus's metamorphosis; Pergusa, where "Dis caught her [Persephone] up"; and Gargaphia, where Actaeon came upon Diana bathing. All three myths bespeak the continuity of
the vital universe, as does the line "The pines of Takasago grow with the
pines of Isé," added in holograph after line 70. This image exemplifies Pound's
gradual preparation of a palette of "emotional colours" in MS A. Pound never
translated the Noh play *Takasago*, but he knew it and remarked to Harriet
Monroe of the *Poetry* cantos, "Their theme is roughly the theme of 'Takasago,' which story I hope to incorporate more explicitly in a later part of the
poem."[21] The play's central image is the twin pines which grow at Takasago
and Suminoye; separated by a great distance, they are inhabited by twin

---

21. Unpublished letter to Harriet Monroe, dated January(?), 1917, in the *Poetry* Magazine
Papers, 1912–1936, University of Chicago Library; cited in Slatin, "A History of Pound's *Cantos*," p. 186.

spirits, and their physical resemblance is seen as testimony to their spiritual union. Pound's line does not allude directly to the play but creates a new image which renders the spirit rather than the letter of the *Takasago* theme, for there are no legendary pines at Ise, and in any case only one of the pines of *Takasago* grows *at* Takasago. Pound's free rendering, which emphasizes the Ovidian quality of the Japanese original, preserves what is important for his purposes: the recurrent perception of continuities in nature, through historical time and across cultures. The subject rhyme, then, derives from Pound's reading of myth as testimony to a "permanent basis in humanity" and to "our kinship to the vital universe, to the tree and the living rock." (SR, 92)

After line 70, Pound returns to MS A with a new idea for the Catullus/Poicebot lines. He first transfers them from MS AA to MS A, embellishing them with details emphasizing the sordid outcome of these amours. To the tag from Catullus 58, "remi nepotes" (alluding to all the sons of Rome whom Lesbia has taken as lovers), he adds "in angiportis" (in alleyways) and other details, including Francesca's line to Dante, "quel giorno più non vi leggemmo avante" (*Inferno* 5.138: that day we read no further). At this point, however, the subject rhyme turns dissonant as Pound moves to a rendering of Catullus's epithalamium (61: "Collis o Heliconii"), contrasting the virgin bride Aurunculeia to Lesbia and the lady Poicebot: "Till Gaubertz found her. / (in angiportis) / But Aurunculeia." Reviewing a recent edition of *Portrait of the Artist* in the May 1918 issue of *Future*, Pound had pointed to Joyce's "swift alternation of subjective beauty and external shabbiness, squalor, and sordidness" as "the bass and treble of his method." (LE, 412) Given the coincidence of dates, it is likely that he had this view of Joyce's technique in mind as he contrasted the epithalamium passage against the earlier parallel.

Although this ironic parallel does not survive MS A, the epithalamium lines continue into the final canto. As with the Takasago lines, Pound transforms his source rather than simply translating it. He first embroiders Catullus's scene elaborately with his own particulars (MS 2A, 45 lines) and then pares these lines to thirteen (in MS A), ending:

> O Hymenaeus! Io, Io, Io, Hymenaeus.
> Saffron, the yellow shoe, O Hymenaeus,
>   Lips like the poppy-leaf, O Hymenaeus,
> Manlius takes a wife, O Hymenaeus.
>   Look to the door-step,
>   Carmina tinula,
> sing out with reedy voice, O Hymenaeus,
> Blue agate casing the sky, sputter the resin,
>   Parthian white the stone, Aurunculeia, . . .

Pound's elaborations include the cook-stall, Crassus's corner (Crassus, the wealthiest Roman of his time, owned an efficient firefighting company which he refused to call out until the owner of a burning building had sold it to him), the agate sky, and the "Parthian white" stone. The history of this last image illustrates the freedom with which Pound handled his sources as well as the suggestibility of his imagination. "Parthian" marble in MS A ("Parthenian marble" in fragment 2A) probably originates in Catullus 61, lines 189–91: "ore floridulo nitens, / alba parthenice velut / luteumve papaver" (shining with blossomy face / like a white daisy / or a saffron-yellow poppy). Poppies brought red to Pound's mind, not saffron-yellow; and "parthenice" (daisy) brought to mind Parian marble, perhaps reminding him also of Sappho's fragment 164: "parthenia, parthenia, poi me lipois apoikhe . . . " (Maidenhead, maidenhead, whither away . . .). In fragment 2A, the flower and stone become an image of nuptial consummation: "Parthenian marble, the one poppy leaf, / flares out its red against the sparkling grain, / flower on stone, ah, so red gleams her mouth." This transfigured image remains in the final text, becoming first "O papaver, / luteum [red leaf of petal gleam on the marble]" in MS B, and then "The scarlet flower is cast on the bleach-white stone" in MS E (MSS C and D omit the image: "bleach-white" ultimately becomes "blanch-white"). Pound had earlier exploited his homophonic suggestibility in his translations, most strikingly in his "Seafarer." Here he again makes use of the poet's receptivity to unstable, virtual meanings that emerge spontaneously from somewhere between sign and sound.

As MS A shows, Pound's method of composition, even after the "subject rhyme" insight, was highly experimental. In his exploratory forays he sometimes hit upon a resonant subject and sometimes labored through lengthy passages only to discard them. The last few leaves of MS A, less a draft than notes with trial divagations, find him casting about for opportunities which might match the Procne/Soremonda and Actaeon/Vidal rhymes or the epithalamium. His original rhyme, the Troy/Auvergne parallel which had fascinated him for years, in the end provided nothing for the final canto (he used it later in Canto V). But before he abandoned it, he followed out a train of associations which led from Cadmus and Peire de Maensac, both creative exiles, to an array of images of disastrous love from the *Metamorphoses*: Procris, murdered accidentally by her husband Cephalus; Pan, eluded by Syrinx; Scylla, who betrays her father's love for Minos; the Cyclops' ill-fated wooing of Galatea; the Sibyl's hard lot of prolonged old age for her refusal of Apollo; and Circe's vengeful transformation of Picus, who scorned her. The draft breaks off in mid-sentence, and of these last lines only Cadmus and the metamorphosis of Cygnus find place in Canto IV. For all its blind alleys, however, MS A was an important stage in the writing of Canto IV, illuminating the "repeat in history" as an interpretation of myth and advancing toward the final form of the poem: a collage—or ideogram—of fragments centered on images of continuity and transformation in history, nature, and language.

In MS B, Pound refines the collage form evolved in the writing of MS A. He composed MS B by gleaning the live material from MS A and then gathering more fragments from the early manuscripts (MSS 1B–5B) and fitting them to his theme. Its first thirty-five lines retain the same structure as the opening of MS A: invocation, Procne/Soremonda, Actaeon/Vidal. At this point, having failed to develop the Catullus/Poicebot and Troy/Auvergne parallels to his satisfaction, Pound is still casting about for a way to complete the canto; and the first image to enter MS B from the early manuscripts expresses anew his anxiety about finding a poetic motive:

> For so the light rains and pours,
> The liquid and rushing crystal,
> > whirling the bright brown sand,
> Air, fire, the pale soft light,
> Artemis, Rose of Cnydus, and the red rust of Mars,
> Topaz I manage, and three sorts of blues,

This image captures at once the poetics Pound is struggling to evolve and his own awareness that he has not yet succeeded. The separate images he is composing in the canto are "emotional colours" like the colors of the spectrum, and the effect he intends is symbolized in the colorless, crystal light into which the whirling colors blend. This image of "light"—given palpable form in the image of seawater, its energy visible in the eddying vortices—recalls the Image, the vortex, the subject rhyme, and the ideogram, all of which are forms of "the word beyond formulated language." (GB, 88) Each of these forms aims at a mode of meaning which transcends the signifying function of words. But Pound, in his own judgment, has not yet achieved this effect: "Topaz I manage . . . "[22] As he completes the structural evolution of the poem in MS C, he comes close enough to his intention that the apology is no longer necessary, and these lines disappear altogether.

After another treatment of the Aurunculeia passage, Pound introduces the Chinese wind poem from fragment 2B, condensing it from thirty-four lines to thirteen and reinterpreting it in keeping with his central theme. The first version of the wind poem belongs to the manuscripts of 1915–16. This text

---

22. The revision of these lines from fragment 1B to MS B reflects their status as metaphor for the poem's structure, for they condense sixty-seven rambling lines of the earlier version. The reticently critical "Topaz I manage" is all that remains of the nervous, self-doubting rhetoric of fragment 1B ("say does it fall, or pour?"; "How does it live"; "Say that I build out the spheres / I've but half seen. . . . / (that I don't see at all").

is a freehand variation on Fenollosa's incomplete translation (MS FN), itself quite different from the original poem as Arthur Waley translates it.[23] As given by Waley, the poem is an exchange between Hsiang, King of Ch'u, and the poet Sung-Yü (in Japanese, So-Gioku). Hsiang bares his breast to the wind, rejoicing that he shares it with the common people. Sung-Yü responds, "This is the Great King's wind," and, when the king objects, describes the wind in natural imagery as fresh, sweet, and soothing. The king then asks about the common people's wind, which Sung-Yü describes as turgid and oppressive; his point appears to be that the king's life is so privileged relative to his subjects' that the very wind cannot touch them in the same way.

Fenollosa's version, MS FN, translates only the first section of the poem, ending with the comment, "This is only the first ⅗ of the poem—the rest describes the wind of the common people which brings dust & sickness to people. Leave out the rest"—Fenollosa being, apparently, more interested in the imagistic beauty of oriental poetry than in its moral allegories. When Pound first came upon it in the Fenollosa notebooks, the poem had a puzzling shape, and his first translation (fragment 2B) shows him interpreting the poet's speeches somewhat uncertainly as flattering sophistry designed to win the king's favor.

Coming back to the wind poem in the midst of composing MS B, however, Pound saw another interpretation sympathetic to his thematic purpose in Canto IV. In MS B, the implication that the king is won over by So-Gioku's adroit flattery disappears, and the king's denials express his awareness of nature's greater power:

> So-gioku answered,
> "This is wind for the king."
>   "This wind roars in the earth's bag,
> it lays the water with rushes."
> "This wind is here for the king,
> "it shakes the imperial water-jets".
>   "Let every cow keep her calf,"
> "This wind is held in gauze curtains."

The contrasting image which follows, of Danaë on the tower, counters this king's respect for nature's power with the futile arrogance of King Acrisius, who imprisoned Danaë when an oracle revealed that he would meet his death by a child she would bear. In MS C, Pound reverses the order of the wind poem's speakers, so that the king refutes So-Gioku's claims, and the scene

23. Arthur Waley, *One Hundred & Seventy Chinese Poems* (London: Constable, 1962), pp. 24–26.

retains this form in the final text. Again, as Pound works his material into its
new shape and meaning, the stylistic features which characterize the canto
recur spontaneously, in anaphoric lines and in the simple, line-long syntactic
patterns repeated with minor variations.

Seven enigmatic lines follow the wind poem in Canto IV:

> Smoke hangs on the stream,
> The peach-trees shed bright leaves in the water,
> Sound drifts in the evening haze,
> > The bark scrapes at the ford,
> Gilt rafters above black water,
> > Three steps in an open field,
> Gray stone-posts leading . . . . .

Lacking the wind poem's dramatic shape, these lines half-sketch suggestive
scenes and landscapes, unspecified places which appear to be grouped together sheerly for their evocative power. A look at their sources, however,
reveals more specific relationships to Pound's theme. The first version of this
passage, in MS B, is considerably longer:

> [The smoke hangs on the laquer]
> The smoke hangs on the stream, the peach-trees
> > shed leaves on the water,
> Past, past the hundred fords, the slow barge.
> loiters, the thousand peach-trees shed their flakes
> into the stream, out of a former time,
> [The Duke heard] Heard the dynastic music
>
> > Blue-black of Venice
> that night, the Loredan, gilt rafters [glare]
> lighted in the first floor rooms,
> > Go down from Angouleme,
> three steps in an open field, grey stone, no yard
> > behind them,
> posts for the vanished gate,
> > in Spain the poppies swim in the air of glass.

Looking through the early manuscripts, Pound came upon fragment 3B, a
brief and rather insipid lament for lost youth in which he compares its sensuality to "the richness of Omakitsu's verses." Line 75 of MS B—"The smoke
hangs on the laquer [sic]"—originates here; and Pound uses a similar image
in a 1919 essay on Remy de Gourmont: "I do not think it possible to over-

emphasize Gourmont's sense of beauty. The mist clings to the lacquer. His spirit was the spirit of Omakitsu; his *pays natal* was near to the peach-blossom-fountain of the untranslatable poem." (LE, 343)

Thinking of Omakitsu in composing MS B, Pound remembered this "untranslatable poem," Omakitsu's "To Gen Ko," or "peach source song," which he had read in Fenollosa's notebooks. He then altered the line to "The smoke hangs on the stream" and added images recalling the beginning of the "To Gen Ko" as presented in Fenollosa's notes (which also suggest why Pound thought the poem "untranslatable"):

> Fishing boat driving water love mountain spring
> Both banks peach flower fold between them departure ford
> Sitting seeing crimson tree not know how far distant   [PA]

In Omakitsu's poem, the speaker recalls a journey he once made to a village "far away from the world of things." There he found people who had fled the cruelty of the Hsin dynasty and, living in seclusion, had been transformed into sennin, or air spirits. Every spring, when the peach flowers lie on the stream, he remembers this mysterious place, the "sennin source" of the "peach flower water." Pound's lines, then, originate in a landscape of metamorphosis and add another "emotional colour" to his spectrum, another eastern testimony to the mythopoeic animation of nature as a "permanent basis in humanity."

Beyond the thematic depth obtained through a look at Pound's source, it is interesting to see that the peach-blossom poem Pound recalls as being so beautiful is apparently just this text, Fenollosa's rough English translation written beneath the Chinese characters with their Japanese pronunciations. Whether intentionally or not, Fenollosa's English preserves the inherent indeterminacy of Chinese syntax, and Pound would not at this time have known enough Chinese to make more sense of the original than Fenollosa had done. But, given the emphasis in his developing poetics on nonsignifying modes of meaning, it is tempting to speculate that his admiration for this poem was only increased by the syntactic obscurity of the text he confronted. The "To Gen Ko" came to Pound with the imaginative distance he kept between himself and his sources already inscribed, and it perhaps brought to his mind a scene the more exquisite for its not being clearly presented. Indeed, his rendering of it in the Canto IV manuscripts simply transposes its ambiguity from syntax to the image itself, a correspondence entirely in keeping with the emerging metamorphic theme and form of the poem.

The origin of the rest of the "Smoke hangs on the stream" passage bears out the connection between fragmented syntax and a poetics based not on words as signs but on their powers of suggestion. Pound's source for these lines is fragment 4B, an early draft written in the mode of "Three Cantos" and, like them, preoccupied with the problem of writing a poem:

> What's poetry?
> > There is a castle set,
> The Auvezere, or its Dordoigne, chalk white and whiteish blue,
> Or Goldring writes "That night, the Loredan"
> And the blue-black of Venice fills my mind
> And the gilt rafters of the first floor rooms
> > Show there above me all a-red, ablaze.
> "I knew it first, and it was such a year,
> "When first I knew it there was such an air"
> Or "This night it will happen". "Further on".
> Or "Down you go, a mile from Angouleme
> And in an open field there are three steps
> Grey stone, they wait, there is no yard behind them,
> Only the stone piers that have held a gate."
>
> Or "The red poppies seem to swim in glass"

For a passage on poetry by a poet who would eventually be acknowledged the preeminent craftsman of his time, the language of 4B is singularly dull. Pound answers his own query not with artful words but with images deliberately fragmented to create a sense of mysterious expectancy—images which, moreover, recall his own travels in the countries of romance: the Auvezere, the blue Dordogne between white cliffs, the Loredan palace in Venice, the stone steps which are all that remain of an old dwelling in Provence.

What is interesting here is the discrepancy between the claims the passage makes for these images and the modesty of their actual effects. Indeed, so far did the force of these images outweigh the defects of literary style in Pound's mind at this time that he could draw the exemplary lines with which he answers his own question, "What's poetry?" from the unremarkable verses of Douglas Goldring. Goldring, Ford Madox Hueffer's assistant on the *English Review*, wrote verse, fiction, and travelogues, and Pound sent some of his work to Harriet Monroe and H. L. Mencken. Three poems which *Poetry* printed in 1914–15 relate to fragment 4B. "Calle Memo o Loredan" (September 1914), a souvenir of Venice, begins:

> We were staying (that night) in a very old palace—
> > Very dark, very large, and sheer to the water below.
> The rooms were silent and strange, and you were frightened, Alice:
> > The silver lamp gave off a feeble, flickering glow.

"Hill House," published at the same time, contains the line: "Then you told me of your dream cities, that Venice was one." The third poem, "Voyages," appeared in *Poetry* in May 1915. It begins:

> To come so soon to this imagined dark—
> More velvet-deep than any midnight park!
> Palaces hem me in, with blind black walls;
> The water is hushed for a voice that never calls.[24]

Just as Pound's lines in 4B fail to convey the magic they apparently had for their author, Goldring's tedious verses would hardly seem likely to have impressed Pound so deeply. But in writing 4B, he was following his characteristic practice of composing not directly from his source but from his memory of it, and what he remembered was not Goldring's words, nor even Goldring's poems, but the beloved places which the poems had called to mind. As he wrote to Harriet Monroe in a letter accompanying the poems, Goldring "succeeded in giving me 'a mood.'" For this he was willing to forgive a good deal in the way of craftsmanly lapses: "Goldring's two things read very well . . . save for the awful Alice in line 3 and the rotten end of the second poem. . . . the Voyages I send herewith have their own atmosphere and do not break it."[25] Goldring's dream cities were also Pound's, and the poet he remembered in thinking of him was not Goldring but the poet he himself was trying to become.

Pound's use of the Omakitsu and Goldring images, then, distills their "spirit of romance," leaving their mimetic content aside. The advance Pound made in his treatment of this material from 4B to MS B was simply to exploit its limitations. As both the incomprehensible Fenollosa text and his remarks to Monroe indicate, he was more attracted to what the words of his sources did not say than to what was there on the page. The images that appear merely threadbare in the discursive context of MS B become effectively enigmatic when shorn of rhetorical trappings. Again, the images themselves do not gratify an interest in representation. Rather, they are an abstract image of "the poetic," a formal rather than descriptive answer to the question, "What's poetry?" As Gaudier-Brzeska, in his "Vortex," had defined sculpture in abstract terms as "masses in relation," Pound here implicitly defines poetry as a relation of words that creates "the word beyond formulated language." (GB, 20, 88)

In the remaining passages of MS B, Pound alludes briefly to the Cyne-

---

24. *Poetry* 4 (September 1914): 217–18, and 6 (May 1915): 79–80.
25. Unpublished letter to Harriet Monroe, dated September 22, 1915, in the *Poetry* Magazine Papers, 1912–1936.

heard story in the *Anglo-Saxon Chronicle* (fragment 5B), introduces the image of Père Henri Jacques and the sennin from MS Ur1, and experiments with recapitulating the canto's main thematic motifs by a rapid series of intertwined allusions which prefigure lines 113–18 of the final poem. He then takes up the Troy/Auvergne parallel in a last, vain attempt to bring it to life:

> The Dauphin wars, and Paris for like cause
> Like cause De Maensac. "Though the church's men
> fought round the Dalfin's walls:"
> > with unlike end.
>
> ....
> "Longa saison ai estat vas amor"
> So sang de Maensac, lackland,
> Venus nec iners, the new Phrygian judge,
> Flame hung on the viol strings, nec torpet lingua,
> [Suasit mater amoris], ... cytherea thalamo,

"Longa saison . . ." alludes to a song by de Maensac, the first two lines of which Pound translates in "Troubadours—Their Sorts and Conditions": "For a long time have I stood toward Love / Humble and frank, and have done his commands." (LE, 97n) The Latin tags (Venus neither idle . . . nor slow of tongue, / The mother of love persuaded . . . the Cytherean bower) come from Paris's seductive letter to Helen in Ovid's *Heroïdes*.[26] In thus linking Paris and Peire, Pound alludes to the spiritual continuity which he wished the Troy/Auvergne parallel to express: Piere's reverent obedience toward his personified figure of love matches Paris's divinely inspired passion for Helen, whom Venus promised him at the Judgment of Paris. Even with this expression of Paris's and Piere's "like cause," however, the "unlike end" of the ensuing wars undermines the parallel, and Pound abandons this theme in his next draft.

MS B ends with seven lines on the Actaeon/Vidal scene, probably a warm-up for the revised version in MS A. Like MS A, it is structurally inconclusive. But even though this draft is more pastiche than poem and contains some heterogeneous materials which Pound later discarded, its collage supplied some "emotional colours" for the fuller spectrum he would arrange in MS C. Further, in MS A and MS B he established the structural conception of the poem as an ideogram of images, achieving an "extensive" form for the "intensive" Image which his "long imagiste or vorticist poem" required.

In MS C, Canto IV reached what was essentially its final shape. This draft draws its material mainly from the two earlier typescript drafts while pre-

---

26. Epistola 16, lines 158, 16, 20 ("nec torpet lingua" does not appear in Ovid's text).

serving their collage form. Pound omitted the Poicebot material, the "Air, fire" lines, the *Anglo-Saxon Chronicle* material, the unsuccessful Troy/Auvergne parallel, and other, more minor details. He added the "Ply over ply" passage, first drafted in fragments c1 and c2, and began to assimilate the elements of the ending, which continued to evolve until 1923.

Pound's addition of the "Ply over ply" passage in MS C is interesting, for it supplants the "Air, fire" lines of MS B. At the point where, in the earlier draft, he had placed an image expressing his failure to achieve the aims of his poetics ("Topaz I manage, and three sorts of blues . . ."), he now writes these lines:

> Ply over ply, thin glitter of water,
> Brook film bearing white petals.
>   "Behold the tree of the visages,
> The forked tips flaming as if with lotus."
>   Ply over ply,
> [behind them the floating images, behind them recurring images]
> [behind them the lasting Gods.]
> Shallow eddying fluid, beneath the knees of the Gods.

Here the fragmented colors disappear and white light and crystalline water appear in their place. The image describes and illuminates the structural principle Pound has found for Canto IV: a "ply over ply" of images, in themselves fictions but revealing through their juxtapositions the "permanent basis in humanity" which the abstract form of Canto IV intends: "Behind them the lasting Gods"—"gods" being his metaphor, as he says elsewhere, for "eternal states of mind." (SPr, 47) Pound's theme of correspondences in nature which communicate an unseen order and meaning emerges clearly here in the structural "rhyme" of petals and faces, a perhaps unconscious rewriting of "In a Station of the Metro." The tree of visages is the tree of life, as fragment c1 affirms ("Ecce arborem vitae"): the petals becoming faces and faces becoming petals enfold death and change within this transformative continuity, expressing "our kinship to the vital universe, to the tree and the living rock" that Pound thought common to myth and troubadour art.

The first draft of this passage, fragment c1, also gave Pound the canto's ending, which becomes in MS C:

>   In trellises,
> over-wound with small flowers, across th' Adige
> in the but half used room, Verona,
> Stephanus pinxit, in the included garden,
> thin film, the early Virgin, age of unbodied gods,

"The virtue risen in heaven", the vitreous
fragile images haunting the mind,—as of Guido—
Thin as the locusts wing.
                              The Centaurs heel
plants in the earth loam.
A jesuit seeks the sennin upon the cusped peak of Ro-ku

The line translated from Cavalcanti—"'The virtue risen in heaven'"—was
one of the exhibits in "Psychology and Troubadours," and its "rhyme" with
the image of the "madonna in hortulo" in Stefano da Verona's painting posits
a correspondence of sensibility like that of Ovid and the troubadours with
which Pound began. It recalls Pound's 1910 introduction to Cavalcanti: "In
reading a line like 'Vedrai la sua virtù nel ciel salita' [thou shalt see her virtue
risen in heaven] one must have in mind the connotations alchemical, astro-
logical, metaphysical, which Swedenborg would have called the correspondences." Pound describes this "virtue" as "a spiritual chemistry" which "both
modern science and modern mysticism are set to confirm."[27] The images of
the centaur, Pound's symbol for poetry, and the Jesuit's metamorphic spiri-
tuality (from MS Ur1) close this draft of Canto IV, recalling his view in
"Psychology and Troubadours" that this sensibility expresses itself in the art
which is a religion, the religion which is an art.

Having completed MS C, Pound made a clean typescript of the poem, MS
D, probably intending it to be the final copy. He finished it shortly before
departing London for a walking tour of Provence in April 1919 and sent MS
C off to his father, writing, "Here is a draft of the fourth Canto. . . . Not to
be shown to anyone (save IWP [Isabel Weston Pound] if she wishes to see
it). Won't be printed until there is another bundle of three; fifth is begun."
(L, ca. April 20, 1919) The typescript text of MS D shows only minor
stylistic changes from MS C. At a later point, however, Pound worked over
the manuscript again, making many more stylistic changes in holograph and
deleting several images. He extended the repetitive technique used so effectively in the Procne/Soremonda section (for example, "air, air," in line 43; "of
nymphs, of nymphs," in line 44; "answered, answered," in line 89). And he
also worked over the canto's opening lines:

                              Beacon from isle to isle.
                              Hear me.

[Rise O thou]
[Come then the smoky palace!] Troy but a heap of

27. Sonnets and Ballate of Guido Cavalcanti, with translations and an introduction by Ezra
Pound (London: Stephen Swift, 1912), p. 3.

[Palace in smokey]   smouldering boundary stones!
ANAXIFORMINGES! [Hear me!] Aurunculeia! Cadmus of Golden Prows:
The silver mirrors catch the bright stones and flare.

Wording the image of the Virgilian burning palace gave Pound some trouble;
it was not until the proof for the 1919 Rodker printing that "Palace in smoky
light" appeared.[28] Meanwhile, he considered another image from MS A, the
beacons which flash from island to island to signal the end of the Trojan War
in Aeschylus's *Agamemnon*. Pound's remarks on Aeschylus's "agglutinative"
syntax seem also to describe the intention of his own agglutination of images
in this passage: "his general drive . . . is merely to remind the audience of the
events of the Trojan war; . . . syntax is subordinate, and duly subordinated,
left out." (LE, 273)

But the most striking feature of the opening, here as in MS A, are the
vexed apostrophes, written, marked out, and rewritten again and again in
the early manuscripts and twice more here. Jonathan Culler has suggested
that the gesture of apostrophe is "perhaps always an indirect invocation of
the muse," an "embarrassing . . . embodiment of poetic pretension: of the
subject's claim that in his verse he is not merely an empirical poet, a writer
of verse, but the embodiment of poetic tradition and the spirit of poesy."[29]
The debated history of Pound's apostrophe, continually suppressed and continually resurfacing, attests to the self-consciousness that attends the modern
poet in the invocational situation, as does the solution which Pound finally
manages. To invoke the Muse is, after all, to claim divine authority for the
poem. Pound, however, is no more willing to assert such authority here than
he was in "Psychology and Troubadours." While the poem's theme of metamorphosis is profoundly religious and its form seeks to express a "permanent
basis in humanity," the success (or failure) of this claim depends entirely
upon the effect of its symbolic form upon the reader. So it is that, having
begun his modern epic with the intention of historicizing epic desire, Pound
appears to find himself "embarrassed" precisely by the conjuring power of
poetic language. His suppression of the vocative mode suggests a fear that
his own poetic sleight of hand builds only castles in the air.

Pound eventually extricates himself from this dilemma by composing an
anti-invocation through the ironic juxtaposition of Pindar's bombastic "AN-
AXIFORMINGES!" (invoking "Ye hymns that rule the lyre!") with the

28. Bradford Morrow, in "A Source for 'Palace in smoky light': Pound and Dryden's Virgil,"
Paideuma 3 (Fall 1974): 245–46, identifies this image as Ucalegon's and Deiphobus's burning
mansions in *Aeneid* 2.417–20. From the labored compositional history of the opening line, however, it seems unlikely that Pound actually had in mind the subtle critique of Virgil's and Dryden's respective verbosities that Morrow suggests; he was struggling too hard with his own.

29. Jonathan Culler, "Apostrophe," *Diacritics* 7 (1977): 63.

name of Catullus's bride. As Walter Baumann remarks, "Since Pound has never ceased to voice his distaste for Pindar's rhetoric, the motive which led to the inclusion of the epithet in Canto IV can only be scorn."[30] The juxtaposition of Pindar and Catullus recapitulates the contrast that *Homage to Sextus Propertius*, draws between the epic Virgil, poet laureate of the Roman Empire, and Propertius, whose "Ingenium nobis ipsa puella fecit" Pound quotes in "Psychology and Troubadours." (SR, 96) The epic poet's claim to divine authority modulates to the "Hear me!" that, Pound implies, is its literal subtext, and the palace is not raised again but left as "smouldering boundary stones," its imaginary historical trace. Pound's anti-invocation deflates epic pretension by deflecting its claims of historical truth from the events it narrates to the poetic impulse. As the historical event is always over before the poem begins, it can only be an occasion for that impulse, and this is true not only for the belated Virgils of the epic tradition but for the legendary Homer himself, blind and far removed in time and place from historic Troy, composing its fantasy from the sounds of words.[31] Pound's resituating of poetic authority in the poet's desire, which qualifies its claims to truth, expresses the modernist tension between history and poetry, "Truth and Calliope." Adrian Leverkuhn in *Dr. Faustus* puts it plainly: "The work of art? It is a fraud. It is something the burgher wishes there still were. It is contrary to truth, contrary to serious art. . . . Pretence and play have the conscience of art against them today. Art would like to stop being pretence and play, it would like to become knowledge."[32] Pound's *Cantos*, at the outset as through its long progress, strives to free itself from poetic "pretension," seeking "a language to think in" (LE, 194) that is also a language of reality.

The last major change that Pound made in the text of Canto IV may be read in light of the dialectic between poetic vision and historical truth which informs its compositional history from the beginning. The evolution of Canto IV did not prove quite complete with MS D, as he had expected; one more typescript draft followed before the poem's first printing in October 1919. In this draft, MS E, he introduced an image which confronts poetic imagining with historical actualities: that of the modern-day religious procession, inserted in MS E between the summary of themes and the Stefano/Guido image:

30. Walter Baumann, *The Rose in the Steel Dust: An Examination of* The Cantos *of Ezra Pound* (Coral Gables, Fla.: University of Miami Press, 1970), p. 21.

31. Cf. Canto II:

> And poor old Homer, blind, blind, as a bat,
> Ear, ear for the sea-surge, murmur of old men's voices:
> "Let her go back to the ships,   [C, 6]

32. Thomas Mann, *Dr. Faustus*, trans. H. T. Lowe-Porter (New York: Random House, Vintage Books, 1948), p. 181.

> Et saave!
> But today, Garonne is thick like paint, beyond Dorada,
> The worm of the Procession bores in the soup of the crowd,
> The blue thin voices against the crash of the crowd
> Et "Salve regina".

This ironic presentation of the modern "spirit of Provence" strikes a discordant note and causes an important shift in the canto's force. In introducing the image of "tawdry light" (fragment e2) into the poem, Pound tears the veil of images which he has so painstakingly woven, "ply over ply," and dispels the illusion, the bright "light," which his years of work had finally created. In the course of composing Canto IV, he had progressed from a desire for a "paradisal" style to its realization, from the dull verbosity of the *Poetry* cantos to a tapestry of images which seem to leave the words behind. The flat statement of the early drafts—"There is a castle set" (4B)—gradually gave way to the anxiously heightened "Rise O thou smoky palace" of the later ones, and finally, deleting absence and desire with the imperative verb, to the vivid "Palace in smoky light" of the final text. The effect of the Garonne image, however, threatens to remove the "ply over ply" of images to an unreachable past. Soremonda's transformation seems irrecoverably distant, the Omakitsu/Goldring lines an artful fabrication, the "vitreous / Fragile images haunting the mind," "out of a former time." This distancing effect is augmented by the last structural change which Pound made in MS F. Retyping Canto IV for *A Draft of XVI. Cantos* (1925), he added the closing lines: "And we sit here. . . . / there in the arena. . . .," which frame the canto's vision, placing its illusion at a double remove, in an arena itself first evoked, then distanced.

The late introduction of these elements shows that, in the body of Canto IV as in the invocation, Pound had no sooner conjured his castles than he hastened to turn them back into words. And indeed, the history of MS E suggests a little allegory which brings us back full circle to the canto's beginnings. A comparison of fragment e2, the first draft of the procession image (see plate 3), with the manuscripts of Pound's letters to his parents indicates that he composed it during the summer of 1919 while on his walking tour of Provence, after the poem had already evolved through MS D.[33] It records, presumably, Pound's response to what he actually saw there, in place of the dream-landscapes of old Provence which he had seen so clearly in his mind's

---

33. The fragment is written in ink on a sheet of graph paper which matches that of two letters that Pound sent to his parents from Montrejeau on July 13 and 16, 1919. These are the only occurrences of this paper both in the manuscripts of 1914–20 and in the letters to his parents of that period.

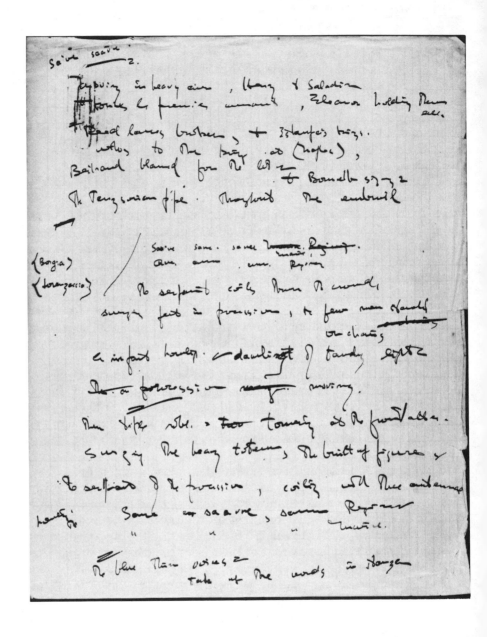

Plate 3. Fragment e2, reduced from 21½ cm × 28 cm. Courtesy of the Collection of American Literature, Beinecke Rare Book and Manuscript Library, Yale University.

eye and evoked so successfully in Canto IV: "*But today*, Garonne is thick like paint" (MS E). In a letter to Homer Pound after the Rodker printing of Canto IV on October 4, 1919, Pound wrote, "The worm of the procession had three large antennae, and I hope to develop the motive later, text clearly states that this vermiform object circulated in the crowd at the Church of St. Nicholas in Toulouse." Remembering Pound's remarks on the verbal paradises of the Latin poets, the troubadours, and Dante, and the desire for an analogous modern language which inspired the Fourth Canto, we may easily read the procession image as prefiguring what the Usura Canto would later term a "thickening" of religious sensibility, of perception itself, in the transition from the medieval economy, underwritten by the Church's ban of usury, to modern capitalism. The muddy paint of the Garonne waters parallels a concomitant thickening of language: "Et sa'ave, sa'ave Regina!" And even this image is prefigured in "Psychology and Troubadours," where Pound distinguishes between "two kinds of religion": ecstatic, which includes early Christianity as well as the Greek mysteries, and "the Mosaic or Roman or British Empire type, where someone, having to keep a troublesome rabble in order, invents and scares them with a disagreeable bogie, which he calls god." (SR, 95) Pound apparently observed the latter, not the former, on his walking tour, and he accordingly wove it into the "thin film of images" which he had so vividly reimagined.

With the procession image, then, Pound allows history to tear through the fabric of the poem; or rather, he allows experience to revise his conception of the history which he had already committed his long poem to "including." Rather than, like Mallarmé, distinguishing the world of the poem from the actual world and knowingly crafting the "fleur . . . absente de tous bouquets," Pound had from the beginning meant his words to be true to the world, and his epic to be a "silver mirrour" reflecting the ruins of history no less than the phantasms of desire. The vision always had to be tested in the world. Pound's tour of Provence necessitated a revision of the poem in which he had painted landscapes of the imagination in order to save it from the aestheticism he so vigorously denounced in *Hugh Selwyn Mauberley*, published the following year.

To a great extent, the linguistic odyssey of Pound's *Cantos* is the history of his desire to make his verbal paradise a *paradiso terrestre*, a modern analogue to Dante's great poem. The continuing dialectic between poetic vision and the experienced world issues from the desire to renounce fancy's cheating and to create a poetic language adequate to historical experience. For this he had, as he put it, no "Aquinas-map," and the failures of his efforts are recorded in the history of our times as well as in the history of the poem. Pound's desire to create the language of an earthly paradise, a language in which poetry and history might coincide, would lead eventually to his defeated awareness that "Le paradis n'est pas artificiel" (C, 468), and finally to a much sadder confession of his failure to "write Paradise." Of this fifty-year adventure, the composition of the Fourth Canto is only one episode, yet by virtue of the dialectics governing its compositional history, it is both beginning and archetype. The ideology of its form and style as initially realized in MSS C and D only transposes the romantic idealism—which his commitment to history would reform—from divine spirit to an elite "body" of poets; rather than bringing the transcendent back to earth, to history, Pound idealizes the (literary) historical. Yet Pound discovered in the very act of writing it his own error of denying actualities in an attempt to shape history to his designs.

Although its project of creating an abstract form which captures transcendence in historical patterns does not succeed on the terms Pound initially imagined, the final canto still accomplishes a great deal. Its break with the closure of story and with iambic pentameter begins that formal critique of the traditional epic that is *The Cantos'* greatest achievement. It succeeds also in creating a live form and language that can embody the contradictions of twentieth-century poetics and the transition from romanticism to modernism even when they cannot resolve them. *The Cantos* succeeds like no other poem of the century in making poetry a living language, and this linguistic success, the kind that matters most to poetry, is inseparable from its historical and visionary purposes as well as from its historical importance. Of all that remains to be understood about *The Cantos*, perhaps most pressing is the odyssey of its style, its risky, resourceful, and tirelessly inventive search for a language that would be at once a paradise and a home—"the essence of religion" as "the *present* tense." (SPr, 70) The composition of Canto IV inaugurates this adventurous wandering, not least because it, too, has no end. Its expectant conclusion—"And we sit here. . . . / there in the arena. . . ."—awaits what is still to occur in the drama of modern history which Pound's epic will record. And its style, too, is beginning only. Though it helped to inaugurate a major vein of the modern tradition, Pound did not find its paradise a home. Going on to Canto V, he continued to seek a reconciliation between the paradisal word and the world, repeating there the moment of doubt which the successes of the Fourth Canto had temporarily denied:

> Air, fire, the pale soft light.
> Topaz I manage, and three sorts of blue;
> but on the barb of time.   [C, 17]

CHAPTER 2

Il Miglior Fabbro:
A Genetic Text of Canto IV, 1915–25

T. S. Eliot, whose *The Waste Land* Pound helped put into final shape not long after he himself had made the formal and stylistic breakthroughs entailed in the writing of Canto IV, dedicated that poem to him with the words Dante had used of the troubadour poet Arnaut Daniel: *miglior fabbro*, "the better craftsman."[1] Probably no one, not even Eliot, has influenced twentieth-century poetry more strongly than Pound, through his practical criticism, both in published essays and in informal collaboration with other artists, through his innovative poetic theory, and most of all through his untiringly exploratory and inventive poetic practice. Eliot wrote, "I cannot think of anyone writing verse, of our generation and the next, whose verse (if any good) has not been improved by the study of Pound's."[2] William Carlos Williams spoke of his "mystical ear"[3] and wrote that Pound "has lifted the language up as no one else has done";[4] and Hayden Carruth—speaking as "one of his thousands upon thousands of disciples: the word is exact, for he has given us our discipline"—writes that "Pound by himself re-invented the poetic line as the unit of poetry, variable and end-stopped" and that "his concept of modern verse measure was clearer and more workable than anyone else's."[5]

Such testimonies tend to draw readers to Pound's workshop with anticipations that the traces left by the act of creation cannot possibly satisfy. Familiar with the finished work, we somehow expect a vantage point behind the scenes to deliver up its secrets, explicating its mysteries as well as its beauties. We anticipate undiscovered treasures not yet brought to light, and we hope for an intimate brush with genius, or at least with inspiration. All these expectations leave us unprepared for the fumblings and gropings, the vulnerable dishevelment and prosaic toil we find recorded in the manuscripts for Canto IV, which bear out Yeats's description of his profession in "Adam's Curse":

1. Dante's actual words are "fu miglior fabbro del parlar materno" (he was a better craftsman of the mother tongue), *Purgatorio* 26.117.
2. T. S. Eliot, "Isolated Superiority," *Dial* 84 (January 1928): 5.
3. Allen Ginsberg quotes Williams on Pound's "mystical ear" in Michael Reck, "A Conversation between Ezra Pound and Allen Ginsberg," *Evergreen Review* 57 (June 1968): 28; reprinted in J. P. Sullivan, *Ezra Pound* (Baltimore: Penguin, 1970), p. 354.
4. William Carlos Williams, *Selected Essays* (New York: New Directions, 1954), p. 111.
5. Hayden Carruth, "On a Picture of Ezra Pound," *Poetry* 110 (May 1967): 104; reprinted in Eric Homberger, ed., *Ezra Pound: The Critical Heritage* (Boston: Routledge and Kegan Paul, 1972), pp. 472–74.

I said: "A line will take us hours maybe;
Yet if it does not seem a moment's thought,
Our stitching and unstitching has been naught.
Better go down upon your marrow-bones
And scrub a kitchen pavement, or break stones
Like an old pauper, in all kinds of weather;
For to articulate sweet sounds together
Is to work harder than all these . . .

Pound was an astute self-critic. He canceled little that merits a place in his published works, and he frugally mined usable lines and images from discarded drafts, leaving few good lines unpublished. Nor does a perusal of the manuscripts behind *The Cantos* suffice to "make it cohere" or the recovery of lost contexts clarify obscurities as often as we might wish. The history of the poem and the insights it offers are not there on the surface of its trail of discarded pages but must be constructed by historical, critical, and interpretive acts, subject to the same limitations as other critical approaches. And finally, poetic genius eludes both historical explanation and technical analysis; it is an indefinable precondition of the poetry, not the fruit of visible labor. As Pound put it in an early essay on poetic craft, quoting from Duhamel and Vildrac's *Notes sur la Technique Poétique*, "'Mais d'abord il faut être un poète.'" (LE, 7)

All these limitations acknowledged, there is still much to interest us in watching the progress of *il miglior fabbro*. "I have never seen a discarded poem that excelled the final form," remarks Karl Shapiro. "On the other hand, no final poem can ever tell as much about the intention of the poet or about the poetic psyche as those worksheets which he almost systematically destroys."[6] Pound's *Cantos* is rooted more intransigently than most poems in its own history, and that history is entangled with the history of our times. Studies of its background, while they cannot resolve all the interpretive and critical questions which surround the poem, make clearer the forms and fields of these questions and open new pathways for exploring them. Ultimately, they assist us in reading *The Cantos*, in understanding its poetics, and in situating Pound's poem including history in literary history.

It is only fair for an editor who is presenting a poet's rejected work to consider how the author would have viewed its publication. Pound would probably have been less than delighted to see his early manuscripts come into public view. One thinks of his expostulations to Homer Pound upon learning that the Hailey, Idaho, *Times-News-Miner* had printed two of his

6. Karl Shapiro, "The Meaning of the Discarded Poem," in *Poets at Work: Essays Based on the Modern Poetry Collection at the Lockwood Memorial Library, University of Buffalo*, ed. Charles D. Abbott (New York: Harcourt, Brace, 1948), p. 121.

early poems "'never yet published, and kindly furnished . . . by the father of
the poet'"[7]: "Goshdratandgoldangitall: Ef you go and dig up enny more of
my infantile productions and print 'em" (L, June 20, 1925); and of his impatient dismissal of the reprinted *A Lume Spento* poems as "stale cream-
puffs."[8] But Pound also shared with other artists an interest in the psychology of the creative process, and, as the existence of the Pound Archive attests,
a commitment to preserving the historical dimension of his art. Picasso imagined "a science . . . which will seek to penetrate further into man through
the creative man. I often think of that science, and am resolved to leave pos-
terity with as complete a documentation as possible. That is why I date all
that I do."[9] And Pound's last statement on *The Cantos*, the foreword to the
Selected Cantos, shows much the same sense of his artistic creativity as a force
larger than himself, of which he is but the medium:

> I have made these selections to indicate main elements in the *Cantos*. To
> the specialist the task of explaining them. As Jung says: "Being essen-
> tially the instrument of his work, he [the artist] is subordinate to it, and
> we have no reason for expecting him to interpret it for us. He has done
> the best that is in him by giving it form and he must leave interpretation
> to others and to the future."

Pound then quoted as "the best introduction to the *Cantos*" the opening lines
of the canceled *Poetry* cantos. This gesture toward the explanatory power of
history and beginnings suggests that he would have approved such studies
as this one with the same generosity to which this foreword, and his preser-
vation of the manuscripts behind *The Cantos*, testify; and, indeed, that he
might have read them with interest in what "the future" is making of that
powerful but difficult text which he, its author, could bring into being but
never read.

A HISTORICAL OVERVIEW, 1915–25

The earliest manuscripts for Canto IV belong to 1915–16, when Pound began working steadily on drafts for his long poem, accumulating many pages
of roughly sketched material. Though the first enabling inspiration for Canto
IV came only in 1918, several of these drafts contributed lines and images to
the final poem (MSS 1B–5B). Pound's first known allusion to a fourth canto
occurs in a letter to his father of December 18, 1915: "my big long endless
poem that I am now struggling with, starts off with a barrelful of allusions

---

7. Quoted by Donald Gallup, *Ezra Pound: A Bibliography*, p. 271.
8. "Foreword (1964)" to *A Lume Spento and Other Early Poems* (New York: New Directions, 1965), p. [7].
9. Quoted by Francis Ponge, "Picasso," *Antaeus* 20–22 (1976): 95.

to *Sordello*. . . . It will be two months at least before I can send it, I suppose, as I don't want to muddle my mind now in the Vth Canto by typing the first three cantos."(L) An examination of the manuscript materials shows that Pound had at this time only the first of the "Three Cantos," which he published in *Poetry* in 1917. The others to which the letter refers are apparently those which comprise the long manuscript of which MS Ur1, the earliest designated "fourth canto," forms part; these were all replaced by new versions as Pound worked on the poem. An earlier draft of this text, typed on the versos of announcements for Miscio Itow's program of Japanese dancing on October 28 and November 2 and 9, 1915, suggests that the version of these two manuscripts was composed and revised between late October and December 18, 1915, the date of the letter to his father.

No references to a fourth canto appear in the letters of 1916–17. During these years, Pound continued composing and revising the several drafts of the first "Three Cantos," and he revised the *Poetry* version for inclusion in the American edition of *Lustra* published in October 1917. In the process, he composed another fragment which he temporarily intended for the fourth canto, MS Ur2. The first typescript draft of this passage was titled "III" in Pound's first typescript draft of "Three Cantos." At the time of this draft, Pound had not yet settled on the divisions of the poem. In the next typescript, this third canto became the fourth, and this retyped version is here transcribed as MS Ur2. Its themes record the dissatisfactions with the early cantos which Pound's three revisions of "Three Cantos" document,[10] and its closing image gestures toward the return to Imagist poetics which eventually freed Pound from the highly self-conscious, Browningesque iambic pentameter of the early manuscripts.

Pound appears to have done no more work on Canto IV until early in 1918, when he drafted MS AA, the pencil sketch which reveals his first inspiration for Canto IV. The manuscript was composed in rapid handwriting on random scraps of paper—a letter from John Quinn of September 21, 1917, two remnants of its envelope, a letter from the Future Publishing Company dated February 21, 1918, a torn leaf of gray account paper, and a leaf of plain paper—and these physical characteristics suggest that inspiration came suddenly. Indeed, the subject rhymes which make up this text gave Pound the thematic and formal seed around which his final Fourth Canto would grow.

The holograph sketch was followed by fragment a, a sketch of the Procne/ Soremonda scene, and then by the first two typescript drafts of Canto IV, MS A and MS B. The physical characteristics and textual interrelationships of these two manuscripts indicate a complicated history which I have conjec-

10. Pound revised "Three Cantos" in 1917 for the American edition of *Lustra*, in 1919 for *Quia Pauper Amavi*, and in 1923 for *A Draft of XVI. Cantos*.

turally reconstructed—not entirely satisfactorily—as follows. Pound began by composing leaves 1, 6, 7, and possibly 8 and 9 of MS A. He then composed MS B, drawing on these original leaves of MS A, on the holograph fragment of the Actaeon/Vidal section, now in Omar Pound's possession, and on nine of the manuscripts of 1915–16, including MSS Ur1 and Ur2. After completing MS B, Pound rewrote the Actaeon/Vidal section in MS A and continued to gather images about his theme, drawing upon MS AA as well as adding new material. This stage of composition resulted in leaves 2–5 of MS A, which he interpolated in the original draft.

Pound's first two typescript drafts diverge after the opening section of the poem to follow different organizational principles. In MS A, he elaborates the classical/Provençal subject rhymes sketched in MS AA and broadens its structural concept to include other forms of mythic correspondence. He also experiments briefly with the technique he identified in Joyce's work, the "alternation of subjective beauty and external shabbiness." In MS B, he uses only the Procne/Soremonda and Actaeon/Vidal parallels, after which he returns to the manuscripts of 1915–17, carving images out of them for the ideogram of Canto IV. Both MS A and MS B contributed to the composition of MS C. Manuscript B supplied its basic structure, and Pound drew images from MS A as he had drawn them from the early manuscripts in writing MS B. In addition to synthesizing the experiments of the first two drafts in MS C, Pound incorporated the "Ply over ply" lines from fragments c1 and c2 and reworked the ending, completing the basic structural evolution of the poem.

Pound made the fourth typescript of Canto IV, MS D, from MS C without major changes or additions, mainly tightening the poem's structure and polishing its style. He completed this draft shortly before departing London on April 22, 1919, for a walking tour of Provence and sent MS C off to his father, writing that he was now at work on Canto V. Canto IV, he said, would not be printed "until there is another bundle of three" (L, April 20, 1919), implying that at this time he considered MS D to be the final draft. The walking tour, however, gave him new perspectives on the imaginary landscapes of the poem he had just completed. While in France, he composed fragment e2, the lines on the modern-day religious procession, and, returning to London and his typewriter on September 11, 1919, revised it (fragment e3) and incorporated it in MS E, the last typescript draft of Canto IV before its first printing at John Rodker's press on October 4, 1919.

The first printing of "The Fourth Canto" at Rodker's Ovid Press seems to have been the idea of a moment and the labor of a few hours. A list found in the Pound Archive of items forthcoming from the Ovid Press in that year makes no mention of it, and Pound had told his father he did not intend to print the canto until the fifth and sixth were ready. The letters available for this period show only one brief mention of it in a letter of October 6 to John

Quinn, in which Pound enclosed a proof.[11] At any rate, as far as its author was concerned, the Ovid printing did not constitute publication: on the setting copy which he sent to the *Dial* he wrote, "forty copies *privately* printed, for author's convenience, NOT published." (The *Dial*, of course, would not have been able to print the poem had it already seen "book" publication.)

The Rodker text had quite an eventful history for so small an edition. A single sheet folded twice to form a title page and three pages of text, it exists in at least four states: a proof with Pound's corrections, now in the Pound Archive (P); the corrected rough proof which Pound sent to the *Dial* as setting copy for their 1920 publication of the poem (ScDial); the first state, the printed text of which differs from that of the *Dial* setting copy only in the deletion of a comma after line 101, in which the title page is printed for the first time (019a); and the second state, in which the colophon is reset and a total of twenty changes are made in the text, four substantive, eleven punctuation, and five indentation and spacing (019b). The three revisions of the Rodker text, with their many alterations of punctuation and spacing, indicate that Pound watched over the printing process and read the text with a careful eye for detail; and the fact that the corrections marked on the proof (P) were not systematically incorporated into the later stages of the text suggests that Pound may have changed his mind about some of them as he watched Rodker at work. By the time he prepared the setting copy for the *Dial*, however, he had apparently forgotten the many small changes made in the second state of the text. Of the eleven punctuation changes, only one was made in the *Dial* setting copy. Five more were incorporated in *Poems 1918–21*, and three in the setting copy for *A Draft of XVI. Cantos*, leaving only two uncorrected for the remainder of the canto's printing history.

The *Dial* text of 1920 probably served as Pound's setting copy for the 1921 publication of Canto IV in *Poems 1918–21*, in which no revisions occur. Two years later, in preparing the setting copy for *A Draft of XVI. Cantos*, Pound revised the ending of Canto IV (fragment xvi) and made a new typescript, probably copying from the *Poems 1918–21* text. Besides the revised ending, the setting copy manuscript shows several other variants, both accidental and substantive. The text of this final draft proceeded into print in William Bird's handsome deluxe edition of *A Draft of XVI. Cantos* without adventure.

PRESENTATION OF THE TEXT

This genetic text of Canto IV presents all of the available manuscripts relating directly to the composition of Canto IV from its beginnings to the first

---

11. Quoted by Daniel D. Pearlman in Appendix A of his *The Barb of Time: On the Unity of Ezra Pound's* Cantos (New York: Oxford University Press, 1969), p. 300.

publication of the final text in 1925. These manuscripts are transcribed or collated in full except for fragments 1B, 4B, and 5B, which excerpt material related to Canto IV from longer texts (note ellipsis dots). MS FN transcribes Fenollosa's annotations and translation as well as the Chinese characters (see plate 4). The manuscript materials for Canto IV are extensive and diverse, comprising two false starts, one holograph sketch, six typescript drafts, and seven fragments relating to these drafts. In addition, seven other manuscripts which Pound had accumulated while composing "Three Cantos" (1917) provided lines for the first two typescript drafts of Canto IV, and the Fenollosa notebooks contain a translation of So-Gioku's wind poem, Pound's source for this vignette in Canto IV. These manuscripts, listed according to the sigla which I have assigned them and by which they are designated in the textual notes, are described in the List of Manuscripts and Editions. The list is followed by a stemmatic diagram which schematically represents the relationships among the various manuscripts and printings.

The volume of manuscript material for Canto IV makes a full collation of it infeasible. At the same time, collation is preferable to complete transcription for those later manuscripts that are close enough to the final text to permit it. For this reason, the presentation of the manuscript material for Canto IV takes two forms. First, the two discarded versions and the drafts, fragment, and manuscript sources through the second typescript (MS B) are transcribed as Preliminary Manuscripts, 1915–18. The order of the manuscripts in this section follows that of the List of Manuscripts and Editions except for those drafts and fragments (c1–xvi) removed to the Collation and to the Supplementary Textual Notes. The remaining manuscripts, proof, and editions to 1924 are collated with the 1925 text of "The Fourth Canto" from *A Draft of XVI. Cantos*. Transcriptions of the six fragments associated with the collated manuscripts follow the Collation as the Supplementary Textual Notes (STN) and are cross-referenced in the Collation at the appropriate line numbers. The Preliminary Manuscripts, the Collation, and the Supplementary Textual Notes are followed by the Explanatory Notes, which gloss those references and allusions not found in the final text of Canto IV.

In transcribing the Preliminary Manuscripts and the later fragments I have aimed to record all the features that are significant to the evolution of the text of Canto IV with minimal editorial mediation. The siglum for each manuscript appears in the upper right-hand corner of each page. I have numbered the lines of each draft and fragment at the left margin. The numbers in parentheses at the right margin refer to the Explanatory Notes. Cross-references to other manuscripts and to the final text are placed at the bottom of the first page of each transcribed manuscript.

I have used standard type to transcribe Pound's typescript and italic type to transcribe his holograph. Significant irregular holograph markings have been drawn in. Pound's holograph sign " ⊇ " is transcribed as a dash, its

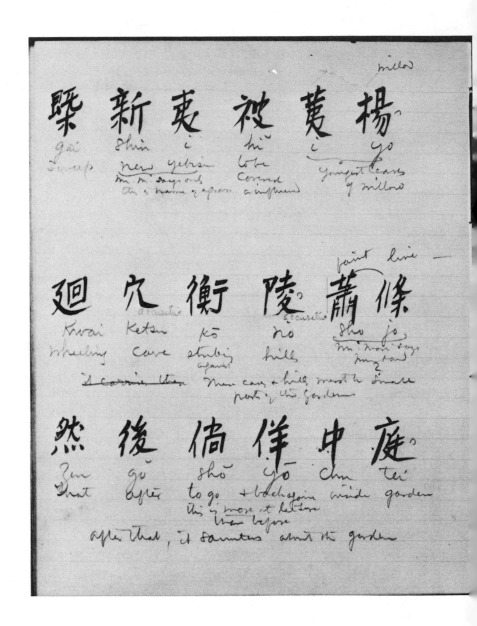

Plate 4. Double page from Ernest Fenollosa's notebook of translations from "Okakura, Sogioku and others," reduced from 32 cm × 20 cm. Courtesy of the Collection of American Literature, Beinecke Rare Book and Manuscript Library, Yale University.

— these characters are often used to describe an autumn field - say "field & shops & *** & *** *** can reach" Calm as here - solitary

衆芳。

Shu ho
many sweet smell

?

北上玉堂。

hoku jō Gioku do
North climbs gem palace

as climbs at the jewel palace with North.

functional equivalent. Page divisions and recto/verso divisions within a manuscript are indicated by a broken line (_ _ _ _ _). Square brackets enclose words deleted in typescript; and angle brackets, words deleted in holograph. The transcriptions maintain Pound's vertical spacing, lineation, and indentation. Pound habitually typed multiple spaces between words and before punctuation marks, but as this characteristic is irrelevant to the printed form of his texts, I have used standard horizontal spacing. Pound's handwriting is often rapid, omitting or eliding letters. When the word intended is clear, I have supplied the missing letters. Illegible words are indicated by the sign xxxxx, the number of x's approximating the number of letters in the word; questionable readings, by a question mark preceding the word, for example "?green." I have silently corrected typographical and spelling errors which Pound himself corrected in the same draft while allowing uncorrected misspellings and typographical errors to stand.

Cross-references are provided, first, between the fragments, the holograph draft, and the sources and MSS A and B; and second, between fragments and sources and the final text. Correspondences among the six typescript drafts (A–ScXVI) and the final text are not noted.

The numbers referring the reader to the Explanatory Notes are placed beside the line containing the allusion or reference glossed. When an allusion or reference is repeated from a draft appearing earlier in the Preliminary Manuscripts, the same number is given as in the earlier occurrence to avoid needless repetition.

The text of "The Fourth Canto" from the Three Mountains edition of *A Draft of XVI. Cantos* serves for the copy-text for the Collation of Later Manuscripts and Printed Texts, 1919–1925. I have numbered the lines at the left margin. The four reference tags in the margin (Itys, Actaeon, Hymenaeus, Danaë) occur only in the copy-text (TM25) and its setting copy (ScXVI).

The record of variants employs the standard system of line number, lemma, right square bracket, variant, and siglum or sigla. Where no lemma appears, the reading given is understood to replace the entire line. A dash between two sigla indicates that all texts in the direct line of descent between the sigla, as shown in the stemma, inclusive of the sigla, agree with the variant given. Any texts not listed are understood to agree with the Three Mountains text. It should be noted that the setting copy for the *Dial* text, being a rough proof of the Rodker text, is placed in the stemma according to its position in the printing history and not directly before the *Dial* text. The sign *ScDial–D20* thus includes both 019a and 019b. Variants are given in roman type and editorial comments in italic.

Spelling and punctuation variants are recorded except for the following: misspellings corrected by Pound in the same or a later draft; variants in the number of dots used to indicate an elision; and variants in lineation and spacing which do not affect the disposition of words within a line, for example, indentations and verse paragraphing.

Here, as in the Preliminary Manuscripts, Pound's holograph is transcribed in italic type and his typescript in roman, with angle brackets indicating hand-marked deletions and square brackets indicating deletions by typed overstriking. Pound's irregular horizontal spacing in the typescript drafts has been normalized; illegible words are indicated by the sign xxxx and doubtful readings by a question mark preceding the word.

Two signs record punctuation variants: a wavy dash (~) replaces a word when the variant occurs in an attached punctuation mark, and a caret (ˆ) notes deletions of punctuation marks. Thus, "flare,] ~ˆ C" indicates that the comma after "flare" is deleted in MS C.

LIST OF MANUSCRIPTS AND EDITIONS

Manuscripts and Manuscript Sources, 1915–23

Discarded Versions

Ur1   IV.   But whats all this to us? The modern world . . . . !"

98 lines. Typescript, 4 leaves, purple ribbon on legal-size wove paper with author's revisions in pencil. An earlier typescript of lines 1–84 (4 numbered pages, purple ribbon on versos of printed announcements of Miscio Itow's program of Japanese dancing on October 28 and November 2 and 9, 1915) suggests that this was the fourth canto implied in a letter Pound wrote to his father on December 18, 1915: "I don't want to muddle my mind now in the Vth Canto by typing the first three cantos" (L).

Ur2   IV   'What do I mean by all this clattering rumble?'

40 lines. Typescript, 2 pages numbered 29 and 30. Blue ribbon on wove paper watermarked "Imperial Strong IIII," with author's revisions in pencil; about 3 inches have been torn from the bottom of page 30. These pages originally followed a 28-page typescript draft of "Three Cantos" which Pound made in late 1916 or early 1917.

Three other early manuscripts in the Pound Archive relate to this draft: leaf 74 of the holograph draft of "Three Cantos," probably composed in 1916, a rough draft of lines 13–17; an earlier typescript draft of lines 1–21, titled "III." (1 leaf, blue ribbon on laid paper); and an earlier, longer typescript draft of lines 22–40 (two leaves, black followed by blue ribbon on wove paper watermarked "Imperial Strong IIII").

Drafts and Fragments

AA   Stumbling, stumbling along

83 lines. Holograph, pencil, 6 leaves. Leaf 1: verso of letter from
the Future Publishing Company dated February 21, 1918. Leaves
2 and 6: fragments of large envelope addressed to Pound from
John Quinn. Leaf 3: verso and recto of a fragment of heavy gray
account paper with Pound's Holland Place Chambers address
stamped on verso. Leaf 4: light wove paper. Leaf 5: verso of letter
from John Quinn dated September 21, 1917.

These leaves appear to comprise a continuous draft, which
probably dates from early 1918. A holograph draft of "Langue
d'Oc," published in the *Little Review* in May 1918, was written
on the same kind of paper as leaf 3. As Pound seldom used this
paper for drafting poems, it is likely that MS AA was composed
between late February and early May of 1918.

a   And she said: The swallows are

22 lines. Holograph, black ink on wove paper, 2 leaves.

A   IV   Rise, O thou smoky palace,

194 lines. Typescript with author's revisions in pencil and ink, 9
leaves. Leaves 1, 4–9: green ribbon. Leaf 2: purple ribbon. Leaf
3: lines 1–3 purple, lines 5–7 green ribbon. Leaves 1, 5, 6 on
lightweight wove paper; leaves 2–4, 8, and possibly 9, on me-
dium-weight wove paper; leaf 7 on paper watermarked "Excelsior
Superfine British-Make." Leaf 4 is cut in half.

The leaves here arranged and designated MS A do not appear
to form a continuous draft, unlike MSS B–E, and bear a complex
relationship to MS B. Leaves 1–3, the top half of 4, and 5–6 were
found in order in a folder in the Pound Archive. The bottom half
of leaf 4 and leaves 7–9 were found elsewhere in the Pound Archive and assembled with the others. Leaves 1–5 appear to be
consecutive. Leaf 6 elaborates the "Aurunculeia" motif which ends
leaf 5. Leaves 8 and 9 are placed at the end; they treat related
motifs and have similar physical characteristics, but there is no
clear indication of their original position in the draft.

Leaves 1 and 6–9 appear to have been written before MS B,
and leaves 2–5 to have followed MS B.

B   Canto IV.   Rise, O thou smoky palace, Ἀναξιφορμιγγες!

133 lines. Typescript, 6 leaves. Purple ribbon on wove paper with
author's revisions in pencil and ink.

c1   ply over ply—

30 lines. Holograph, 2 leaves (3 numbered sides), pencil on heavy

wove paper watermarked "Bilston Extra Strong" which matches that of MS C. The line on page 3 was used in "The Alchemist," first published in *Umbra* in 1920, dated 1912.

c2 Ply over ply, thin glitter of water

15 lines. Typescript, 1 leaf, blue ribbon on heavy wove paper which matches that of c1 and C, with pencil memo at bottom.

C IV Come then the smoky palace! Troy but a heap of smouldering

135 lines. Typescript, 6 leaves. Blue ribbon on heavy wove paper with author's revisions in pencil. Pound sent this manuscript to Homer and Isabel Pound in April 1919, shortly before departing for France.

D FOURTH CANTO Troy but a heap of smouldering boundary stones!

125 lines. Typescript, 5 numbered pages, blue ribbon on wove paper watermarked "Bilston Extra Strong" with author's corrections in pencil and ink. Pound completed this manuscript about April 20, 1919, shortly before departing for France, and then sent MS C to his parents.

e1 "Haunt of Urania's son. . . .

9 lines. Typescript, 1 leaf, blue ribbon on same wove paper (watermarked "Bilston Extra Strong") as D and e3, with author's revisions in pencil and ink and note for Rodker printing on verso.

e2 Sa've sāave—

21 lines. Holograph, 1 leaf, ink on graph paper. The paper and ink of this manuscript match those of two letters which Pound wrote to his parents from Montrejeau, dated July 13 and July 16, 1919. As these are the only occurrences of this paper in the 1915–20 manuscripts and family letters, it is likely that fragment e2 was composed about this time.

e3 Et:

SAAve, saave, saave régina,

17 lines. Typescript, 1 leaf, blue ribbon on paper watermarked "Bilston Extra Strong" (cf. D and e1), with author's revisions in ink and pencil.

E FOURTH CANTO Troy but a heap of smouldering boundary-stones,

128 lines. Typescript carbon (purple), 5 leaves (2–4 numbered), on wove paper. Pound probably made this typescript in Septem-

ber 1919, after his return from France. This appears to be a carbon of the MS used for setting copy for John Rodker's Ovid Press edition, now lost.

xvi Procession,—

11 lines. Typescript with author's additions in blue ink and pencil, one leaf. Purple ribbon on wove paper. Incorporated in ScXVI in 1923. Bird Collection, Ezra Pound Archive.

Early Manuscript Sources

1A Or pierce the cosmos,

14 lines. Typescript with author's additions in pencil, one leaf. Blue ribbon on wove paper watermarked "Imperial Strong IIII." The date August 9, 1915, appears on contiguous leaves of matching paper and ribbon color.

2A All from the genii's bottles, all this talk,

43 lines. Typescript with author's revisions in ink and pencil, 2 leaves. Purple ribbon on wove paper watermarked "Unity Bank: Strength and Security," a paper Pound was using in mid-1916.

1B Iamblichus light,

59 lines excerpted from a typescript of 6 numbered leaves, black ribbon on wove paper watermarked "Imperial Strong IIII" with author's corrections in pencil. I have excerpted only pages 3–6, which include all the lines used in MS B.

2B Wind-poem for Canto IV

33 lines. Typescript with author's revisions in pencil, 2 leaves. Red ribbon on wove paper watermarked "Imperial Strong IIII."

3B When you find that feminine contact

17 lines. Holograph, pencil on wove paper watermarked "Imperial Strong IIII," 1 leaf.

4B What's poetry?

20 lines excerpted from an early typescript of 71 lines. 1 leaf. Purple ribbon on legal-size wove paper (cf. Ur1 and 5B). A version of this text precedes the MS Ur1 text in the earlier typescript of 1915 (see description of MS Ur1).

5B Nam Sygebryht his rices, on Westsaexna wiotan,

22 lines excerpted from an early typescript of 41 lines on 2 leaves. Purple ribbon on legal-size wove paper (cf. Ur1 and 4B). This fragment may be contemporary with a letter to Milton Bronner dated September 24, 1915, in which Pound writes: "There are

two people who are dying for me to do an epic of AngloSaxon times" (University of Texas Library).

FN   wind kind of poem by So-Gioku

47 lines on sixteen double pages of one of Ernest Fenollosa's notebooks (file 17, Fenollosa Papers, Pound Archive). Professor Mori's calligraphy and Fenollosa's holograph transliteration, translation, and commentary, with "30" in Pound's hand in blue pencil at upper right of first double page. Jiajun Jiang, who transcribed the Chinese, points out that "ko" in line 45 is an error for the character "sho" (as in line 34) and that the "tan" character in line 12 is erroneously written.

Manuscript Not Consulted

A manuscript for Canto IV belonging to Omar Pound was exhibited at the Sheffield University Library, Sheffield, England, from April 23 to May 13, 1976. The catalogue, entitled *Ezra Pound: The London Years*, describes it thus:

(2) Manuscript draft of part of Canto IV.

By comparing the manuscript with the printed version one can notice the changes, usually in the form of further condensation and economy of phrase, that EP made before reading his final version. Study of the manuscript also seems to suggest that he thought and composed in short phrases—these are usually marked off at the end of or between lines by a double dash. These short phrases thus separated in the manuscript are sometimes linked together to form a longer line in the final version.

(3) Further pages of the manuscript draft. These deal with Vidal, Actaeon, the nymphs bathing in water, and the church roof in Poitiers. All the manuscript material we have hence relates to Provence.

Philip Grover, who organized the exhibit, described the manuscript thus in response to my query:

[I]t is holograph and in heavy pencil. It covers, approximately, the lines "And by the curved, carved foot . . ." to "pool . . . pool of Salmacis." There are a number of variants. . . .

Omar Pound could not make the manuscript available for this study but added that it is written on thick scraps of paper and that it was given to him by a family friend in the early 1950s.

Proof, Setting Copy, and Editions, 1919–25

A list of the texts which document the history of Canto IV from Pound's completion of MS E in September 1919 through the 1925 edition follows. This list is based largely on Donald Gallup's indispensable *Ezra Pound : A Bibliography*, to which I refer the reader for complete descriptions of the published texts. In this list, the siglum that I have assigned the text appears at left; the title, place, and date of publication, and the number assigned the text in the *Bibliography* appear on the right, followed by any additional information relevant to the history of the text.

P
: Page proofs for 019a, with author's corrections and additions in ink and proofreader's corrections in pencil. Four pages glued onto a folded sheet of heavy gray account paper.

019a
: THE FOURTH CANTO. (London: privately printed by John Rodker at the Ovid Press, October 4, 1919). A16a (First state).

019b
: THE FOURTH CANTO. (London: privately printed by John Rodker at the Ovid Press, October 4, 1919). A16b (Second state, with substantive changes in 4 lines, 5 changes in spacing, and 11 changes in punctuation).

ScDial
: Rough proof of THE FOURTH CANTO with author's corrections in ink, sent to the *Dial* as setting copy for D20; on deposit in the Beinecke Library at Yale University. On the blank first page, Pound has written, "Canto IV by Ezra Pound/forty copies *privately* printed for author's convenience NOT published." The printed text is that of 019a with a comma added after line 101. Three of the four substantive changes made on 019b are inserted in the text by the author. In addition, six alterations in spacing and a regularizing of elision dots are marked in pencil, apparently by a *Dial* editor.

D20
: THE FOURTH CANTO. *Dial* 68 (June 1920): [689]–692. C579.

P21
: THE FOURTH CANTO in *Poems 1918–21* (New York: Boni and Liveright, December 8, 1921). A21.

ScXVI
: IV in setting copy for 1925, dated January 6, 1924. Author's typescript, 6 pages numbered blank, 2, 3, blank, 5, 6, in improvised binding with other cantos. Purple ribbon on wove paper with revisions in ink and pencil by author and editor.

TM25
: THE FOURTH CANTO in *A Draft of XVI. Cantos* (Paris: Three Mountains Press, late January 1925). A26.

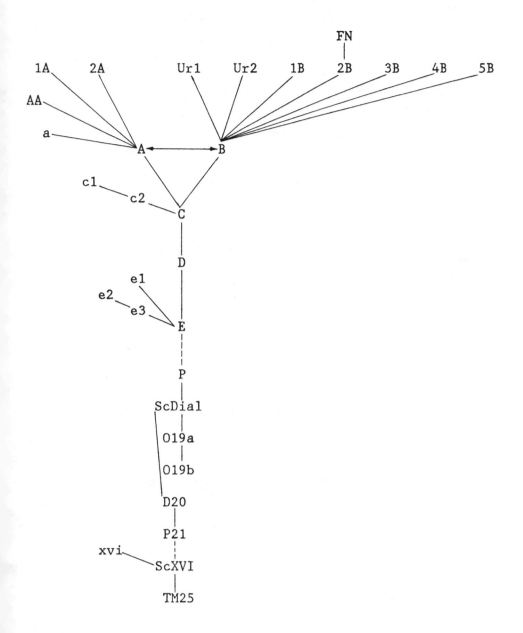

Figure 1. Stemma for Canto IV: Schematic representation of the relationships among the texts of Canto IV from 1915 to 1925. Broken lines indicate indirect or uncertain descent.

PRELIMINARY MANUSCRIPTS, 1915–18

MS Ur1

IV.

But whats all this to us? The modern world . . . . !"

Here is your modern world, ⌊and I'm no Stendhal⌋ :
     in the   *near*
"Napoleon lands from Elba, north <upon Lake> Come

<And ignorant boy sets out ... how wild the fire ran,>
    starts
5 Fabrice, falls upon Waterloo, <(Chartreuse de Parme,   (1)
the first eleven chapters.)>
                      Then there's the Parma court,
stupidities.

A dinner table, up our Campden Hill, five men,   (2)

10 Five women, a bullet-headed fellow

               (wrote me from Liverpool five years ago
                    sole
, to find fault with phrase in my [best] Ballad,)

This comes out in the talk, he fidgits in his kakhi,

is spurred up and begins:
            Well when I got to
15   <Begin in> Posen, <I know>   (3)
        <that I escaped,>

<Cant tell it all, unless from the begining,>

    better a poem than story, mostly feeling,

Posen resists kultur, millions like water

20   poured out to make them German,

Poles have their cafes, germans still have theirs,

The place a fortress, people <u>will</u> talk polish,

Children beaten in school, but <u>will</u> talk polish,

The place a fortress.

25   <Oh,<u>I</u>> sopped up kultur,

   I <u>liked</u> it, I <u>liked</u> germans. Got <moved up a peg>

Lines 77-81: cf. B.93, IV.111-12.

                              went through
          Moved on to Jena, \<took> the doctorate,

                              Oh well that's all over.
                                        a visit.
          When the show began,? In Hungary, \<stopped with>

30   a puplis' people,

          Couldn't think <u>we</u>'d come in.

                         Family', boys' mother and some other
                                children,

          Excited by war, the "russian invasion",

                    I ran the estate,

          - - - - -

35   \<The atmosphere, slow, change, I liked the>
                         \<german people,>

          Then one morning   "

                              "I wish you'd go." pause,
          The
           Embarassed mother "The Children, ... we like you"

          \<"Your'e different>, They'll get a wrong impression

40   of englishmen"

          We two alone at breakfast, talking it out.

                         hungarian
          A neighbor,\<ing> count, said he would take me and keep me,

          She wouldn't have it. told me to stay a while,

          And I stayed on and on.

45   and then one midnight,

          Packed up and went.

                         Oh? atmosphere.
                                   rat-run prison
          Arrested in Salzburg, put in a \<ratty dungeon,>

          fished out, decently treated, half trusted,

50 Oh I was *a* pro German, told 'em I was. I was,
                                                        we
            god damn it all, <I> couldn't see how could fight.
                                                    ∧
      I'd nothing but german versions.

                Got loose, got my head cropped,

      I can look fairly german, Connivance, I think,

55 I think they let me go,

      Wandered about, hiding, begging my food from peasants,

      Finally got to the Swiss border, our consul at X
      a   *a note*
      (german) gave me £5./ hoped I would mention him

            here, when war was over.

60 The Exglishman at Y. [gave m] sniffy and cold,

                until I mentioned Cambridge,
                                he forked up 2 quid--
                        then <I got £2 from him.>

            <Then in> the train. small boy, waving a flag,

            , tea basket, mother, anglo-indian, col's wife.

            - - - - -

                    it 'twas
65 All in a heap<;> England. Just England. I dont know.
            to the kid,   *I've been in*
      I said <"Boy. [I've just] Just out of> a german prison.

      "Mummy, <here's a> man just from a german prison,

      <Then she> took charge of me. \ <Still I'd> no thought of

                        enlisting, \ *talked all the way to Paris*
                        then.
70 And all the time in Paris I had no thought of <enlisting,>
      Got to   *it.*
      <and> ⟨half-an hour after⟩ <I left> [the] Victoria,

                    ⟨ I <was> joined up, <and did> six months in
                                        Flanders,

      The train that did it. The people no longer hostile.
      But   *I didn't think about,*
      <But> still <no thought of enlisting.> I dont know.

75 Six months at the front, now in the the information,

              The modern world:

    Sen-sei Pere Henri Jacques *(ex-jesuit father)*

        Talks with the sennin near the summit of Rok-ko,

    <Who will follow all the ex-jesuit fathers.>

80 <I know [the] a man who has seen Jacques' hermitage,>

          <talked with this modern frenchman.>

    The ?gracile ?Banker of Japan-- cheap theatre--xalxx-dramatist.
        told me about him   Kalimohon

    withstood the idols of his native village,

    Wouldn't bow to high-priest who'd spoiled a poor man's
                                    marriage,

85 You'd dig this up, talking with orientals,

        Plain, manufactured, "well-taught" orientals,

    talking of Emerson and Hoffmansthal

                Cezanne and Neitzche.

    And women's quarters, with ancient ceremonies,

90 Suburrian suburburbs with long courtesies.,

    Day's of long waiting, stately [and] tacit receptions,

    One day to gaze, another to speak words,

              courtship of sorts, deliberate ceremony.

    "Going at last, Japan turns european.

95   Beef bones at brahmin's doors, that's scarilege.

    Ghose's saw the young bucks do it in his village.

    - - - - -

    So the world wakes and turns.
                      art's but
          <And [art's]> integrity
              <art's>

Margin annotations:

Loyalty is
hard to
explain.

Thus (4)
saith
Rihaku

(5)

(6)

dinar
=

(6)

29

_____IV_____

'What do I mean by all this clattering rumble?'

Bewildered reader, what is the poet's business?

To fill up chaos, populate solitudes, multiply images

Or streak the barren way to paradise

5   <(Here was the renaissance)>
                              up
To Band out fine colours, fill the void with stars

And make each star a nest of noble voices.

Let <the> undines hear me, and in cool streams   *faut un*
                                                      bois aux   (7)
Redeck the muses' gardens, green herbs and cress   *rossignols*

10   And water-drinking flowers ....

[Rumble again?   'What are the muses' gardens?']

Oh, take a heaven you know, and make the starry wood

Sound like a grove well filled with nightingales,

And call lights 'souls',

15   And say: The lights ascending ... like a covey of partridges.

Thus much I saw above me, and beneath, looking into the water,

Beheld the turret as a pillar of fire reflected,

And thence to God,

To the ineffable, trashumanar non si potria per verba.   (8)

20   The soul starts with itself, builds out perfection,

Confucius, Dante.

                    Or the best man killed in France,   (9)

Struck by a Prussian bullet at St Vaast

_____

Line 9: cf. B.58.

With just enough cut stone left here behind him

- - - - -

                                                                30

25   To show a new way to the kindred arts,

     Laying a method, quite outsdie his art,

     Vortex, dispersal, throw it at history.

     <Say that the prose is life, scooped out of time,>

     <A bristling node ... and I am all too plain,>

30   Too full of footnotes, too careful to tell you

     The how and why of my meaning   "here was the renaissance,

     Venus intaglio'd in the papal gem.]]

     Lewis with simpler means   (10)

     Catches the age, his Timon,

35   Throws our few years onto a score of pasteboards,

     Says all our conflict, edgey, epigrammatic,

     This Timon lived in Greece, and loved the people,

     And gave high feasts, and dug his rabbit barrow.

     "And Ka-hu churned in the sea,   (11)

40   [Churning the ocean,] using the [sun] for a churn-stick.
                                         moon

MS AA

Stumbling, stumbling along

  muttering, muttering Ovid--

Ity & Polignat et ter flebiliter--   (12)

  flebiliter. Ityn--

5 *& and she went to the window*

   & cast her down--

     Gaubertz upon the round--   (13)

       at Poicebot--

   ?monked in his own ?despite--

10   *enfes--*   (14)

   - - - - -

   past in an ?image

   war<s>--

   Dalfin for Priam   (15)

     & an <wa>

15 *<was> no walls*

   Torn down--

   ———————————

   "She stood <of>   (16)

     above them

       all"

   ———————————

   ——————

Lines 1-10: cf. A.56-60, 67, 94; 11-16: cf. A.157-70, B.102-04; 17-19:
cf. A.70; 20-75: cf. A.71-83, 92-111; 78: cf. A.78, 85, 88, 89, 91.
Lines 1-2: cf. IV. 64-65; 3-6: cf. IV.17-18; 20-25: cf. IV.21-23, 113.

20 *The Lord of Polhonac*   (12)

   killed Cabestang in

     the hunt--

cooked up his vitales--

  served the stuff

25   *in a pie--*

- - - - -

his neighbors hang'd him--

Vidal--ran mad--Gaubertz, returning,   (13)

found-- <_____> his girl in a <pub> pub--

They ?came--there's a woman--

30   *will serve you with all you want--*

The second turning--close to the wall--

  an old bitch guarding the entry-- --

"è trobet ella"   (17)

   Mauleon-- gifts--   (18)

35 *his first youth, his*

   first harness--

put off the monk's hood

- - - - -

felt the air upon him--

  --drawn on the teeth--

40 *mid-spring--the night*

  all full of <women's> women--

clinging unseen--putting soft

   hands upon him--

- - - - -

```
        & the high clear head--

45          Quel giorno piu non vi leggemo avante,                   (19)

        era enfes--child of a castelan,                     (14) (20)

        in S. Leonart--made monk &

      learned to sing--

                      Broke vows--

50 sang through the courts--

            <& she refused him-->

      <Savairic made him knight-->                              (18)

              <she not>

              <she took him then-->

55    & she refused him--

      Savairic made him knight--                                (18)
               _____

            runs to this ending--

      - - - - -

      "era enfens"                                            (14)

      child of a catelan                                       (20)

60        <in San Leonart   made monk-->

      <& learned to sing>

      Took her to wife--

            e tenc en gran honor--                            (20)

                  (& left for Spain)

65                        but why--

      <Then ?England>

      & a chevallier--of England--

            <la> tenc la long temps                           (20)

                  per druda ]
```

70 *e pois la laisset malamen anar]*

        --

    Thus Gaubertz found her (13)

\- - - - -

a child--found out--

"and he returned from Spain"--

Remi nepotes-- (21)

      ————————

75 *& Cadmus of golden prows--*

  no ?time for Helen-- (22)

     not (*?alm_____*) *plot--*

to cheat the fates, & Mars

     of his due spoils--

80 *Austors & castle &*

    Piere took the singing-- (23)

made the new local

    Troy--

And she said: The swallows are

crying <u>Ityn</u>.

Procne. Procne.   (24)

And he said--<How is the dish?]>

5   *How do you like <the flavour>*

the meat I have set before you

And she said--it pleases me--

<and she-->
10   *and he said-- Cabesteyn's*

heart might taste

so--

& looked up

it was true

15   *and she--*

so well have

I liked the flavour of

- - - - -

this food   that I will

not spoil it with other:

20   *and walked by him to*

the high tower window

& cast her down.

Cf. A.11-20, IV.16-32.

MS A

IV

<Rise, O thou smoky palace<.>,>

   <"Troy<'s> but a heap of smouldering boundry stones">

<Rise, O thou smoky palace!>

   Silver mirrours catch the bright stones and flame,
        <in the> *?cloud palace*
5 Dawn to our waking, / drifts in the green cool light,

  Light foot <with> the /goat-foot alternate,
  [And there]
  The
  [Dew haze] Dew haze blurrs) [round the ankles]
             [round, their ankles in the grass,]
<<in> the grass, pale ankles moving.   *sunk in the <h> maze of dew* --

10   A black cock crows in the sea-foam. (<Cytherean!>   (25)

       . . . .

  <Itys and Polhonac>:   *Ityn*
                       <Ityn>
        <Flebiliter,> et ter flebiliter [Ityn],

  "And she went toward the window, and cast her down."

  "And she went toward the window ... the swallows crying ...

15   "How like you the dish" he said,

  And she "None better.",
&   is   *dish"*
He said:"It [was] Cabestan's heart [you have] in the <flavour>."
       its suits my   *ste*
& *said* "So well, my taste, that I will ta<ke> of none other"

   <Will spoil that taste with none other,>"

20   <Walked past him and cast her> down.
     & walked to the high arched window & cast

        [Actaeon, Vidal.]   *her down.*
     <Ityn, et ter flebilier, Ityn,>

       the swallows
       crying on high ⑩

- - - - -

Line 6: cf. 1A.4,8; 56-60, 67. 94: cf. AA.1-10; 70: cf. AA.17-19; 71-83,
92-111: cf. AA.20-75; 78, 85, 88, 89, 91: cf. AA.78; 113-26: cf. frag. 2A;
157-70: cf. AA.11-16.

the swallows   Vidal goes
crying an   to south
?orison   <of the>

25 <Itys and Polhonac, Acteon, Vidal>:

<*in*>"A valley thick with trees,

  "With trees, the sunlight,

  "glitters atop, glitters, glitters atop

  like a fish-scale roof

30 like the church roof [at] in Poictiers ⟨...⟩ if it were gold

  And beneath it, beneath it, not a ray, not a sliver,

  not a spare coin of sunlight,

  not a spot on the black, soft water,

  Goddess Diana! ... lucida sidera,   (26)

35 Bathing, the body of nymphs

  gathered around her, air shaking,

  air alight with the goddess, fanning their hair in the dark,

  lifting and waffing

  Pholoe, Niceas, leap in the pool of Diana,   (27)

40 Ivory dipping in silver,

  Shadowed, o'er shadowed, ivory dipping in silver,

  Not a splotch, not a bubble of sunlight,

  Hither, hither, Acteon!

  And the pale hair of the Goddess,"----

45 Vidal, Vidal, it is Vidal speaking, Old Vidal,
  Old groggy Vidal
  Stumbling along through the wood,

  Not a patch, not a shimmer of sunlight,

  The dogs, dogs, leap on Acteon,

50 Spotted stag in the wood,

  The dogs leap on Acteon.

  - - - - -

Gold, gold, and a sheaf of hair, thick like the

        wheat swath

blaze, blaze in the sun.

55   The dogs leap on Acteon.

<Gaubertz come home from Spain,>   (13)

       <desire of women,>

<L'Engles had left her there,>   (28)

   Stumbling, stumbling along
60   *muttering, muttering Ovid--*
  <Pool of>   *<Pool> <Pool of> Salmacis*
          <Sh>
      <Seek of> out the pool--
    <Procne & Tereus,!>   (24)
    Pergusa. --
65   *Pool of Gargaphia--*
        Seek out Salmacis' pool.

- - - - -

    Stumbling, stumbling along, muttering, muttering Ovid:

"Pergusa, Pool of Gargaphia"

    seeking Salmacis' pool.

70 "She stood [out] above them all."   (16)

       "The pines of Takasago grow with the Pines
                     of Isé"
<The Lord of Polhonac killed Cabestang in the hunt,>   (12)

    <Cooked up his vitals, served up the stuff in a pie.>

<His neighbors hanged him.>

<Vidal ran mad,> Gaubertz returning   (13)
    (&)
75 Found his girl in a pub. They said "there's a woman,

Will serve you with all you want. The second turning

Close to the wall. An old bitch guarding the entry.

E trobet ella.   (17) (21)

<*(Remi>*   (18)
Mauleon's gifts, His first youth,

80   first harness, put off the monks hood,

felt the air upon him, drawn on the teeth,

mid spring, the night all full of women,

Clinging unseen, putting soft hands upon him.

[Gripping him in the]
                                "Remi nepotes"   (21)
85   [Unheeding Azalais.]   (29)

                 Crushed all together--bursting the ring of
                                              fire--

                 ————

                 jagged blue-lights--
                                "Remi nepotes"   (21)

- - - - -

                                "Remi nepotes"   (21)

90   Crushed all together, bursting the ring of fire,

Jagged blue lights! "Remi nepotes."   (21)

And the high, clear head.

               "Quel giorno piu non vi leggemo avanti"   (19)

Era enfes.   (14)

95   Child of a castelan,   (20)

In Sain Leonart made monk, and learned to sing,

Broke vows, sang then through courts

          walking the turning ways, roads by the rivers,

by the squared out fields,

100   hedge where a slut combs out her beggars lice,

sits in mid field with her legs V's apart,

      Talks with doddering men about about the inns,

Gathers the the gabble, meets with Savairic,   (18)

   The girl refused him, Savaric gives him clothes,

105 Horese and knighthood, and he takes the girl,

     holds her in honour,

                         but goes off to Spain.

     [Tert] Third what, an English rider, us cavaliers Engles,   (28)

     supplies his functions, tenc la lonc temps per druda,   (20)

110 e pois laisset la malamen anar,

                         Till Gaubertz found her.   (13)

                             (in angiportis)   (21)

     But Aurunculeia

     - - - - -

     Glare through the Roman streets, black shadows lap the
                                         facade,
                        slop
115 The long-locked cressets <glare> on a cook-stall,*'s flicker*--
                        as
     <& We pass> Cr<oe>sus' corner.   (30)

                 (Fire-insurance, 60 to 80 slaves)

         O Hymenaeus! Io, Io, Io, Hymenaeus.

     Saffron, the yellow shoe, O Hymenaeus,

120   Lips like the poppy-leaf, O Hymenaues,

     Manlius takes a wife, O Hymenaeus.   (31)

             Look to the door-step,

                         Carmina tinula,

     sing out with reedy voice, O Hymenaeus,

125 Blue agate casing the sky, sputter the resin,

             Parthian white the stone, Aurunculeia,

     Aimar of Roussac could not pay his rent,   (32)

             Bariols, lost dicing, and died south in Spain,

     and all he gained, whent with dice and women,

130   Roussac plays viel, is no more a knight,

        - - - - -

                        in angiportis,   (21)
        But Aurunculeia.

                        ─────

        Cadmus of golden prows. Again Auvergnat.   (15)
        The Dalfin holds against the Church and all,
135   De Maensac keeps the girl.
                                "Paris to judgement!"   (33)
        Menelaus howls.
                        ///
        Fought with a man of stone, and stfling him,
        Empty the armour,
140   only downy cygnet, grey [dust-brown]

        fluff half turning feather, flacks loose,
                and up, lights upon Neptune's heave,   (33)
                        streaks in the swirling water,
                        cirlcing with foam trails, spotted and
145   white ringed water.

                        //
        has   & his tabletalk--
        Nestor <babbles of> Centaurs, <and's of the> beauty of Cyllarus   (34)

        [a tawny bird oaring the liquid air ....]

        Sea-beacons from isle to isle pass on Troy's fire   (35)
                And the news of Troy,
150   <And> sea-grils cry to <stom->wracked Odysseus
                    "We know the tale of thy deeds,
                     We know thou art Odysseus
                     Bringer of arrows,
                Stealer of Pallas' idol, bearing the shield of Achilles   (36)

155   Who knows thy tale as we know it,
        Who shall sing with our voices.

        ?cross.waves
             on ?wat.

        - - - - -

        It is worth a cast of the dice, said young DeMaensac,   (23)

        If you win I shall keep the house,

        We shall neither botch at two trades,

160   Let one of us take the singing,

Let one of us fatten himself, keep bounds to pig styes,

  Settle the tenants brawls, aforest land,

Rear up the trees for lisses, squabble at boundry stones;   (37)

One keep a fiddle in tune,

165   "The castle to Austors, and Pieire kept the   (23)
                        singing"

And Tyndarus plotted to keep off war, strove with   (38)

       spinning women,
                 Harks to [Odysseus]. Laertes' son,   (38)
[crafty in handling suitors, planned an allegiane.]

170   "Of all who sue, swear to obey the victor".

- - - - -

Nymphs wail their drying wells, by gateless Thebes,

goats lick the parched rock,

Procris is dead, Pan mourns and his great hound,

Scylla boasting her conquests,   (39)

175 Cyclops rakes his hair and slicks it down,

and hacks with a pruning-knife against his beard,

More white than primrose leaf, more bright than glass,

more clear than ice, Galatea,

Smoother than sea-worn shells, and hard,

180 deaf deaf as the wind, Galatea,

Lift thee from Acis lap.

        Sybil scorner of Apollo.

       Nec amata videbor, nec placuisse deo Apollo,   (39)

      Sed iam felicior aetas terga dedit,

185   venit aegra senectus,   (39)

        vocem mihi fata relinquent.

    Circe's seanymphs, sorting their Lethey flowers.

    A face to lure the nymphs from Latian hills,

                    Picus and Venilia,
190   singing Venilia,

                Picus and the shadowy boar, falleth in   (39)

        Circe's net.

        What surned woman can, and she be Circe,
                    Circe Titania,

Canto IV.

<Rise, O thou smoky palace, Ἀναξιφόρμιϩϩεs!>

<Troy's but a heap of smouldering boundry stones,>

<The> silver mirrours catch the bright stones and flare,

Dawn, to our waking, drifts in the green cool light,
   The
5 <The> dew-haze blurrs, in the grass, pale ankles moving.

The black cock crows in the sea foam.

       "Ityn, et ter flebiliter, Ityn, Ityn,"

And she went toward the went toward the window,

        ----   the swallows crying   ---

10 "It is Cabestan's heart in the dish."

"I thought as much."

     and she went toward the window in Polhonac,

And held to the [cetrla] slim white stone-bar

Breaking the window arch,

15 And the wind out of the hills by Rhodez

      caught the turn of her sleeve,

        --- the swallows crying ---

Ityn! Acteon:
              [with trees]
The valley is thick with trees, [the sunlight]
20   with trees, the sunlight<,>

Lines 39-49: cf. frag. 1B; 49-57: cf. frag. 2A; 58: cf. Ur2.9; 59-71:
cf. frag. 2B, MS FN; 75-76: cf. frag. 3B.6-7; 82-88: cf. frag. 4B.4-16;
89-92: cf. frag. 5B; 93: cf. Ur1.77-81.

glitters, glitters atop,

[leaves] like the fish-scale roof,

Like the church roof in Poictiers .... if it were gold,

And beneath it, beneath it, not a ray, not a sliver
                                            <of sunlight>
25   , not a spare coin of sun<light>,

not a spot on the black soft water.

- - - - -

Bathing, the body of nymphs,

gathered around her, air shaking,

air alight with the goddess, lifting, and waffing

30   wind, the air alight with the goddess,

Ivory dipping in silver.

Vidal, stumbling along through the wood.

The dogs, leap on Actaeon.

Gold, gold, hair-sheaf thick like a wheat-sheaf,

35   The dogs leap on Actaeon. . Salmacis comes to the pool.

The cygnet moves in the empty clattering armour. *Stones*
                                                    can feel
"We know the tale of they deeds," Odysseus.   *no blows*
                                                  <The>
Odysseum bringer of arrows."

And thus? And thus.

40 For so the light rains and pours,

The liquid and rushing crystal,

        whirling the bright brown sand,

xxxxxx Air, fire, the pale soft light,
                         and
Artemis, Rose of Cnydus, the red rust of Mars,   (40)

45 Topaz I manage, and three sorts of blues,

The orange banners, sparks whirl in the saffron gold,

                    /// The scared beasts huddle

crouching beneath cold rain, ///

Caelestis intus .. blue agate casing the sky,   (41)

50 Truth's in the lot. So true Aurunculeia.

- - - - -

The saffron sandal gleams on the slender foot,

"Tiller of Helicon, Urania's sons".   (42)

Bring out the flamy cloak, bright amaracus,

The boys run crowing the song, O papaver,

55 luteum, [red leaf of petal gleam in the marble]

[sun], the cressets gleam, flare on the corner's

                    cook-stall,

Light melts in the clash of light,

            green   muses
                cress for the <water>-garden<s>,

                                                            Ranti
                                        upon the palace of
    The pine-wind moves <blows across> [So-gioku's garden,]
<cross-wind> Ranti
60 And [So-gioku] opened his collar,

            "This much I can share with the people"

    "The birds nest in the lemon-tree, so this wind

    "nests in the palace,"

                        So-gioku answered,<">

65 "This is wind for the king<">."

                    "This wind roars in the earth's bag,

it lays the water with rushes."

"This wind is here for the king,

"it shakes the imperial water-jets".
                       her
70   "Let every cow keep<er> calf,"

"This wind is held in gauze curtains."

- - - - -

So on the gilded tower in Ecbatan,

    Danae! Danae!

The camel-drivers gabble about the stairs,

75 [The smoke hangs on the laquer]

<The smoke hangs on the stream, the peach-trees>

   <shed leaves in the water,>

<Past, past the hundered fords, the slow barge,>

<loiters, the thousand peach-trees shed their flakes>   (43)

80 <into the stream, out of a former time,>
       <Heard the>
    <[The duke heard] dynastic music">   (44)

         <Blue-black of Venice,>

<that night, the Loredan, gilt rafters [glare]>   (45)

<lighted in the first floor rooms,>

85   <Go down from Angouleme,>   (46)

<three steps in an open field, grey stone, no yard>

       <behind them,>

<posts for the vanished gate,>

          <in Spain the poppies swim in the air of glass.>

Cynewulf drove Sigebriht into the Kentish weald,   (47)

90 And Cyneheard caught him,, faught long about the gate,

all killed save one, no terms,

Cyneheard then slaughterd.

- - - - -

Pere Henri Jacques, talks with the sennin on the summit of Rok-ku,

Acteon hunted with dogs and can not call their names,

95 Dumb stag, torn down,

                        and Vidal dumb

Clenching a stubborn mouth, fled from the dogs

For Loba.   (48)

            And Procne, flittering   (24)

100 Cries a crime, like crime in Polhonac,.   (12)

The Dauphin wars, and Paris for like cause   (15)

Like cause De Maensac. "Though the church's men

fought round the Dalfin's walls:

                        with unlike end.

105 Poor knight of Alverne, was Pierre de Maensac,   (23)

Austors his brother, one castle, with place for one,

[Toss coin for luck]

One viol, maybe, song enough for one,

Set on the toss of a crown-piece, Austor's the castle,<()>

110 [Maensac, and the song] Maensac, not the song,

[En Bernart de Tierci,   golden Menelaus,]   (15)

                    [of Atreus house,]   (49)

            [line of Atreus,]

                [had Leda] mated with Leda's fledgling,   (50)
115 The lord of Tierci,

Cries out and raises the host like Menelaus,

"Longa saison ai estat vas amor"   (51)

So sang de Maensac, lackland,   (23)

- - - - -

Venus nec iners, the new Phrygian judge,   (52)

120 Flame hung on the viol strings, nec torpet lingua,

   S   *A*
  suasit mater amoris, ││....   cytherea thalamo,

out from the curtained room,

                           [(Tierci, or Tyndarus,]
       L
      lady of Tierci, daughter of Tyndarus,

125   Auvergnat shakes, ab lo gran guerra que fan,   (15)

Auvergant holds despite the church and war ....

"Glitters, glitters a-top,
 L
"like the church roof in Poictiers ...

                    glitters against the ray,
           <? band ?before>
130 <"Niceas,> Diana's <nymph,> dip<s> in the silver pool,"   (27)

Vidal, Vidal, stumbling along through the wood,

Mutters, mutters, "Dogs leap on Actaeon,
S
spotted stag in the wood,"

Or pierce the cosmos,

           you've a dozen visions,

Of spear heads interlaced, a shower of embers,

or fauns and nymphs, swift in alternate dancing,

5   keeping the one same tread, the one quick measure,

Pink, in a place of trees, sweet trees with

       blossomy branches,

The goat-foot and the light foot alternate.

Or Nike springs from her sphere.

                soft ?green, &
                          bright--   (53)
                <A> <the> <?lamf-->
                      *the lanes_*

10   Your microcosmos?

       ?knowledge--   *the inner zodiac--?*   (54)

           Freud-   *psyco-analysis--*

       Well- then.
               The data:

Lines 4, 8: cf. A.6, IV.7-10.

All from the genii's bottles, all this talk,

Great heads bear up the carpet, heeling along,

we float out of the lecture rooms, over the city,

truth's in the lot?

5   You think so, pass along,

        the
Smoke from high brick chimneys, stream puffs, mingling

          and rising,

     blue agate casing the sky, blurred smoke,

              soft patterns,

10 truth's in the lot,

          "so true this speculation,"

                 the
     Or true, Aurunculeia". Which is truth,

The saffron sandal gleams on the slender foot,

       Hymen, Hymenaeus,

15 Tiller of the Heliconian hill, Unrania's son,   (42)

       Hymen, Hymenaeus,

Take up the flamey cloak, bring amaracus,   (42)

See where the boys run, crowding, lifting the song,

    "Venus moved so, before the Phrygian judge"   (52)
        upon the
20 Drayad moved so <among the> sylvan dew,   (55)

            Hymen, Hymenaues,

Mind there!, the threshold<s>,!

       Careful!   Hymenaues,

- - - - -

Cf. A.113-26, B.49-57, frag. e1, IV.82-88.

Parthenian marble, the one poppy leaf,

25   flares out its read [and] against the sparkling grain

, flower on stone, ah, so red gleams her mouth,

        Hymen, Hymen Hymenaues,

thus   (31)
Manlius takes [her his] a wife,
                  bear
      sing out you boys, [take] up the toarches,
      their
30 shaking [the] flame[s],
                            e
           cressets (long-locked), glar<ing> through
the
Roman stretets, black shadows) <licking the>
                     the long-locked cressets--
                          cook-stalls,
        facade
   lap<ping> the <palace front>, Croessus' that corner,

Here now is Caesar's stair, [t]
                        glare on the
35   taken the girl home,
                         ?sestare
               Hymenaeus,
      Io, io, io, Hymen Hymenaeus,

Sing out with reedy voice,
                       We pass
           Hymenaeus,
                     Crassus'   (30)
40 down the far strret, fainter the voices passing,
                     corner--
      Hymen hymenaeus,

Fainter the resined toarch, Hymeneaues,   --

                       (Fire insurance

Et ominis intellectus omniformis ....   (56)

        60 or 80 slaves--)

- - - - -

```
                          . . .

             Iamblichus light,                          (57)

    say does it fall, or pour,?

                 the crystal fluid

    <That> spouts up through the mind,

5                    whirling its bright brown sand

    How does it live.  How does it spurt and start.?


    Like air that thrust in through the fishes tank

                 to keep them lively?



    Your omniformis omnis intellectus?                  (56)


                    ///////////////

10                        Say I bulid out the spheres

    I've but half seen.

                    Air, fire, the pale

                        soft light.

    <of> Artemis, <the> rose of Cnydus,                 (40)

15                        and the rust red Mars,

    (that I dont see at all,

                    Topaz I manage,

    and three sorts of blues,

    - - - - -
                                            4.
    And filled the whole with stars and images,

20  with orange banners, with transparent forms,
```

Cf. B.39-49. Lines 3-5: cf. IV.69-81.

(borrowed, half borrowed, for Old Agnolo   (58)

shouted that passage at me seven times,

spat on the marble, "Pape! spurcu 'iu!!   (58)

Cant the fools <u>see</u> They take your lattin messes.)

25 His better or his equal ......"

                              you have heard him.

"There is <u>your</u> field,"

                        [It is neither in paint nor casting. .]

                            Nile North you say?

                    ////////

30 That was the way I saw it.

                        I can see fire,
                            the
Weave, with its points, <and> line, gold, saffron, yellow,

, red like burnt points of stick.

                    and [fr] gracile figures,

35 stiff, placid, air-light lepidoptera,

gracious in form, not god-like,

            persisting in wind, not blown,

but frail,, unvigorous, seeming at loss for will.

                take
Where does it get one?
                lead

- - - - -
                                                        5
            //////// 3.

40   Not like scared beasts

Crowching beneath the rain, dark night, wind

wallowing in the trees, leaves, drops thgether,

swishing, articulate, talking their frightening talk,

You have cut down your fears?

/////// 4.

45   But jungles, horrors?

You see these also.

                              ? Vyasa--   (59)
                                   then
                                   sax.

                         . . .

- - - - -

                                                        6

                    //////// 3

Genii, and giants?

                    ///// I have ridden the carpet.

I can not the least explain. Yet these things happen.

50 Not that my corpus moved. Unreasoning feeling.

What?

     Four huge headed figures, one to a corner,

Ugly, I think you'd say, benevolent.

               Gnomes are small luck,

55 trouvailles. you find nine maravedis.

                    [think fortune's], finding is pleasure.

Dear fellow, try.

          Think your're at peace with Nature.

          //////////// 3

That's what you mean with your caelestis intus?   (41)

                    . . .

Fragment 2B

Wind-poem for Canto IV

"Is there an end to debates,? So Gioku

  painted his poem [to] of the wind

"so-jo-O
went to the palace of Ranti,

5 And I, So Gioku and Keisa went with him,

  and the pine-wind came bearing upon us

  Then the King looked [on] into the wind, oppened his collar,

  Said "This at least I can share with the people"

  To whom So-gioku,

10   No sire, this is the great king's
                        wind,

  The pople don't share it,
                          hold it
  And the King "Nonsense, I can not \<shut it up> in a
                    sack,
  So-gioku tai etsu   (60)

      "sire we have the tradition

15 Small holes in the lemon-tree's trunk

      are a fine place for nesting, and by the same
              token,

An⌐cave⌐\<that> hollow⌐ makes winds,"
                        the
  That is Liu Che, \<its> old nonsense, but \<our>   :   (60)
                sophists,
                      what it \<strik>
  \<Say that>: wind changes according to \<that which it>
                     \<blows on>,"   *blows on*
           its nature--

- - - - -

Cf. MS FN, B.59-71, IV.89-99.

20 And the king

                "every cow has its calf,

    The wind <belongs to the fellow> who made it"
                      is his   *rather,*

                                    '*s*
    Yes your high ness, <the> wind <comes up> from the earth.

            <where> green water and rushes <are> mingled,
                                            set up the wind--
25 Doubtless it drifts up the valleys,

            it roars in the earth's bag,

        <It> flames and shakes in the mountains,

        [and shakes out the]

   & <It> strikes through <the> water-jets,
        But   *here, sifted among*
30 <Also> when it comes <through the> gauze curtains,
                              it's   *wind*
            Then <it beomes the wind of the> palace', <*way*>
        <your wind Sire."*>
        You own the palace--

                An argument's not to convince.

Fragment 3B

When you find that feminine contact

  has no longer the richness

  of Omakitsu's verses,   (43) (44)

Know then, o man,

5   *that the Cytherean has turned from you,*   (25)

      <fugges!>   (61)

When the smoke no longer
      hangs
<clings> upon the laquer,

When the night air no

10   *longer clings*

               to your cuticle,

When the air has in it no

        mystery about her,

- - - - -

Know then that the days

15   *of your adolence are*   (62)

               ended

    fugaces, fugges, fugus   (61)

———————

Cf. B.75-76.

What's poetry?

   There is a castle set,

The Auvezere, or its Dordoigne, chalk white and whiteish blue, (63)

Or Goldring writes "That night, the Loredan"   (64)

5 And the blue-black of Venice fills my mind

And the gilt rafters of the first floor rooms

   Show there above me all a-red, ablaze,

"I knew it first, and it was such a year,

"When first I knew it there was such an air"

10 Or "This night it will happen". "Further on".

Or "Down you go, a mile from Angouleme   (46)

And in an open field there are three steps

Grey stone, they wait, there is no yard behind them,

 Only the stone piers that have held a gate."

15 Or "The red poppies seem to swim in glass"

That's Spain, your dusty France

    holds half the colour back,

Your temperate eyes .....

     "Arles gray, what gary?   (65)

20 "The church of St Trophime."

    . . .

Cf. B.82-88, IV.108-10.

Fragment 5B

Nam Sygebryht his rices, on Westsaexna wiotan,   (66)

Rough wood, rough wood, Cynewufl, king,   (47)

Reft from Sygebryht his rule, for his harsh deed,

All save the shire of Hampton,

5 And Sygebryht lived there but killed off the neighboring

              head men

Then Cynewifl drave him on to Andred forest,

A sawin of Cumbran's pushed on there and slew him,

For 30 years king Cynewulf warred with Brit-welsh

And strove to drive out Cyneheard, Sygebryht's brother,   (47)

10 Who head the king lay undefended, near to Merton,

        lay with his mistress,

And thither Cyneheard, and [lay] set on the bower,

  Ere the kings men were ware,

The King uprose from bed, went to the door,
           warily
15   nobly defended himself until he spied

           the athling Cyneheard,
and he rushed out on him and micle wounded him,

      But all were fighting there about the king

         until they slew him,
         . . .

20   And all fought round the gate, till it

          burst in,

And all that were with ythe athling died save one,

     the aldorman's god son that was often wounded.

Cf. B.89-92.

風賦 宋玉
fu   *fu*   by So-gioku
wind   kind of poem

楚 襄 王 遊 於 蘭 臺 之 宮
Sŏ   *jō*   *o*   *yu*   *ŏ*   *ran*   *dai*   *shi*   *kiu*
name of   name of   king   play   to   orchid   storied 's   palace
country   king   wander   house,
                                  name of villa
Jo, King of So, went to the palace of Rantai

minister   minister

宋 玉 景 差 侍
So   *Gioku,*   *Kei Sa*   *jĭ*
name   name   wait on
Sogioku & Kei Sa waited upon him

有 風 颯 然 而 至
yu   *fu*   *satsu*   *jen*   *jĭ*   *shĭ*
was   wind   sound of   so it is   in   come or reach
             autumn
             wind in   -ly
             pine trees
there was a wind soughingly coming in

- - - - -

             hand
             skin

王 乃 披 襟 而 當 之 曰
5 *o*   *dai*   *hĭ*   *kin*   *jĭ*   *to*   *shĭ*   *etsu*
king   then   opened   breast   and   face   this   said
                  part of   correspond
                  garment
The King then opened his collar and facing it said

快 哉 此 風
kwai   *sai*   *shĭ*   *fu*
pleasant   !   this   wind
How pleasant, this wind!

Cf. frag. 2B, B.59-71, IV.89-99.

xxhan--also used by kings for "I"--or by some lords

that ——————————————————————————— which

寡　人　所　與　庶　人　共　者　邪

ka | jin | shǒ | yo | shǒ | jin | kio | sha | ya
little | man | what | with | many | people | partake | what | ?
or one who | | (rel.) | | common
has not
much　　King & Emperor
　　　use it for I

Is this what I partake of with the common people?

- - - - -

lit. = opposite

宋　玉　對　曰

So | Gioku | tai | etsu
---------- | | respond | said

Sogioku responded & said

此　獨　大　王　之　風　耳

Shi | doku | dai | o | shǐ | fu | jǐ
This | only | great | king | 's | wind | lit. = ear

This is the wind of the Great King only
　　　　　　　　you

庶　人　安　得　而　共　之

10 Shǒ | jin | an | toku | ji | kio | shǐ
Common | people | how | <can> | and | partake | this
　　　　　get

How can common people get & partake of it

- - - - -

some
very dignified　　"wa"
introduction

王　曰　夫　風　者　天　地　之　氣

o | etsu | fǔ | fu | sha | ten | chǐ | shǐ | kǐ
King | said | well | wind | nom. | heaven | earth | 's | breath
　　　　　　end

The King said, "Well, this wind is the breath of heaven & earth"

溥　暢　而　至
tan   chō   jĭ   shĭ
universal prolong and come
       expand
universally expanding it comes

不　擇　貴　賤　高　下　而　加　焉
fŭ   taku   kĭ   sen   ko   gĕ   jĭ   ka   hen
not select noble poor high low and add   blow on
                      low
It cares not for noble or poor, high or low, but blows on them

－ － － － －

        sometimes
          = you
        used for Mr. = Koshi

今　子　獨　以　爲　寡　人　之　風
kon   shĭ   doku   ĭ   ĭ   Ra   jin   shĭ   fŭ
now   son   alone emphatic make &   's   wind
      = you   my
And now you alone make out that this is a wind of mine

                              = interjection

豈　有　說　乎
                              =ah!
15 gai   yu   setsu   kŏ
   perhaps is   opinion ?   so far is introduction
   Is there an opinion (of yours) possibly?

宋　玉　對　曰
So   Gioku   tai   etsu
----------   answer   ----

－ － － － －

   I when one
   speaks to lord

臣　聞　於　師
shin   bun   ŏ   shĭ
subject heard from teacher
Your subject heard this from his teacher (Kutsuga)

tachibana bloom is fragrant

枳　句　　來　巢

shǐ ——— kō　　sai　　sō
small fruit　hole at　to make　nest
lemon　　　the elbow of　come
　　　　　a tree branch
the old holes in the lemon trees make come nests
　　　　　　　　　　　　are a good place for

空　穴　來　風

ku　　ketsu　　sai　　fu
empty　cave　makes　wind
　　　　　come
and empty caves induce wind

- - - - -

其　所　託　者　然

20 ki　　shǒ　　taku　　　　sha　　jen
That　what　rely upon　　---　　so--
The breath of wind becomes different　　　　　?

則　風　氣　殊　焉

Soku　　fu　　ki　　shǔ　　en
then　wind　breath　different ?
according to what it relies upon

王　曰　夫　風　始　安　生　哉

O　　etsu　　fǔ　　fu　　shǐ　　an　　sei　　sai
King　said　well　wind　first　where　grow　?
The King said Well then, where was the wind first born?

- - - - -

宋　玉　對　曰

So　Gioku　tai　etsu

fŭ fu sei ŏ chi
Now, wind grows from earth
      is born in
Well, the wind is born in the earth

okiru

25 kĭ ŏ sei hin shĭ batsu
start from green water 's end
       weed
       floating
It starts from the end of the green water weeds.

In Konzan Ken there is a big Mt.
with a cave called "Wind well"

shin in kei koku sei   dŏ ŏ dŏ nō shĭ ko
flow on moisten pass valley flourishing get in earth bag 's mouth
slowly   angry
         violent   cave?
It flows on slowly, refreshing, thro' passes & valleys, and gets violent in
         the mouth of the Mt. caves--

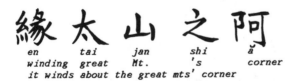

en tai jan shi ă
winding great Mt. 's corner
it winds about the great mts' corner

kashiwa

fŭ ŏ shō haku shi ka
dance in pine oak? 's under
it dances under the pines & cedars

- - - - -

friend side

飄 忽 淜 滂 　激 颺 熛 怒

hio katsu hō hō geki yo hyō dŏ

quick water violent

floating lightly in air | sudden | sound made by water striking against rock in spring | rise in the air | flame | get angry

surges

from floating light it suddenly with a "Ho! Ho!" <rises> violently up like an angry flame.

ear & broad
used for sound

耾 耾 　雷 聲 迴 穴 錯 迕

ko ko rai sei kwai ketsu saku gŏ

noisily

sharp striking on the ear (onomatopoeia) | thunder voice | to wheel cave (whirlwind) | interchange mix

With a thundering "Ko Ko!", it wheels and churns itself together

蹷 石 伐 木

ketsu seki batsu boku

suddenly to fall from a standing position | stone | beat | tree

<it makes> it tears out stones and blasts trees

- - - - -

梢 殺 林 莽

shō satsu rin bō

beat | kill | forest | (shoots)

it beats down and kills the forest leaves

when ... it is!!

至 其 將 衰 也

shĭ kĭ sho sui ya

come | that | (future) going to | to lose <its> power | (when)

in some texts this line is omitted. Mr. Mori thinks better omit.

<open> *rising line*   *level line*
          open separate
               rhyme

被 麗 披 離 衝 孔 動 楗
hi *ri*   *hi* *ri* *sho* *ko* *do* *ken*
(only for sound) *(meaning also)* *strike* *small* *move* *door locked*
                against *hole*
(shrieking) hi ri hi ri, it strikes against holes and moves locked doors
(scattering light in 4 directions) it beats in through

- - - - -

                   Every character in this
                   strong line must be separately
                   studied
                   must be far bigger thoughts

            scattering
dazzling interchange *color* *brilliancy*
                of flame

35 眴 渙 粲 爛 離 散 轉 移
  ken *kwan* *san* *ran* *ri* *san* *ten* *i*
               separate *scatter* *revolve* *change*
                          place
accumulation of sound & meaning both
increasing the idea of brilliancy--
shows wind is very clean, carrying no dust
  (comment says this)

                   These lines are probably not
                   written out in correct metre
                   not according to rhyme
                   must recast the lines

故 其 清 涼 雄 風
kŏ *kĭ* *sei* *yo* *yu* *fu*
therefore *that* *clear* *cool* *male* *wind*
             mighty
So that clear cool mighty wind

則 飄 舉 升 降
Soku *hiŏ*   *kiŏ* *shō* *gō*
Then *floating very* <rise> *rise* *fall*
  lightly in the *raise*
      air
floating lightly it lifts itself, rises & falls

- - - - -

to climb
higher than
clouds

蔡　陵　　高　城

jo　　rio　　　ko　　　jŏ
ride　*to climb*　*high*　　*castle*
climb　*high*
rides climbing up to high castle

入　于　深　宮　　邸　華　葉　　而　振　氣

nin　　u　　shin　　kiu　　tei　　ka　　yo　　ji　shin　ki
enter　*to*　*deep*　*palace*　*touch*　*flowery*　*leaves*　*and*　*shake*　*breath*
　　　　　　　　　　　　　　　　　　　　　　　making itself mighty

wall

徘　　徊　　於　桂　　椒　之　　間

40 hai　　　kai　　　ŏ　kei　　　shō　　shĭ　　kan
go moving　*come back*　*in katsura*　　*pepper*　*'s*　*interval of place*
wander　　*to same*　　　|　　<some sweet smelling>　*places where these are*
　　　　　place　　*palace*　　*some pungent*
　　　　　　　　built with　*powder mixed*
　　　　　　　　kei wood　*with the plaster*

- - - - -

翺　　翔　於　激　　水　之　上

ko　　　sho　　ŏ　geki　　sui　　shĭ　jŏ
run in the　*lofty*　*in*　*violent*　*water*　*'s*　*top*
air　　　　　　　　*high spouting water*
　　　　　　　　　　from a fountain

　　　　soar
and soars up to the tip of the fountain's jet

- - - - -

fuyo flower

將　擊　芙　蓉　之　精

sho　　geki　　fu　　yo　　shĭ　　sei
take lead　*beat*　*(husband)*　*(appearance)*　*'s*　*essence*
　　　　　　　　finest of fuyo
it is about to press out the essence of the fuyo
　　fuyo may here be lotos.

獵　蕙　草　離　　秦　衡
rio　kei　so　ri　　shin　kō
hunt　fragrant　grass　influence　a kind　flower like
to seek　?　　　of sweet　an iris
　　　　　　　　　　grass

- - - - -

　　　　　　　　　　　　　　　willow

槩　新　夷　被　　夷　楊
gai　shin　i　hǐ　　i　yo
sweep　new yebisu　to be　youngest leaves
　　　　　covered　of willow
　　Mr. M. says only　or influenced
　　this is name
　　of a grass

　　　these characters are often used to describe an autumn
　　field--say "field is shojo as far as eye can reach"
　　　　　　　　　　calm and sere--solitary
　　　　faint line |

迴　穴　衡　陵　蕭　條　眾　芳
　　accusative　accusative
45 kwai　ketsu　ko　rio　sho⌒jo　shu　ho
wheeling　cave　striking hills　Mr. Mori　many sweet smell
　　　　against　says
　　　　　　?mustard
　　　　　　?
<it carries then> These caves and hills must be small
　　　　parts of the garden.

然　後　徜　徉　　中　庭　北　上　玉　堂
Zen　go　sho　yo　chu　tei　hoku　jo　gioku　do
That after to go & back again inside garden north climb gem palace
　　this is more at leisure
　　　　than before
After that, it saunters about the garden and climbs up the jewel palace
　　　　　　　　　　on the North.

- - - - -

sometimes
in or *to*   *lit.=cave*

躋 于 羅 幬　經 于　洞　房

sai	u	ra	i	kei	in	do	bo
ford	acc.	thin cloth	curtains	pass	all	deepest chamber from front	chamber private

It fords through the gauze curtains, and gets through to the inner chamber.

乃 得 爲 大 王 之 風 也

dai	toku	i	dai	o	shǐ	fu	ya
the	can	become	great	king	's	wind	<to make sure> to be sure--

And then for the first time it can become the great king's wind, for sure.

This is only the first 3/5 of the poem--
the rest describes the wind of the common
people which brings dust & sickness to people.

Leave out the rest.

COLLATION OF LATER MANUSCRIPTS
AND PRINTED TEXTS, 1919–25

THE FOURTH CANTO

Palace in smoky light,
Troy but a heap of smouldering boundary stones,
ANAXIFORMINGES! Aurunculeia!
Hear me. Cadmus of Golden Prows!
5   The silver mirrors catch the bright stones and flare,
Dawn, to our waking, drifts in the green cool light;
Dew-haze blurs, in the grass, pale ankles moving.
Beat, beat, whirr, thud, in the soft turf
                        under the apple trees,
10   Choros nympharum, goat-foot, with the pale foot alternate;
Crescent of blue-shot waters, green-gold in the shallows,
A black cock crows in the sea-foam;

Title: IV *C, ScXVI*   FOURTH CANTO *D*   FOURTH CANTO *E*   *The* FOURTH
CANTO *P*   THE FOURTH CANTO. *ScDial*

1 *Come then the*   ⟨*?last*⟩
   ⟨Rise, O thou⟩ smoky palace! Troy⟨'s⟩ but a heap of smouldering boundry stones. *C*

⟨*Rise O thou*⟩   *Beacon from isle to isle. Hear me.*
⟨Come then the smoky palace!⟩   Troy but a heap of
[*Palace in smokey*]   smouldering boundary stones! *D*

Not in E.   The palace in smoky light: P   Palace] *with ornamental P in ScDial-019b, TM25.*

   2 *C, D: See 1.*   Troy] Troy's *P*   boundary stones] boundary-stones *E–P21; new line in
ScDial-019b.*

   3 ANAXIFORMINGES,⟩‾hear me!⟩Aurunculeia!⟩(*transposition deleted*) Cadmus of Golden
Prows.! *C*

⌈ANAXIFORMINGES!⟩⟨Hear me!⟩⟩Aurunculeia! Cadmus of Golden Prows: *D*

ANAXIFORMINGES! Aurunculeia! Cadmus of Golden Prows: *E*

ANAXIFORMINGES! Aurunculeia! *hear me*
                        Cadmus of Golden Prows⟨;⟩. *P*

   4 *C–P: See 3.*   Prows!] Prows; *ScDial–D20*
   5 mirrors] mirrours *C–E*   mirro⟨u⟩rs *ScXVI*   flare,] ~ ⌄ *C*
   6 Dawn,] ~ ⌄   waking,] ~ ⌄   light;] ~, *the C*
   7 blurs] blurrs *C–P21*   blur⟨r⟩s *ScXVI*   Dew-haze blurs,]~ ⌄~   ~ ⌄ *C*   pale ankles
moving. *dropped one line in C–P.*
   8–9 *ScDial: marked by editor to be run on.   D20–P21: run on*   trees,]~ ⌄ *D*
   10 goat-foot,] goat ⌄foot ⌄ *C*   goat-foot ⌄ *D–P21*   alternate;] ~. *C*   ⟨[⟩~ *P (turnover),
turnover in ScDial–019b, marked by editor to be run on in ScDial.*
   11 Sea crescent bends blue-shot waters, green in the shallows. *C* ⟨Sea⟩ *C*rescent ⟨bends⟩ *of*
blue-shot waters, green-*gold* in the shallows. *D*   waters,]   ~⟨,⟩ *behind them,*   shallows,]
⟨[⟩~⟨,⟩. *P(turnover)*   ~ ⌄ *ScDial–D20, turnover in ScDial–019b, marked by editor to be run on
in ScDial.*
   12 sea-foam] ~ ⌄~ *C*

And by the curved, carved foot of the couch,
      claw-foot and lion head, an old man seated,
15 Speaking in the low drone . . . :
               Ityn!   Itys
Et ter flebiliter, Ityn, Ityn!
And she went toward the window and cast her down,
      "All the while, the while, swallows crying:
20 Ityn!
          "It is Cabestan's heart in the dish."
          "It is Cabestan's heart in the dish?
          "No other taste shall change this."
And she went toward the window,
25   the slim white stone bar
Making a double arch;
Firm even fingers held to the firm pale stone;
Swung for a moment,
               and the wind out of Rhodez
30 Caught in the full of her sleeve.
             . . . the swallows crying:
Ityn, Ityn!
      Actæon . . . . .   Actæon
      and a valley,
35 The valley is thick with leaves, with leaves, the trees,

---

13 And by] By *C* ⟨*And*⟩ *And* By *D* curved,] ~ ‸ *C–P21* couch,] ~ ‸ *C* ~, *D*
14 seated,] ~ ‸ *C–P21*
15 drone . . . :] ~ ‸: *C, D (added in holograph in C)* ~: . . . *E–P21*
16 "Ityn, *C* *of* "Ityn, *D* "Ityn! *E–P21* Itys] *to right of line 13 in ScXVI.*
17 Et] "~ *D–P21* flebiliter,] ~. *P–P21* Ityn!] ~,⟨"⟩ *C* ~! *D*
18 And] "~ *C–P21 (added in holograph in C)*
19 "All] "all *C* "all *D* crying:] crying: *C*
20 "Ityn," *C* "Ityn!⟨"⟩ *D* "Ityn! *E–D20* "Ityn!" *P21*
21–22 *Holograph underline in C; italic in D–P21.* "It] ""~ *D–P21 (each line)* dish?]
~." *D* ~⟨"⟩ *P*
23 *Holograph underline in C; italic in D–P21.* "No] ‸no *C* ""~ *D–P21* this."]
~." *D* window,] ~, *D*
24 And she went toward the window, [and cast her down] *E*
24–26 *Initial holograph quotation mark in C.*
25 stone bar] stone-bar *D*
26 arch;] ~, *C* ~⟨,⟩; *D*
27 Firm] ⟨The⟩ firm *C* stone;] ~, *C–D*
30 Caught in the] Caught the *C, D*
31 crying:] ~. *C*
32 Ityn! Ityn. *C* ⟨"⟩Ityn! Ityn! ⟨"⟩ *D* "Ityn! Ityn!" *E, P21* Ityn! Ityn!" *P–D20*
33 Actaeon. *C* ⟨*And*⟩ Actaeon. . . . . *D* *Tag line at left margin in TM25.*
34 and] And *C–P21* ⟨*And*⟩ And *(at margin:)* ⟨*a valley*⟩ *cliff-crag & valley-slope. D*
35 the] with *C–D* leaves,] ~, *P*

The sunlight glitters, glitters a-top,
Like a fish-scale roof,
    Like the church roof in Poictiers
If it were gold.
40   Beneath it, beneath it
Not a ray, not a sliver, not a spare disc of sunlight
Flaking the black, soft water;
Bathing the body of nymphs, of nymphs, and Diana,
Nymphs, white-gathered about her, and the air, air,
45 Shaking, air alight with the goddess,
    fanning their hair in the dark,
Lifting, lifting and waffing:
Ivory dipping in silver,
    Shadow'd, o'ershadow'd
50 Ivory dipping in silver,
Not a splotch, not a lost shatter of sunlight.
Then Actæon: Vidal,
Vidal. It is old Vidal speaking,
    stumbling along in the wood,
55 Not a patch, not a lost shimmer of sunlight,
    the pale hair of the goddess.

 The dogs leap on Actaeon,

---

36 a-top,] ~ˌ C–D a'top, ScXVI
37 roof,] ~. C ~; D
38 church roof] church-roof P–P21
40 Beneath] & Beneath C And ⟨B⟩beneath D, P
41 sliver] slivver C–P21 sliv⟨v⟩er ScXVI disc] ⟨coin⟩ disc C disk P–P21
42 water;] ~, C
43 the] ⟨the⟩ the of nymphs, of nymphs,] of nymphs, C of nymphs, of nymphs, D
44 Nymphs,] nymphsˌ C ~ˌ D, E, 019b air, air,] airˌ C air, ⟨air⟩ D
45 Shaking] shaking C goddess,] ~, C ~ˌ E–P21
46 dark,] ~ˌ C
47 Lifting] lifting C waffing:] ~, C, D
48 Not in 019a; inserted in holograph in ScDial without comma. silver,] ~; D
49–50 Not in C–E; inserted in P: Shadowed, oershadowed, / Ivory dipping in silver, / Pholoe. Niceas, no splotch / no lost shatter. o'ershadow'd] ~, 019b [Shadowed, oershadowed] Shadow'd, o'ershadow'd ScXVI
51 shatter] patch C ⟨patch⟩ shatter D sunlight.] ~, C ~: D Not a ... not a] no⟨t a⟩ ... no⟨t a⟩ P, and see 49–50
52 [And] Then ⟨and⟩ Actaeon. C Vidal dropped one line in C, D Vidal,] : Vidal C ~. D ⟨~,⟩ P
53–54 C, D: run on. Vidal. It is] It is C, D wood,] ~; D ~ˌ E–D20
55 lost shimmer] shimmer C ⟨shimmer⟩ lost ⟨shatter⟩ shimmer D sunlight,] ~. C ~: D
56 Not in C–E; inserted in holograph in P. goddess.] ~, ScDial–D20
57 "Dogs, dogs, leap the dogs on Actaeon. C
 "⟨Dogs, dogs, leap⟩ the dogs leap on Actaeon, D

"Hither, hither, Actaeon,"
Spotted stag of the wood;
60   Gold, gold, a sheaf of hair,
        Thick like a wheat swath,
Blaze, blaze in the sun,
        The dogs leap on Actæon.

Stumbling, stumbling along in the wood,
65   Muttering, muttering Ovid:
        "Pergusa . . . . pool . . . . pool . . . . Gargaphia,
"Pool . . . . pool of Salmacis."
        The empty armour shakes as the cygnet moves.

Thus the light rains, thus pours, *e lo soleils plovil*
70   The liquid and rushing crystal
        beneath the knees of the gods.
Ply over ply, thin glitter of water;
Brook film bearing white petals.
The pines
        at Takasago
75   grow with the pines of Isé!

---

58 *Not in C–E; inserted in P: hither hither actaeon.*

59 wood;] ~, *C*

61 Thick] thick *C*

62 sun,] ~. *C, D*

63 Actaeon.] ~." *C, D*

65 Ovid:] ~. *C*

66 "Pergusa, pool, pool of Gargaphia" *C, D* Gargaphia"] ~. *D* ~ˏ *E–D20*

67 "Pool . . . .] ˌ~, *C, 019b* ˌ~,? *D* "~, *E, P21* '~, *P–019a, D20* pool] Pool *D* Salmacis."] ~.ˏ *C–019a, D20*

68 moves.] ~" *C* ~, *D20*

69 Thus] (⸗Thus *C* ⟨Thus⟩ ⟨And⟩ ⟨The⟩ Thus *D* rains, thus] rains and *C* thus pours,] ⟨and pours⟩ ⟨thus rains, thus pours⟩ *D* *e lo soleils plovil*] *added in holograph in C* plovil] ~, *C– P21*

70 The liquid] liquid *C* *The* ⟨L⟩liquid, *D* The liquid, *E–P21* The liquid⟨,⟩ *ScXVI* and] ⟨and⟩ ⟨the⟩ *and D*

71 whirls up the bright brown sand. *C–P21* whirls] Whirls *D* ⟨Whirls up the bright brown sand.⟩ *beneath the knees of the gods. ScXVI*

72–81 *See also STN, fragments c1 and c2.*

72 water;] ~, *C*

73 petals.] ~ˏ *E–P21*

74–75 *Not in C, D.* ("The pines of Takasago grow with pines of Ise") *E–D20* Ise] ~. *E* ("The pines of Takasago grow with the pines of Ise") *P21* the pines] pines Ise] Isé *P21* The pines
        at Takasago,
         grow with the pines of Isé! *ScXVI (spacing marked by hand)*

The water whirls up the bright pale sand in the spring's mouth.
"Behold the Tree of the Visages!"
Forked branch-tips, flaming as if with lotus.
      Ply over ply
80 The shallow eddying fluid,
        beneath the knees of the gods.

Torches melt in the glare   Hymenaeus
      Set flame of the corner cook-stall,
Blue agate casing the sky (as at Gourdon that time)
85   the sputter of resin,
Saffron sandal so petals the narrow foot: Hymenæus Io!
Hymen, Io Hymenæe! Aurunculeia!
A scarlet flower is cast on the blanch-white stone.

And So-Gioku, saying:

76 *Not in C–P21: see 71. Inserted in holograph in ScXVI.*
77 Tree] tree   Visages!"] visages,ᴧ *C, D* ~, *D* ~.ᴧ *E* ~." *P–019a, D20, P21* ~,"
019b Quotation marks inserted in holograph in ScXVI.
78 The forked tips flaming as if with lotus." *C–P21* The] ⟨The⟩ *The D* lotus."] ~." *C*
~.ᴧ" *D* ~,ᴧ *E–019a, D20, P21* ~.ᴧ *019b. Hyphen added in holograph in ScXVI.*
79 ply] ~, *C* ~— *D*
after 79 [behind them the floating images, behind them recurring images / behind them
the lasting Gods.] *C*
80–81 Shallow eddying fluid, beneath the knees of the Gods.*))* *C* The shallow] *The*
Shallow   gods] Gods *D Run on, marked for separation in D* fluid,] ~.ᴧ *E–P21*
82 Light melts in the flare, *C* ⟨For the L⟩light⟨s⟩ melt⟨s⟩s in the flare, *D* Aurunculeia,
torches melt in the glare, *E* ⟨The shallow eddying fluid Aurunculeia,⟩ *Torches melt in the glare*
P glare] flare *019a* ⟨f⟩glare *ScDial* ~⟨,⟩ *ScXVI*
83 Set flame] The glare *C* ⟨The⟩*The* glare *D* cook-stall,] ~, *C*
84 *Not in C–E. Inserted in holograph in P:* Blue agate casing the sky, a sputter of resin; *P–*
P21 resin;] ~.ᴧ *P*
85 *Not in C–E. P–P21: see 84.*
86 The saffron sandal petals the slender foot, Hymenaeus! *C–P21* The] ⟨The⟩ *C* ⟨The⟩
a ⟨the⟩ *a D* petals] ⟨empetals⟩ ⟨em⟩*petals D* foot, Hymenaeus!] foot, *C* foot; *D* slender]
tender *P–D20* narrow *P21*
87 *Not in C, D.* Io Hymen, Io Hymenaee! *E* Io Hymen, Io Hymenaee! Aurunculeia,
P–P21 Aurunculeia,] *Aurunculeia, P* ~.ᴧ *ScDial–D20* ~! *P21*
88 *Not in C, D.* A] The *E–P21* blanch-white] bleach-white *E* ⟨beach⟩ *blanch*-white *P,*
ScDial beach-white *019a* stone.] ~, *E–019a, D20, P21 See also STN, fragment e1.*
after 88 "Helicon, Helicon, haunt of Urania's son / Bright Amaracus.!" *C* "⟨Helicon! Helicon! "Haunt of Urania's son . . . / "Bright Amaracus.!⟩ *D* Amaracus, [Haunt] Hill of Urania's
Son, *E* Amaracus⟨,⟩! Hill of Urania's Son⟨.⟩! *P* Amaracus, Hill of Urania's Son. *ScDial–*
P21 Amaracus] Armaracus *P21*
89 And *then* So Gioku answered: *C* ⟨And then⟩ *&* So Gioku, *the mumbler,* answered⟨:⟩,
answered: *D* Meanwhile So-Gioku: *E, ScDial–P21* Meanwhile So-Gioku⟨:⟩ *answered, P*

90   "This wind, sire, is the king's wind,
             This wind is wind of the palace,
    Shaking imperial water-jets."
             And Ran-ti, opening his collar:
    "This wind roars in the earth's bag,
95   it lays the water with rushes;
    No wind is the king's wind.
             Let every cow keep her calf."
    "This wind is held in gauze curtains . . . . ."
     "No wind is the king's . . . ."

100   The camel drivers sit in the turn of the stairs,
            Look down on Ecbatan of plotted streets,
    "Danaë! Danaë!   Danaë
            What wind is the king's?"
    Smoke hangs on the stream,
105   The peach-trees shed bright leaves in the water,
    Sound drifts in the evening haze,

---

90 "This wind is the king's("). *C* "This wind is the king's⟨,⟩ *wind— D*
91 This] "~ *C* this *D–P21* palace,] ~ₐ *C–P21*
92 Shaking] "~ jets.] ~, *C Period added in holograph in ScXVI.*
93 Ran-ti,] ~ₐ *C* Ran-Tiₐ *D–P21* opening] opened *C* open⟨ed⟩*ing D* collar:] ~⟨.⟩: *C*
94 *Quotation mark added in holograph in ScXVI.*
95 it] "~ *C* rushes;] ~, *C*
96 *C, D: transposed with 97.* No] "~ *C, E–P21* wind.] ~" *C* ~." *D*
97 *C, D: transposed with 96.* Let] "~ *C* calf."] ~.ₐ *C, D*
98 curtains . . .] ~ₐ *C* ~. *D* wind is] wind[is the king's wind] is *ScXVI*
99 "No] ₐ~ *P–019a, D20* king's . . . .] kingsₐ *C* ~. *D*
100 The] ⟨The⟩ *While P* 'The *ScDial, 019a, D20* sit in the turn of] sitting upon *C* ⟨The⟩ camel-drivers ⟨sitting upon⟩ *in turn of* the stairs *D* stairs,] ~ₐ *C–E, ScDial–D20*
101 look to the terraced tops of Ecbatan. *C* look ⟨to the terraced tops of⟩ *up toward* Ecbatan; *D* [looking to E] look down to Ecbatan of plotted streets *E* Look] look on] to *P– P21* streets,] ~ₐ *019a*
102 "Danaë!] ₐ~, *C* ₐ~! *D* "Danae! Danae! *E–P21*
103 king's!"] ~?ₐ *C–019a, D20*
104 The smoke hangs on the stream; the peach-trees *C, D* ⟨boughs⟩ *C*
105 Shed bright leaves in the water, *C, D* water,] ~; *D*
106–08 slow barge, past a thousand fords, / The peach flakes fall in the water, / music out of old time / ⟨d⟩Drifts in the haze of evening; / ⟨clavicords⟩ *old instruments,* Loredan, gilt rafters / Above black water; *C*

⟨slow-⟩barge, past a thousand fords; / The peach flakes fall in the water; / ⟨music out of old time⟩ / Drifts ⟨*of sound*⟩ in the haze of evening; / ⟨old instruments, and Loredan,⟩ gilt rafters / Above black water; *D*

The bark scrapes at the ford,
Gilt rafters above black water,
Three steps in an open field,
110 Gray stone-posts leading . . . . .
As Cavalcanti had seen her.
Père Henri Jacques,
On Mount Rokku between the rock and the cedars,
Polhonac,
As Gyges on Thracian platter set the feast,
115 Cabestan, Terreus,
It is Cabestan's heart in the dish,
Vidal, or Ecbatan, upon the gilded tower in Ecbatan

---

107 bark] barge *E–P21*   ford,] ~. *P–P21*   ~., *E*
108 water,] water[s]; *E*   ~; *P–P21*
109 Three] three *E–P21*   ⟨Three⟩ *D*   field,] ~ˌ *D–P21*
110 By Angouleme, grey stone-posts leading nowhither. *C, D*   By Angouleme] ⟨By Angouleme⟩ *D*   nowhither.] ~; *D*   leading . . . . .] leading nowhither, *E, P*   leading nowhither. *ScDial–P21*
after 110 The Spanish poppies swim in an air of glass. *C–P21* an] *an C*   glass.] ~; *D*   ~, *E*
111 Père Henri Jacques *still* seek*s* the sennin on Rokku, *C–P21*   Père] Pere *E*   Rokku,] ~. *E–P21*   Père Henri Jacques, [on Mount Rokku, between the] *ScXVI*
112–16 *C:*   *Friend Floating Cloud*
                Still seeks the sennin on Rokku,
                Polhon as, Gyges on Thracian platter,
                    set the feast;
                Cabestan: Tereus. It is Cabestan's
                    heart in the dish
                Vidal tracked out with dogs—for
                    glamour of Loba.
                    as Itys on Thracian platter—
                        as Procne Itys
                Polhonac made Gyges feast, ⟨served his wife's lover,⟩
                                ⟨Tereus⟩
                ⟨Procne and the son Itys, served to King. . . . .⟩
                                Itys   ⟨of Thrace⟩
                    ⟨As Procne server her son to Tereus.⟩
                Vidal, hunted ⟨with⟩ *tracked out, the unleashed* dogs for ⟨love⟩
                                praise of Loba.
margin: ⟨*Cabestan as Itys to Tereus queen   Cabestan as Itys on*
            Thracian ⟨*platter*⟩ *dish*⟩
112 *D:* ⟨Friendly with Floating Cloud, / *Past time in orders Jesuit* / Still seeks the sennin on *upon* Rokku. *The sennin and Floating Cloud*⟩ *Not in E–P21. Comma added in holograph in ScXVI.*
113–14 *D: run on.*   As] as *D*   platter] ~, *D–P21*   feast,] ~; *E–P21*
115–16 *D: run on.*   Terreus,] ~. *D–P21*   dish,] ~; *D*   ~. *E–P21*
after 116 Vidal, tracked out with dogs . . . for glamour of Loba; *D–P21*   Vidal,] ~ˌ *D*
117 Upon the gilded tower in Ecbatan *C–P21*   Ecbatan] ~, *C*

Lay the god's bride, lay ever, waiting the golden rain.

By Garonne. "Saave!"
120   The Garonne is thick like paint,
Procession,—"Et sa'ave, sa'ave, sa'ave Regina!"
Moves like a worm, in the crowd,
Adige, this film of images,
Across the Adige, by Stefano, Madonna in hortulo,

---

118 Lay the god's bride, lay ever / Waiting the golden rain. *C–P21* Lay] lay *C, D*   ever]
~, *C, D*   Waiting] waiting *C*   rain.] ~: *D*
119 *Not in C, D.* Et saave! *E–P21*   saave] sāāve *P*
119–22 *See STN, fragments e2, e3 and xvi.*
120 *Not in C, D.* But today, Garonne is thick like paint, beyond Dorada, *E–P21*   today]
to-day *D20, P21*
121 *Not in C, D.* The worm of the Procession bores in the soup of the crowd, *E–P21*
crowd,] ~ʌ *P21*   ⟨[⟩~,] *P (turnover),* turnover *ScDial–019b*   Regina!"] ~!"— *ScXVI*
121–28 *See STN, fragment xvi.*
122 *Not in C, D.* The blue thin voices against the crash of the crowd / Et "Salve rè-
ginà." *E–P21*   rēginà] regínà REginà *P*   regina *ScDial, 019a, D20, P21*   REGinà *019b*
crowd,] ~,⟨.⟩ *ScXVI*
123–25 *Not in C, D; instead:*

> In trellises,
> over-wound with small flowers, across th'Adige
> in the but half used room, Verona,
> Stephanus pinxit, in the included garden,
> thin film, the early Virgin, age of unbodied gods,
> "The virtue risen in heaven", the vitreous
> fragile images haunting the mind,—*as* of Guido[,]—
> Thin as the locusts wing.   *C*

D: first words of lines capitalized.   trellises,] ·-ʌ   Stephanus pinxit] ⟨Stephanus pinxit⟩ *margin
near* gods: *Stephanus pinxit*   half used] half-used *D*   "The virtue risen in heaven",] ⟨"The virtue risen in heaven",⟩ Guido,] ~ʌ *D*

Not in E–P21; instead:

> Stephanus pinxit:
>   In trellises
> Wound over with small flowers, beyond Adige
> In the but half-used room, thin film of images,
> 5   Age of unbodied gods, the vitreous fragile eikons
> Thin as the locust's wing
> Haunting the mind . . . as of Guido . . . .
> Thin as the locust's wing.

Stephanus pinxit] ⟨Stephanus pinxit⟩ *P; omitted ScDial–P21*   images,] images, *(by Stefano)*
eikons] ⟨eikons⟩ *P   line inserted after 4:* (by Stefano)   eikons] images *ScDial–P21*
123 this] thin *ScXVI*
124–25 *See STN, fragments c1 and c2.*

125   As Cavalcanti had seen her.

The Centaur's heel plants in the earth loam.

And we sit here . . . .
      there in the arena . . . .

125 As Cavalcanti had ⟨thought of⟩ *seen* her, / [xxxx xx xx] *ScXVI*

126 *((*The Centaurs heel / plants in the earth loam.*)) margin: He Cabestan—tricking killed in hunting— C*   The Centaur's heel / Plants in the earth-loam. *D–P21   Run on with* Thin as the locust's wing *in E–P21*   earth-loam.] ∼, *E*

after 126 A jesuit seeks the sennin upon the cusped peak of Ro-ku *C, D* Ro-ku] Rokku. *D* on Rokku / A jesuit seeks the gods. *E, P; marked for deletion in P* on] ⟨O⟩n *P*   seeks] seek *D*   seek⟨e⟩s *P*

127–28 *Not in C–P21*   here . . . .] ∼---- *ScXVI*

SUPPLEMENTARY TEXTUAL NOTES

Fragment c1

```
    ply over ply--
              thin glitter              1.
    of water--
       brook-film bearing white petals.
5   Behold the tree of the visages--
    Ecce arborem vitae--  <divine>                    (67)
              The forked tips
    flaming as if with lotus--
              Divine Love runs in the branches--

10  Behind them the lasting images.]
      ply over ply--behind them the
    floating images      behind them the
                    recrossing images,
    behind them the lasting gods--
15  Zeus set on Olympos, Pelion & Ossa                (68)
                for his foot-rests
                Truth caught in a
                      fever
```

```
                                        2.

    enfevered--
20      wholly
    strike thru with the
       centaur's heel

    [Stefano da Verona]                               (69)

    Mary trellised in orto
25  <fli> film of blooms & trellace--

       del quaglia,
```

```
    a shallow eddying fluid
       below the knees of the
          gods
```

```
                                        3.

30  Below them the leaf-brown colourless             (70)
```

Lines 1-18, 27-29: cf. IV.72-81; 21-22: cf. IV.126; 23-26: cf.
IV.124-25.

Ply over ply, thin glitter of water

Brook film bearing white petals

Behold the tree of the visages, Ecce arbor vitae   (67)

the forked tips flaming as if with lotus

5   Divine love runs in the branches,

           Behind this the lasting images, ply over ply

behind them the floating images, behind them the recurring im
                                    images

Behind them the lasting Gods,

           Zeus set on Olympos, Pelion and Ossa for his footrests   (68)

10   truth caught in a fever.

A shallow eddying fluid blow the knees of the Gods,

strike thru with the centaur's heel,

           beneath that the leaf-brown colourless,   (70)

       stefano da verona,   , Mary trellis, film of boughs in trellis

15 quaglia.   (69)

Lines 1-11: cf. IV.72-81; 12: cf. IV.126; 14-15: cf. IV.124-25.

"Haunt of Urania's son ....   (42)
<Bright> Amaracus"

"Throw the nuts!"   "Hymenaeus,"

Flow of bright robes over feet,

5 "Bright Amaracus,"   the scarlet popply

                veining the blanch-white stone,

     Auruncuľeia

          come thru the

          <wa> ?stone-dabbed

                street

_____

Cf. IV.88.

Sa've saave.   (71)

───────

Moving in heavy air, Henry & Saladin   (72)

& toutes la premia amant, Eleanor holding them all.

Reed lances broken, & Estampe's kings.

5   *xxxxx   to the king at (Naples),*

Bertrand blamed for the lot--

& Bornelh singing--

The Tennysonian pipe. Throughout the embroil

[Borgia]   Saa've save, savee <Maria> <Regina>.   (73)
[Lorenzaccio.]   Marie,
   10   Ave, ave, ave Regina

The serpent coils through the crowd,

surging feet in procession, the few men standing
<on chairs>
on chairs

an infant howling--?bawling of tawdry light--

15 *<The> a procession <moving> moving.*

───────

Then triple robe--towering at the front altar.

swinging the heavy totem, the built up figure--

The serpent of the procession, coiling with three antennae

Lowering the   Saave saavve, saave Regina--   (71)
   20   "   "   "   Marie.

The blue thin voices--

take up the words in stanza

- - - - -

───────

Lines 1, 19-22: cf. IV.119-22.

but today

Et: *et saave*   (71)

SAAve, saave, saave régina,   *& ?single*
Ave, ave, ave Mária,

The worm of *the* procession, bores in the soup of the
                    crowd,

5 The triple robe<s> towers in triple tier,
   The blue thin voices agains the crash of the <horde>,
       Flaked candles, [the] and the chief totem   *crowd.*

   brandished above the swirl.

                        <dark>

                        <haze>

            <3 antennae of procession>

10 *Robe over robe--*

             the flaked light

                  of candles--

        above the soup of the crowd--

     *
 Shaking of the*

15   *chief totem*

             along the

                soup of the crowd

Cf. IV.119-22.

Procession, -- *"Et sa'ave, sa'ave, sa've Regina!*--   (71)

Moves like a worm in the crowd.

Adige, thin film of images,

<The> Centaur's heel, in the earth-loam.
<The>
5   *The*

                across the adige
                  by Stefano--   (69)
            madonna in hortulo--
                as Cavalcanti
                    had thought of
10   *her.*

    And we sit here -- there in the arena:
          —   —

Cf. IV.119-28

EXPLANATORY NOTES

1. *Stendhal*: Pound saw in Stendhal's *La Chartreuse de Parme* (1839) a stylistic mastery which modern writers might profitably emulate; he wrote to Harriet Monroe in 1915, "I think an ambition to write as well as . . . Stendhal a great ambition" (SL, 55). He recommended "the first eleven chapters" of *La Chartreuse de Parme* to Homer Pound and to Iris Barry in 1916. Fabrice is Stendhal's protagonist.

2. *Campden Hill*: South Lodge at 80 Campden Hill, the Kensington home of Violet Hunt, novelist and suffragist, and Ford Madox Hueffer (later Ford Madox Ford), author and editor of the *English Review*. South Lodge was an important literary center in prewar London, and Pound was a frequent guest there.

3. *Posen*: Poland.

4. *Rihaku*: The Japanese name for the Chinese poet Li Po (c. 700–762), some of whose poems Pound read in the Fenollosa notebooks.

5. *I know a man . . .* : Possibly Miscio (or Michio) Itow or Tami Koumé, two Japanese artists whom Pound saw often during this period.

6. *Kalimohon; Ghose*: Kalimohon (or Kali Mohan) Ghose, pupil and translator of Rabindranath Tagore, with whom Pound became acquainted in 1912.

7. *faut un bois . . .* : "You need a wood with nightingales."

8. *trashumanar non si potria . . .* : Pound is remembering Dante's "Trasumanar significar per verba non si poria" (The transcendence of the human cannot be told in words), *Paradiso* 1.70.

9. *the best man*: Henri Gaudier-Brzeska, killed on July 5, 1915.

10. *Lewis*: Wyndham Lewis, whose series of paintings *Timon of Athens* (1912) Pound judged "the most articulate expression of my own decade" (GB, 93).

11. *And Ka-hu churned . . .* : Cf. lines 5 and 29–30 of Canto II (first written and published as Canto VIII in 1922): "So-shu churned in the sea"; "And So-shu churned in the sea, So-shu also, / using the long moon for a churn-stick." Though Pound's work on the Fenollosa notebooks almost certainly suggested this line, they contain no direct source for it.

12. *Polignat; Polhonac*: Héracle III, Viscount of Polignac. The references to "Polhonac" at AA.10–17, A.72–74, B.100, and C.112–16 all indicate that Pound had confused the Viscount with Raimon de Castel-Roussillon, Soremonda's husband in the *vida* of Guillem de Cabestan.

13. *Gaubertz*: Gaubertz de Poicebot, a monk of Provence who became a troubadour, married, left his wife and went to Spain, and returned to find her a prostitute. Pound translates his *vida* in "Troubadours—Their Sorts and Conditions":

> The monk, Gaubertz de Poicebot, "was a man of birth; he was of the bishopric of Limozin, son of the castellan of Poicebot. And he was made monk when he was a child in a monastery, which is called Sain Leonart. And he knew well letters, and well to sing and well *trobar*. And for desire of woman he went forth from the monastery. And he came thence to the man to whom came all who for courtesy wished honour and good deeds—to Sir Savaric de Mauleon—and this man gave him the harness of a joglar and a horse and clothing; and then he went through the courts and composed and made good canzos. And he set his heart upon a donzella gentle and fair and made his songs of her, and she did not wish to love him unless he should get himself made a knight and take her to wife. And he told En Savaric how the girl had refused him, wherefore En Savaric made him a knight and gave him land and the income from it. And he married the girl and held her in great honour. And it happened that he went into Spain, leaving her behind him. And a knight out of England set his mind upon her and did so much and said so much that he led her

with him, and he kept her long time his mistress and then let her go to the dogs (malamen anar). And En Gaubertz returned from Spain, and lodged himself one night in the city where she was. And he went out for desire of woman, and he entered the *alberc* of a poor woman; for they told him there was a fine woman within. And he found his wife. And when he saw her, and she him, great was the grief between them and great shame. And he stopped the night with her, and on the morrow he went forth with her to a nunnery where he had her enter. And for this grief he ceased to sing and to compose."

[LE, 95–96]

Pound also tells Gaubertz's story in Canto V (C, 18) and refers to him in Canto XLVIII (C, 243).

14. *enfes*; *era enfes*: "A child"; "he was a child." The words are from Gaubertz's *vida*. Jean Boutière and A. H. Schutz, *Biographies des Troubadours* (Paris: A. G. Nizet, 1964), have "era enfans."

15. *Dalfin*; *Priam*; *Auvergnat*; *Bernart de Tierci*: When Peire de Maensac courted and won the wife of Bernart de Tierci, the Dalfin d'Alverne (or Dauphin d'Auvergne) sheltered him against de Tierci and a war ensued, with the church on de Tierci's side. Pound's translation in "Troubadours—Their Sorts and Conditions" runs:

And he took her to the castle of the Dalfin of Auvergne, and the husband, in the manner of the golden Menelaus, demanded her much, with the church to back him and with the great war that they made. But the Dalfin maintained him (Piere [*sic*]) so that he never gave her up.   [LE, 97]

Pound uses this material in Canto V (C, 18) and in Canto XXIII (C, 108–09). Cf. also "Provincia Deserta," first published in March 1915:

> I have thought of the second Troy,
> Some little prized place in Auvergnat:
> Two men tossing a coin, one keeping a castle,
> One set on the highway to sing.   [P, 122]

16. *"She stood above them all"*: This line is placed after the pool images at line 70 in MS A and replaced with "The empty armour" image at line 36 in MS B, which suggests that it alludes to the Judgment of Paris, the cause of the Trojan war. See also n. 52.

17. *è trobet ella*: "and found her"; from Gaubertz's *vida*. Boutière and Schutz have "e trobet la soa moiller" ("and found his own wife"); their list of textual variants does not give "è trobet ella."

18. *Savairic*; *Mauleon*: Savaric Mauleon, the Provençal nobleman who made Gaubertz a troubadour and knighted him. See also n. 13.

19. *Quel giorno piu . . .*: *Inferno* V.138: "'quel giorno più non vi leggemmo avante'" (that day we read no further), from Francesca's speech to Dante. Landor, whom Pound had read with Yeats at Stone Cottage in 1916, highlights this line in his "Pentameron":

At last she [Francesca] disarms him [Dante]: but how?
"*That* day we read no more."
Such a depth of intuitive judgment, such a delicacy of perception, exists not in any other work of human genius.

20. *catelan*; *castelan*: "squire" (Boutière and Schutz: "castellan"); *e tenc en gran honor*: "and held her in great honor" (Boutière and Schutz: "e tenc la a gran honor"); *tenc . . . anar*: "kept her as his mistress for a long time, and then villainously abandoned her." All these phrases are from Gaubertz's *vida*.

21. *Remi nepotes*: "nephews of Remus"; *in angiportis*: "in alleyways," both from Catullus 68,

to which Pound alludes in "Three Cantos" (1917), p. 182. Both phrases refer to Lesbia's promiscuity, and Pound uses them as tags signifying debased sexual love in the early drafts for Canto IV.

22. *Helen*: Helen of Troy.

23. *Austors; Piere; DeMaensac*: Pound translates from La Tour in "Troubadours—Their Sorts and Conditions":

"'Piere de Maensac was of Alverne (Auvergne) a poor knight, and he had a brother named Austors de Maensac, and they both were troubadours and they both were in concord that one should take the castle and the other the *trobar*.' And presumably they tossed up a *marabotin* or some such obsolete coin, for we read, 'And the castle went to Austors and the poetry to Piere, and he sang of the wife of Bernart de Tierci. . . .'" [LE, 96–97]

and thus "made the new local Troy." See also n. 15.

24. *Procne*: Philomela's sister, Itys's mother, Tereus's queen.

25. *Cytherean*: Venus.

26. *lucida sidera*: "starry lights." Diana is goddess of the moon and of night, and Pound uses the words to underline the sunless quality of her grove. Though the source is irrelevant to Pound's use here, the words occur in Horace's *Ode* 1.3.2 (To Virgil Departing for Greece): "Sic te diva potens Cypri, / sic fratres Helenae, lucida sidera, / ventorumque regat pater," etc.: ("May the goddess who rules over Cyprus, / may Helen's brothers, gleaming fires, / and the father of the winds guide them . . ." [trans. C. E. Bennett, Loeb]).

27. *Pholoe, Niceas*: Pholus was a centaur after whom Hercules named Mount Pholoe. I have found no relevant reference for "Niceas," which seems to be a name Pound invented to signify a nymph, desiring to recall the *choros nympharum* of the opening lines of the poem. Cf. "Nicea" in Canto VII, and cf. the Rodker proof (P), lines 49–50.

28. *L'Engles; us cavaliers Engles*: "the Englishman"; "an English knight," both references to Gaubertz's *vida* (see n. 13). Boutière and Schutz have "us cavalliers d'Angleterra" (a knight of England) and do not list this variant.

29. *Azalais*: Possibly Lady Azalais of Porcairagues, a troubadour of Montpellier; or Lady Azalais of Rocamartina, who, thinking the troubadour Folquet of Marseilles had betrayed her love, refused him her favors.

30. *Crassus*: Marcus Lunius Crassus (d. 53 B.C.), the wealthiest Roman of his time, who owed much of his worth to his ownership of a large fire-fighting company which he would employ only after the owner of a burning building had sold it to him. Pound had read his story in Sallustio's *Histories*, and he momentarily confused his name with that of Croesus, a Lydian king in Herodotus's *Histories*.

31. *Manlius*: Manlius Torquato, the groom in Catullus's epithalamium (61: "Collis o Heliconii"). Fragment 2A is a free re-creation of Catullus's poem, from which Pound takes the epithalamium passages in MS A and MS B. *Carmina tin[n]ula*: "the ringing song."

32. *Aimar of Roussac*: No troubadour of this name is to be found in Boutière and Schutz, *Biographies*. In "Troubadours—Their Sorts and Conditions," Pound writes: "The razos have in them the seeds of literary criticism. The speech is, however, laconic. Aimar lo Ners was a gentleman. 'He made such songs as he knew how to.'" (LE, 99) Perhaps Pound was thinking of this Aimar, his mediocrity being the reason he "could not pay his rent." *Bariols*: Again, I have found no reference. Pound may have been thinking of Peirol, "a poor knight who was fitted out by the Dalfin of Auvergne" whom he mentions in "Troubadours—Their Sorts and Conditions."

33. *"Paris to judgement!"*: This phrase, recalling the Judgment of Paris which precipitated the Trojan War, refers to Menelaus's vengeful single combat with Paris, whom Aphrodite spirits away from the battlefield in *Iliad* 3.299–354. Similarly, Cygnus's father *Neptune* transforms him into a swan as he battles Achilles in *Metamorphoses* 12.74–145.

34. *Nestor*; *Cyllarus*: Nestor's "babble of Centaurs" occupies Ovid's *Metamorphoses* 12.209–356. Cyllarus is a centaur whose beauty Nestor remarks.

35. *Sea-beacons* . . . : Cf. the opening scene of Aeschylus's *Agamemnon*.

36. *Bringer of arrows . . . bearing the shield of Achilles*: References to Odysseus's contest with Ajax for the armor of Achilles in *Metamorphoses* 13.1–402. *Stealer of Pallas' idol*: Pallas's idol was "the famous Palladium, the Luck of Troy": "So long as it was preserved Troy was safe. Ulysses and Diomedes stole it," as recounted in *Metamorphoses* 13.335–56 (Frazer, Ovid's *Fasti*, Loeb, 350).

37. *lisses*: plural of *liss* or *lis*, an old Irish word meaning a circular enclosure having an earthen wall, often used as a fort. Yeats uses the word in "The Secret Rose": "He that drove the gods out of their liss."

38. *Tyndarus*: Helen's stepfather. *Laertes*: Odysseus's father.

39. This passage alludes to several episodes of love travails in the *Metamorphoses*. *Procris*, suspecting her husband of infidelity, hides in the forest to watch him as he hunts, and he unknowingly kills her with his spear (*Met.* 7.690–865). *Pan* mourns because Syrinx eludes him (*Met.* 1.681ff.). *Scylla's* boasts may refer to her betrayal of her father Nisus for love of Minos, Nisus's enemy, in *Met.* 8.8ff., or to the many ships she wrecks on her deadly rocks in the Straits of Messina (*Met.* 14.71–73). Lines 162–68 are based on *Met.* 13.740ff., the story of the *Cyclops'* wooing of *Galatea*, who loved *Acis*; lines 164–68 translate phrases from the Cyclops' song to Galatea. Line 169–73 are taken from *Met.* 14.142ff., the *Sybil's* story of the long years of old age to which *Apollo* condemned her when she refused his love. The Latin phrases translate: "nor anyone, seeing me, would think I had been pleasing to the god Apollo"; "but now my happier days are over"; "feeble old age comes on"; "the fates leave me my voice."

Lines 174–81 also come from *Met.* 14: Circe's nymphs sort the herbs and flowers by which she works her magic in 14.265–69, and 14.321ff. recounts the story of Circe's passion for the handsome *Picus*, who loved *Venilia's* daughter. Circe fashioned a phantom boar to lead Picus into her net, but he refused her, and in vengeance she transformed him into a bird and his companions into beasts.

40. *Artemis*: Virgin goddess of the hunt, the moon, and the night. *Cnydus*: Cnidus, ancient Greek city in Asia Minor which possessed Praxiteles' statue, the Aphrodite of Cnidus. *Mars*: God of war.

41. *Caelestis intus*: "the heaven within," the first words of "De Poeti," a poem by Aurelius Augurellus. Pound quotes its opening lines in "Poeti Latini" in *The Spirit of Romance*, and translates: "An inward celestial power arouseth the bard and ever moveth him toward the 'beyond'" (p. 239); and again in *Gaudier-Brzeska*: "I passed my last *exam.* in mathematics on sheer intuition. I saw where the line *had* to go, as clearly as ever I saw an image, or felt *caelestem intus vigorem*" (91).

42. "*Tiller of Helicon*"; "*Urania's son*": Epithets for Hymen in Catullus's epithalamium, 61. *Amaracus*: an aromatic plant. *O papaver luteum* (Catullus: luteumve papaver): "O saffron-yellow poppy," a metaphor for the bride Aurunculeia's face.

43. Lines 76–80: Cf. the opening lines of Fenollosa's rough translation of *Omakitsu's* "To Gen Ko," or "peach source song," which Pound found in the Fenollosa notebooks:

> Fishing boat driving water love mountain spring
> Both banks peach flower fold between them departure ford
> Sitting seeing crimson tree not know how far distant

44. *Heard the dynastic music*: Cf. Pound's letter to Margaret Anderson of early 1918: "I am, for the time being, bored to death with being any kind of an editor. I desire to go on with my long poem; and like the Duke of Chang, I desire to hear the music of a lost dynasty. (Have managed to hear it, in fact)" (SL, 128).

In "Remy de Gourmont: A Distinction followed by notes," first published in the *Little Review* in February/March 1919, Pound wrote: "I do not think it possible to overemphasize Gourmont's sense of beauty. The mist clings to the lacquer. His spirit was the spirit of Omakitsu; his *pays natal* was near to the peach-blossom-fountain of the untranslatable poem" (LE, 343).

The image recurs in Canto LXXXIV: "that T'ao Ch'ien heard the old Dynasty's music / as it might be at the Peach-blossom Fountain / where are smooth lawns with the clear stream / between them, silver, dividing," (C, 538).

45. *Loredan*: Palace of the Loredan family in Venice.

46. *Angouleme*: Capital city of Charente, a department in western France.

47. *Cynewulf; Sigebriht* (or Sygebryht); *Cyneheard*: Warring nobles of medieval England whose deeds are recorded in *The Anglo-Saxon Chronicle*, 754ff.

48. *Loba*: The lady whom Vidal loved.

49. *Atreus*: Father of Menelaus and Agamemnon.

50. *Leda*: Helen's mother.

51. *"Longa saison . . . amor"*: First line of a song by Peire de Maensac. Pound quotes the song's first two lines in "Troubadours—Their Sorts and Conditions" and translates thus: "For a long time have I stood toward Love / Humble and frank, and have done his commands" (LE, 97n).

52. *Venus nec iners . . . nec torpet lingua, / Suasit mater amoris, ...cytherea thalamo*: "Venus neither idle . . . nor slow of tongue, / The mother of love persuaded,. . . .the Cytherean bower," from Paris's letter to Helen in Ovid's *Heroïdes*, Epistola 16, lines 158, 16, 29 ("nec torpet lingua" does not appear in Ovid's text). *The new Phrygian judge*: De Maensac, who plays Paris's role in the Provençal reenactment of the Trojan drama. Bribed by the promise of Helen, Paris judged Aphrodite more beautiful than Hero and Athena in the Judgment of Paris. The *Lady of Tierci*, similarly, is "daughter of Tyndarus" as Helen was (his stepdaughter). *ab lo gran guerra que fan*: Boutière and Schutz's text of Peire de Maensac's *vida* has "e com gran guerra que·n fetz," which Pound translates in "Troubadours—Their Sorts and Conditions" as "and with the great war that they made" (LE, 97).

53. *Nikè*: Goddess of victory.

54. *Freud*: None of the manuscripts for the first thirty cantos elaborates on this mention of Freud. Pound was scornful of Freudian psychology in the thirties and later, but this early reference suggests an interest in relating Freud's theories to the artist's visionary and creative powers, the "inner zodiac."

55. *Dryad*: Pound's name for Hilda Doolittle.

56. *Et ominis* [omnis] *intellectus omnformis* [est]: "and every intellect is omniform," said by Michael Constantine Psellus, eleventh-century Neoplatonist. Cf. Canto V, line 18, and Canto XXIII, lines 1–2.

57. *Iamblichus*: Greek Neoplationist (fl. A.D. 330); see Canto V, line 17.

58. *Old Agnolo*: Michelangelo Buonarroti. The passage alludes to his several altercations with Pope Julius, who commissioned the famous Tomb of Saint Julius from him. Pound read his letters, and his story is told in William Roscoe's *Life and Pontificate of Leo X*, the source for some of the Italian historical material in the early cantos. *Pape! spurcu 'iu!!*: "Pope! (or, Father!) dirty dog!!" (Sicilian dialect).

59. *Vyasa*: Poet of the Indian epic, the *Mahabharata*; the early manuscripts for *The Cantos* include a passage on this theme. *Sax*: The *Anglo-Saxon Chronicle* draft (fragment 5B) which Pound used in MS B.

60. *So-gioku tai etsu*: So-Gioku answered. *Liu Che*: Chinese poet and painter, d. A.D. 1375. See Canto VII, line 25. This fragment is based on Fenollosa's translation of part of So-Gioku's poem, which Pound found in the Fenollosa notebooks (see MS FN).

61. *fugges*: Pound appears to be punning on forms of the Latin verb *fugere* (to flee) here and

in line 16 to express nostalgia for youthful sensuality. He may be remembering Horace's *Ode* 2.14.1: "Eheu fugaces, Postume, Postume, / labuntur anni" etc.: "Alas, O Postumus, Postumus, / the years glide swiftly by. . . ." (trans. C. E. Bennett, Loeb).

62. *adolence*: adolescence.

63. *Auvezere*: A river near Altaforte (or Hautfort) in Old Provence, site of Bertran de Born's castle.

64. *Goldring*: Douglas Goldring (1887–1960), author of travel books, fiction, and poetry. He was Ford Madox Hueffer's assistant on the *English Review* during Pound's early London years. Pound met him at this time and sent some of his work to Harriet Monroe and to H. L. Mencken. Two poems, "Calle Memo o Loredan" and "Hill House," were published in *Poetry* 4 (September 1914), and a third, "Voyages," in *Poetry* 6 (May 1915).

65. *Arles*: A city in southeastern France, once a flourishing Roman town, later a center of Provençal culture. The Church of St. Trophime was begun there in the eleventh century.

66. *Nam Sygebryht . . . wiotan*: "And Sygebryht his kinsman ruled the kingdom of Wessex," from *The Anglo-Saxon Chronicle*, 754 [756]. The ensuing passage translates part of 755 [757]. This fragment may have been done about September 24, 1915, when Pound wrote to Milton Bronner, "There are two people dying for me to do an epic of AngloSaxon times" (unpublished letter in the University of Texas Library).

67. *Ecce arborem* (or *arbor*) *vitae*: "Behold the tree of life."

68. *Pelion and Ossa*: Mountains in Greece.

69. *Stefano da Verona*: The Italian painter Stefano di Giovanni da Verona (1374 or 1375-ca. 1438). *del quaglia* (or *quaglia*): "of the quail" (ungrammatical Italian). Pound was apparently remembering the quail pictured in Stefano's painting of the *Madonna del Roseto* (Madonna of the Rose Garden), which he refers to as the madonna *in orto* and *in hortulo* (in the garden). The painting is now in the Castelvecchio in Verona, on the river Adige.

70. *Below them* (or *beneath that*) *. . . colourless*: This line appears in "The Alchemist," first published in *Umbra* (1920), where it bore the date 1912:

> Out of Erebus, out of the flat waste of air, lying
>   beneath the world;
> Out of the brown leaf-brown colourless
>   Bring the imperceptible cool.   [P, 76]

71. *Sa've Saa've . . . Regina*: I.e., "Salve Regina," from the Roman Catholic hymn to Mary, "Queen of Heaven"; here sung in a procession in honor of the Virgin.

72. *Henry*: Henry II of England (1133–89; king 1154–89). *Saladin*: Sultan of Egypt (1137?–1193), opponent of the Crusaders. *Eleanor*: Eleanor of Aquitaine (1122–1204); *toutes le premia amante*: "all loved the queen." Henry was Eleanor's second husband. An old legend has it that Saladin was her lover while she was married to Louis VII, a historical improbability. *Estampe*: Battlefield of the Crusades. *Bertrand*: Bertran de Born, famous for stirring up strife between neighboring kings and nobles, notably between Henry and his three sons. *Giraut de Bornelh*: Troubadour poet. He left many crusading songs and was a more public poet than de Born, hence *the Tennysonian pipe*. This theme was omitted from Canto IV and expanded in Canto VI.

73. *Borgia*: Cesare Borgia (ca. 1475–1507), rumored to have murdered his brother Giovanni. *Lorenzaccio*: Lorenzo de Medici, rumored to have murdered his cousin Alessandro. These murders are the main subject of Canto V and were never drafted into Canto IV.

PART II

CHAPTER 3

The Pound Error:
The Limits of Authority
in the Modern Epic

*A man of genius makes no mistakes—his errors
are volitional and are the portals of discovery.*
—Stephen Dedalus, Ulysses

A foot-print? alcun vestigio?
    thus was it for 5 thousand years

thus saith 🦆 ⬛ *(Kati).*
and as for the trigger-happy mind
        amid stars
        amid dangers; abysses
going six ways a Sunday,
                how shall philologers?
                —Canto XCIII

The text of *The Cantos of Ezra Pound* poses one of the most complex editorial tasks in modern literature. The manuscripts for the Fourth Canto give some idea of how intricate the compositional history of Pound's long poem is, and its history of publication is no less so. Composing his epic over a period of fifty years, Pound published individual cantos, completed sections, and collected editions at intervals in England, the United States, France, and Italy. This long and complicated history provided frequent opportunities for errors of every description to enter the text. Printer's errors, of course, occurred at almost every step of the way, but these are only the beginning. As the genetic text of Canto IV shows, Pound himself sometimes made copyist's errors as he typed and retyped his drafts, and at some points, in preparing setting copy for a new edition of a canto, sent a less finished state rather than the final state of an earlier publication to the printer. Further, the British and American editions of the individual sections through *The Pisan Cantos* were typeset from different setting copy, the later edition usually incorporating authorial revisions and corrections, and the British and American texts were revised independently. As a result, there exist two authoritative editions of *The Cantos* which differ from one another in hundreds of lines. A third authoritative text of *A Draft of XXX Cantos*, edited in consultation with Pound, came into existence in the English text of Mary de Rachewiltz's bilingual Italian edition, published in 1961.[1]

While so elaborate a history of composition and publication would be unusual in any period, most of the textual problems to which the branchings of Pound's *Cantos* from its various roots have given rise are familiar enough, and the traditional procedures for treating them suffice. But *The Cantos* also contains an unusual editorial problem caused by its pervasive references and allusions to many sources in various languages: errors and divergences made by Pound himself with respect to these sources as he composed the poem. These include errors of fact such as misremembered names and dates, misquotations, mistranscriptions, misspellings, and transliterations of Greek and Chinese produced by local or otherwise nonstandard principles. Canto IV contains several such errors on the part of the author. As noted earlier, lines 113–14, "Polhonac, / As Gyges on Thracian platter, set the feast," stem from Pound's confusion of the Viscount de Polignac with Raimon de Castel-Roussillon, Soremonda's husband in Cabestan's biography.[2] Hence the reference to Polhonac in the final poem was not intended to introduce a new element but simply to recall the Cabestan story; and the Viscount of Polignac is entirely irrelevant to Pound's poem. This mistake strongly suggests that the associated allusion to "Gyges" may be a similar misremembering:

> Polhonac,
> As Gyges on Thracian platter set the feast,
> Cabestan, Tereus,
> > It is Cabestan's heart in the dish. [ll. 113–15]

This ideogram or subject rhyme brings to mind not Gyges but Astyages, another character in Herodotus, who served up Harpagus's son to him as punishment for Harpagus's failure to carry out one of his commands. If Pound could confuse Polignac and Castel-Roussillon, he might well have confused these two names as well. Achilles Fang notes two other errors. "Ran-ti," the name of the king in the wind-poem vignette (lines 88–99), "is a mistake for Ran-tai . . . which is not the name of a person but a terrace (Orchid Terrace)." And, he adds, in the lines "Père Henri Jacques would speak with the sennin, on Rokku, / Mount Rokku between the rock and the cedars," Pound also departs from fact, for "Rokku is not a mountain. The correct name should be Tai-haku."[3] Similar errors, or apparent errors, abound throughout the

---

1. For a history of the text of *The Cantos* from 1925 to 1975 and fuller documentation of Pound's variable response to proposed corrections, see my "Groundwork for an Edition of *The Cantos of Ezra Pound*" (Ph.D. diss., University of Chicago, 1977), chaps. 1, 3, and 4.

2. See chapter 1, p. 25, and chapter 2, MSS A.10–17, A.72–74, B.100, C.112–16.

3. Achilles Fang, letter to the editors, quoted in *The Analyst*, ed. Robert Mayo, no. 2 (September 1953), pp. 8–9.

poem. For example, Hugh Kenner explains that the last line of Canto I, "Bearing the golden bough of Argicida," "comes from *habens auream virgam Argicida* in the previous [Homeric] hymn, apparently a mistake of Pound's since though Aphrodite is speaking the bearer of that wand is Hermes."[4] The text of Cantos XXXI–XLI contains such errors of fact as "1815" for "1813," "adopted" for "adapted," and "ten years" for "six years." Early printings of Canto LXII have it that a baker's boy instead of a barber's boy incited the riot that led to the Boston Massacre.[5] And John Espey notes Pound's divergence from Bede's Latin in Canto XCV: "Tempus est ubique, / non motus / in vesperibus orbis" (Time is everywhere, / not motion / [ungrammatical:] sphere among evening stars), writing that the "absurd" "vesperibus" is an error for "in vepribus orbis," "sphere among thorn bushes," which Pound probably coined "to suggest the evening star (Vesper/Hesperus/Venus) as enduring center, echoing the canto's opening word, LOVE."[6]

All such errors and/or divergences, because they affect the substance of the words on the page and not merely accidental features such as spelling and punctuation, constitute a textual problem of a different order from printer's errors and variants due to branching recensions. While some may seem to be of slight importance—what difference does it make whether it was a barber's boy or a baker's boy who taunted the British sentinels?—others can lead the exegete far afield. For example, Pound's misremembered "Polhonac" and the likely error of Gyges for Astyages in Canto IV inevitably mislead some readers to interpret an "ideogram" of Canto IV that its author never conceived.[7] There is no question that such errors affect what we read, for they *are* what we read. Yet the problem of defining an editorial policy for treating them is complicated by several factors. First, as in the case of my Gyges/Astyages speculation, we frequently cannot be certain that an apparent error is an actual error. It is possible, for example, that Pound never read Astyages' story, just as it is possible, given the importance of Aphrodite in the poem, that in the "Bearing the golden bough of Argicida" line of Canto I Pound was deliberately reshaping his sources to his own purposes.[8] Now that the possibility of consulting the author is past, there is no way to distinguish positively between intentional divergence and unintentional error.

4. Hugh Kenner, *The Pound Era* (Berkeley: University of California Press, 1971), p. 361n.

5. Mary de Rachewiltz suggests a possible source for Pound's confusion of barber's and baker's boys in a baker's boy (*garzone di fornaio*) named Balilla, who threw stones at Austrian soldiers as they were being chased out of Genoa during the Risorgimento. The fascists, she says, took Balilla as a symbol; boy fascists were called Balilla, and there was a popular song about *l'intrepido Balilla* who *lancia il sasso* (threw the stone).

6. John Espey, "Notes and Queries," *Paideuma* 4 (1975): 181–82.

7. See, for example, Guy Davenport, "Ezra Pound's Radiant Gists: A Reading of Cantos II and IV," *Contemporary Literature* 3, ii (1962): 63–64, and Baumann, *The Rose in the Steel Dust*, pp. 135f.

8. The first draft of the Argicida line does suggest that Pound's turn from the second Homeric hymn to Aphrodite to the first was deliberate; there he wrote,

Even if we could determine which readings are certain errors, however, we would still meet complications in formulating an editorial policy for them. An edited text is ordinarily conceived as one which realizes the author's intentions, that is, which produces exactly the words that the author intended. In most cases, the concept of "authorial intention" is a relatively straightforward means of ruling out printer's errors and other historical accidents. But in Pound's case, as Hugh Kenner has pointed out,[9] the "author's final intention" becomes a fountainhead of ambiguity, for this concept is grounded in notions of correctness, orthographical and other kinds, to which Pound did not consistently and completely subscribe. While it is sometimes clear that he "intended" to write a word other than the one that appears on the page, it is equally true that he did not always wish to correct an error once it had made its way into print. The history of Pound's text shows that he took pains to correct his manuscripts and proofs during the various stages of the poem's publication; whatever the reason for the errors, it was not sheer carelessness. At the same time, mistakes were matters of relative importance to Pound, to be weighed against other considerations. He did not always prefer a "correct" reading but treated the errors in the text eclectically. For example, a letter of March 6, 1927, to Olga Rudge finds him balancing over whether

----

> nigras palpebras, O thou with dark eyelids, sweet-voiced
> [Be thy voice]
> "Bearing the golden bough of Argicida."

This first sketch presents the line as a fragment of Aphrodite's speech rather than mistaking it for one of her attributes, thereby preserving its status in its original context. The emphasis on Aphrodite's voice makes this a highly interpretable moment in *The Cantos*. In the first hymn, the line occurs in a passage narrating Aphrodite's appearance to Anchises, with whom she has fallen in love. Anchises, seized with awe, addresses her as a goddess; and she, aware of mortals' fear that to sleep with an immortal is to risk impotence and death, dissembles her own divinity. Pretending to be the mortal daughter of King Otreus, she says to Anchises, in Dartona's Latin translation,

> Nunc autem me rapuit habens auream virgam Argicida,
> Ex cæto Dianæ aureum collum habentis sonoræ.

(Argicida [Hermes] with his golden wand has just snatched me from the choral dance of noisy Artemis with her golden neck; the Greek text refers to Artemis's distaff of gold [chryselakatos], not to her golden neck.) The quoted line alludes, then, to a seductive lie, and the wand to which Aphrodite alludes—or, in the later text, which she carries—is "proof" of her yarn. Later, in cantos XXIII and XXV, Pound makes the point more clearly by substituting an allusion to King Otreus for the wand. In light of its compositional history, then, the image appears to be not an error but a compressed allegory of the seductions of beauty—specifically, in the context of the *Poetry* cantos, the seductions of *style*—Georgius Dartona's "florid mellow phrase." (III, 202)

9. See Hugh Kenner's introduction to Barbara C. Eastman, *Ezra Pound's Cantos: The Story of the Text* (Orono: University of Maine Press for the National Poetry Foundation, 1979), pp. xi–xii.

the pleasing sonorousness of a possible error in Canto XX outweighed the dubious authority of the only reference work at hand:

> O yes sent off the epreuves of XX, with let us zope his [Pound's] igno-
> rance finally concealed under umpteen corrections, including 2 c's in
> Boccata, who probably ends in an i, but demd if I am going to spoil the
> sound on the authority of a picture post card when his name isn't in
> Baedeker   [L][10]

Some errors mattered and some did not. Thus, examining *A Draft of XVI. Cantos*, he wrote to William Bird, "Vurry noble work. And up to date *no* misprint of any importance—only an *i* for an *o* at the end of Piccinini, where it don't matter a cuss" (SL, 195); and later to Homer Pound, "Only one error that matters. 'Head' should be 'heads' on p. 58, l. 10: heads rose, snake heads not the single head of Medusa herself" (L, January 28, 1925). Regarding even so large an error as the printer's accidental repetition of two whole lines at the end of Canto XIII (first appearing in 1925; corrected in 1971), Pound could surprise routine editorial expectations. Editing his 1958 anthology, *The Art of Poetry*, Hugh Kenner asked Pound whether to correct these lines:

> And even I can remember
> A day when the historians left blanks in their writings,
> I mean for things they didn't know,
> But that time seems to be passing."
> A day when the historians left blanks in their writings,
> But that time seems to be passing."

Pound replied, "Repeat in XIII sanctioned by time and the author, or rather first by the author, who never objects to the typesetter making improve-ments."[11] Yet another justification of error, perhaps the most surprising, oc-curs in Pound's correspondence with Eliot about the Faber edition of *The Pisan Cantos*. Here Pound reverses his earlier desire that his ignorance be "finally concealed under umpteen corrections": "D[orothy] says créees takes three blinkin eee's. I don't care which way it is printed. A little saving igno-rance on the part of the bard might allay venom"; and "even the double ll in balladines can stay as sign of author's iggurunce."[12] Later, he enlarged upon

10. This letter is misdated March 6, 1928, in the Paige collection.
11. Kenner, introduction, *Ezra Pound's* Cantos: *The Story of the Text*, p. xiv. Cf. Norman Holmes Pearson, "Proposed Procedure for Establishing the Text of the *Cantos*" (unpublished paper, 1963, Beinecke Library), p. 1.
12. Unpublished letter to T. S. Eliot dated February 23, 1949; photocopy, Pound/Faber correspondence, Yale Collection of American Literature, Beinecke Library. I am grateful to Peter du Sautoy of Faber and Faber for his help in procuring copies of this correspondence.

this defense of textual error, writing to Norman Holmes Pearson regarding the editing of *The Cantos*, "'Fang-Pearson' text as accurate as the natr of the goddam author permits. WotterELL, CIV/N aint a one man chop."[13]

In Pound's case, then, the concept of "authorial intention" is, at the least, lacking in neatness. As almost all the documents that point to its complications are not yet published, however, the scholars who have worked on his texts have naturally enough tended to assume without question the desirability of an error-free text and have proceeded accordingly. The first editorial project to be brought to conclusion was John J. Espey's text of *Hugh Selwyn Mauberley*, first published in 1955 and revised in 1974. Engaged in the background studies which Pound's poetry necessitates, Espey noticed a number of differences between Pound's poem and its sources, for which he, through Hugh Kenner, submitted corrections to Pound in St. Elizabeths. Pound's response, however, was unexpectedly selective: he accepted most of the changes, added one ("trentuniesme") of his own, and rejected two. These were the spelling "Bloughram" for Browning's "Blougram" and "vacuos exercet aera morsus" for Ovid's "vacuos exercet in aera morsus"—the first for its sound, Espey thought, and the second as having a more direct, however erroneous, correspondence with his own compressed translation, "Mouths biting empty air."[14] Espey, unfamiliar with the expansive range of criteria Pound habitually invoked in considering errors in his texts, was naturally puzzled by Pound's eclecticism. He himself continued to prefer the correct readings. When his book appeared, he began a correspondence with Pound, who explained himself further:

> I am unconvinced re/ CERTAIN sorts of accuracy. Vid. the spellings in the REAL text of Guido, my Marsano, paleog/ edtn. in confronto the ed/ pr/ after Medici editing. . . . I think both Yeats and Fordie also resisted the grammarians. . . . I shd/ be grateful for manifestation SINGular, and for the 31st. I resist the other two EspeyRontos ["Blougram" and "in aera morsus"].[15]

The author's clearly expressed, if idiosyncratic, preferences notwithstanding, the errors in the text continued to pain and puzzle his critics. Pound's way-

13. Unpublished letter dated March 5, 1956, Norman Holmes Pearson Papers, Yale Collection of American Literature, Beinecke Library. I am grateful to Donald Gallup, Pearson's literary executor, for permission to examine the documents of Pearson's work on the text.

14. I am indebted to John Espey for providing me with background information about his edition of *Mauberley* in *Ezra Pound's Mauberley: A Study in Composition* (Berkeley: University of California Press, 1955) in a letter of April 15, 1977, and for photocopies of his correspondence with Pound about the text.

15. Unpublished letter dated March 23, 1955. As for Yeats and Ford having "resisted the grammarians," Pound ought to have known: he himself was the grammarian in those early days. See Richard Ellmann, *Eminent Domain: Yeats among Wilde, Joyce, Pound, Eliot, and Auden* (New York: Oxford University Press, 1965), pp. 64–65.

ward texts embarrassed many scholarly readers, and they continued to advocate corrections. Later on, when Espey's edited text was reprinted in a German edition under Eva Hesse's supervision, both of the rejected corrections were made without asking Pound's approval. According to Espey, once the corrections were in print, Pound "apparently approved them tacitly," and Espey incorporated them in the second American edition of his book in 1974.

Other editorial work on Pound's poetry has proceeded on much the same presumption of the value of a corrected text. J. P. Sullivan, editing the text of the "Homage to Sextus Propertius," suggested a number of corrections to Pound, some of which he accepted ("Citharaon" to "Cithaeron" in I.44; "Atalic" to "Attalic" in VI.16; "Cytharean" to "Cytherean" in II.32; "Cerulean" to "cerulean" in IX.7; "Ranaus" to "Tanais" in XI.5; "'neath . . . shade" to "'neath . . . shade'" in XII.41) and others of which he rejected: "Polydmantus" to "Polydamas" in I.30, even though it was spelled correctly in the *Poetry* and *New Age* printings; "Oetian gods" to "Oetian god" in I.33, because the correction would spoil "the movement of the verse." Sullivan, however, appreciating the "heuristic" method of Pound's translation of Propertius, was less uncomfortable with his "deliberate and obstinate defiance of scholarly standards" and recorded the correct readings in the apparatus instead of changing Pound's text against his wishes.[16]

Editorial work on *The Cantos* has in general also proceeded on the presumption that the ideal text is one which is correct with respect to its sources. Here again, scholars' conception of the poem's "ideal text" has come into conflict with that of its author. For example, Pound's prefatory note to the Chinese Cantos explains that he employs "mainly" French transliterations to signify the fact that "our European knowledge of China has come via latin and french." (C, [254]) Twenty years later, he reiterated this position with respect to the Chinese words in *Section: Rock Drill*. When Achilles Fang, Pound's authority on such matters, suggested that the text be revised to follow standard transliteration of Chinese into English, Pound declined to alter his original readings for reasons he outlined to another correspondent. Through his reading of Frobenius, Pound coined the word "sagetrieb"—literally, "drive to say"; figuratively, tradition—to explain his orthographical rationale:

> I refuse to accept ANY alphabetic display as final/ AND the sagetrieb/ different spellings used to indicate the stream wherethru and whereby

16. See J. P. Sullivan's discussion of "Mistakes and 'Mistakes'" in *Ezra Pound and Sextus Propertius* (Austin: University of Texas Press, 1964), pp. 95–104 (where, in the spirit of the thing, he remarks Pound's stubborn persistence in such errors as "Blougram" in *Mauberley*, himself mistaking the correct reading for the error), and his edited text of the "Homage," pp. 107–71; and Lawrence Richardson, "Ezra Pound's Homage to Propertius," *Yale Poetry Review* 6 (1947): 21–29, who also finds Pound's errors richly interesting and interpretable except for "unpardonable catastrophies [*sic*] like *Citharaon* and *Phaecia*" (p. 23).

our legend came/ latin, portagoose, french. Epos is not COLD history.
got to have emotion, and that from fanatical kungismo.[17]

Fang's suggested changes were never made. However, during the fifties a
number of scholars began working on the text of *The Cantos*, consulting with
Pound about corrections in the text. Although this project was originally
conceived simply as an effort to bring errors in Pound's text to his attention
and to incorporate those corrections which he authorized in later printings
of the New Directions text, economic considerations delayed a full-scale correction of the text until 1970. By that time Pound's health had declined, and
he had lost interest in the editorial project. Proceeding on their own authority, the New Directions committee made more than two hundred changes in
the American printings from 1970 to 1975, which Barbara C. Eastman has
documented in her *Ezra Pound's* Cantos: *The Story of the Text*.[18] While Pound's
approval was obtained at some point for many of these corrections, the inac-
cessibility of the documents necessary to editorial work, the lack of a considered editorial policy and of methodical procedures, and the unmanageable
extent and complexity of the poem conspired against this unsystematic attempt to establish the text of *The Cantos*. Consequently, the changes made
by the New Directions committee cannot be presumed to be authoritative,
but instead constitute newly problematical readings which must be exam-
ined critically in any future attempt to edit the text of the poem.

The current text of Canto IV contains two examples of the editorial committee's corrections. In lines 74–75, the committee altered "The pines at
Takasago / grow with the pines of Isé!" to read "The pine at Takasago / grows
with the pine of Isé!"; and in lines 89–99 they made a number of changes in
the wind-poem passage to make it accord with the original Chinese poem.
In *A Draft of XVI. Cantos*, the first printing of the poem in its final version,
the lines read:

> And So-Gioku, saying,
> "This wind, sire, is the king's wind,
> This wind is wind of the palace,
> Shaking imperial water-jets."
> And Ran-ti, opening his collar:

17. Unpublished letter to Lewis Maverick dated September 2, 1957, Yale Collection of
American Literature, Beinecke Library.

18. See n. 9 above. Eastman discusses the history of the New Directions editorial committee
on pp. 14–16. Pound initially cooperated with the project, Eastman writes, but lost interest
after 1958. Suggestions for corrections came in from many quarters, but "[w]hen the corrections
were eventually made . . . [t]he proposed 'committee' to correct the New Directions text became
Professor Kenner and Eva Hesse, each acting as a consulting editor working directly with the
publishers." (p. 15)

"This wind roars in the earth's bag,
                    it lays the water with rushes;
No wind is the king's wind.
                    Let every cow keep her calf."
"This wind is held in gauze curtains. . . . ."
                    "No wind is the king's. . . ."

Since 1970, the New Directions text has read:

And Sō-Gyoku, saying:
"This wind, sire, is the king's wind,
                    This wind is wind of the palace,
Shaking imperial water-jets."
                    And Hsiang, opening his collar:
"This wind roars in the earth's bag,
                    it lays the water with rushes."
No wind is the king's wind.
                    Let every cow keep her calf.
"This wind is held in gauze curtains . . ."
                    No wind is the king's . . .

In addition to changing the name of the king from Ran-ti to Hsiang and standardizing the transliteration of the Japanese name "So-Gioku," the New Directions text introduces a number of changes in punctuation which alter the structure of the dialogue between the king and the poet So-Gioku. In Pound's original text, So-Gioku asserts that the wind belongs to the king; the king demurs in allegorical recognition of natural powers which surpass his own. The poet answers with an image of the wind held in the palace curtains, again implying the king's possession, which he meets with a second denial: "No wind is the king's." The "corrected" text does not alter So-Gioku's speeches, but the import of the king's responses changes from implied recognition of the limits of his own power to an inconclusive description: "This wind roars in the earth's bag; / it lays the water with rushes." The contradictions of So-Gioku's claims now come from an indeterminate voice outside the dialogue.

While the editors who made these changes undoubtedly meant to realize what they conceived to be Pound's intentions regarding his text, there is no evidence that Pound's approval of these changes was obtained, nor, in view of the value he attached to the historicity of the text, is it likely that he would have given it. It appears, then, that the editors' well-intentioned attempts to correct authorial errors were not informed by the goal of realizing Pound's intentions for the words on the page, but rather projected upon Pound the editors' own presumptions as to the desirability of certain kinds of accuracy in the poem. As the above examples show, the policy for treating Pound's substantive errors is the most important decision an editor makes, for the decision to alter Pound's text to accord with its sources will result in a text very different from that which the decision to preserve these differences will produce. At the same time, because Pound's own treatment is beyond simulation, a particular policy for treating substantive errors will reflect critical, interpretive, and epistemological assumptions which, although they may be unacknowledged, inform the "ideal text" at which the editorial task aims. The disagreement between author and editors as to how Pound's errors ought to be treated brings these assumptions to light and raises interesting questions which concern, finally, not simply the poem or the text, nor Pound's accuracy or lack of it, but assumptions about error and the authority of the printed word which are so deeply engrained in us that they are rarely questioned.

A consideration of the corrections made in Canto IV by the New Directions editorial committee opens up the complexities surrounding the interdependence of critical assumptions and editorial policy. Eastman's history of the New Directions text shows that the editorial committee altered the wind poem with the intention of making the structure of the dialogue between king and poet conform to its structure in the original Chinese poem (pp. 47– 49). A letter from one of the editors notes that in Sung Yü's poem, the poet's argument persuades the king; hence the punctuation changes in lines 96–97 and 99, which silence the king's demurrals.[19] The correction of the Japanese "Ran-ti" to the Chinese "Hsiang" is, of course, another effort to make Pound's text a more accurate reflection of the original poem. However, as we learn from the manuscripts which document the compositional history of Canto IV, Pound's version of the wind poem constitutes not an inaccurate rendering of the original as translated by Waley or Fenollosa, but a deliberate reshaping of Fenollosa's redaction. We recall that the incomplete translation of the poem in the early manuscripts omitted the ending of the original poem and obscured the moral allegory of the dialogue between king and poet. Pound's first version (fragment 2B) interpreted the poet's speeches as flattery; but later, in composing Canto IV, he reshaped the poem to a design of his own, quite different from Sung Yü's original, Fenollosa's partial translation, and his own earlier version. In the context of the Fourth Canto, "Ran-ti"'s denial signifies not a lack of perspective on his own privileged position, as in the original poem as translated by Waley, nor an invitation to flattery, as in frag-

---

19. Letter of March 30, 1977, to me from Barbara C. Eastman, to whom I am indebted for information not included in her text.

ment 2B, but his acknowledgment that nature's power, imaged in the wind, exceeds his own.

Pound's wind poem, then, is far removed from Fenollosa's version and has no historical connection with either the original Chinese poem or any other translation of it. The editors' alterations thus "restore" a relationship between Pound's poem and the original which never existed in the first place. Attempting to "correct" the text, the editors obliterate the traces of the canto's actual source. It is easy to see from the Fenollosa notebook how Pound mistook the word "Ran-ti" for the king's name. Fenollosa's first line reads, "Jo, King of So, went to the palace of Rantai"; above the last word is the gloss, "name of villa." Pound transferred the line into fragment 2B without the gloss; by the time he returned to it in composing Canto IV, he had forgotten the explanatory note, and the syntax of the line made his misreading perfectly plausible. "Hsiang," needless to say, does not occur at all in Fenollosa's translation, which transliterates the Japanese rather than the Chinese pronunciations of the characters. "Ran-ti," then, while clearly an error, also has a historical authenticity, inscribing in the poem not only the Japanese medium through which Pound came to the Chinese poem, but also, in its very mistake, the limiting circumstances of this meeting between East and West. "Hsiang," by contrast, not only fills in the footprints of the word's history but also changes the sound of Pound's line and fits awkwardly with the Japanese "Sō-Gyoku." Though literally correct with respect to the original Chinese poem, with respect to the canto "Hsiang" is a far more egregious error than the one it was intended to rectify. "So-Gioku," while escaping translation into Chinese, is retransliterated into the standard "Sō-Gyoku," erasing the orthographical trace of its origin in the Fenollosa text.

The other substantive change made in Canto IV by the editorial committee, the change of "The pines at Takasago / grow with the pines of Isé!" to "The pine at Takasago / grows with the pine of Isé!" (lines 74–75) appears to have been similarly motivated by a notion that the ideal text in Pound's case is one which perfectly reproduces the details of its sources. According to Eastman nothing in the New Directions files records the reasons for this change, but a glance at the Noh play *Takasago* suggests that, again, the original work was the Procrustean bed to which Pound's text was tailored. In *Takasago*, an old couple personify the spirits of twin pines, one at Takasago and one at Suminoye. Though the legendary pines dwell apart, they are one in spirit in the same way as the old couple who symbolize them. The editorial change, then, was probably an attempt to make Pound's poem more accurate, for in *Takasago*, the single pine of Takasago "grows with" the pine of Suminoye.

Again, however, Pound's text frustrates the scholar's attempt to correct it, for what are the pines (or pine) of Ise, and what have they to do with the pine of Takasago? The only link which the play offers is the fact that the two short poems quoted in the second part come from the *Tales of Ise*, but one would have to go a long way to contrive a specific meaning from this. Perhaps Pound—who never translated *Takasago*—forgot the word *Suminoye* and remembered the word *Ise*, and perhaps he also forgot that there is only one pine in each place. More likely, of course, he simply used the pines, "symbol of the unchanging" as he noted in *Noh or Accomplishment*,[20] and the names Takasago and Ise in a freehand image inspired by the theme of *Takasago*—yet another mythopoeic reading of nature. (We recall Pound's remark to Harriet Monroe that the theme of the *Poetry* cantos was "roughly the theme of 'Takasago.'")[21] In this case, the revision again "corrects" what does not seem to be an error in the sense the editors conceived it to be. With respect to his sources in general in Canto IV, Pound was not concerned with literal accuracy but with nature as a ground for metaphor and with the constancy of metaphorical relations on which his poetic theory depends. It would be absurd to think that Pound "mistook" "Ecce arbor vitae" in fragment c1 to mean "Behold the tree of the visages," its continuation in fragment c2. Rather, this revision resembles the transformative "repeat" of the image in Pound's famous Imagist poem of 1912, "In a Station of the Metro":

> The apparition of these faces in the crowd;
> Petals on a wet, black bough.   [P, 109]

The images are related not by literal translation or metonymic contiguity but by associative metaphor—a creative transformation enacting on the level of word and image the poem's metamorphic theme. To subordinate the words of Pound's poem to the specifics of his sources not only tampers with its history but mistakes the nature of his poetics. He himself did not know or care that, for example, his Mount Rokku is an error, for he explained sanguinely to Felix Schelling, "Rokku is a mountain. I can perhaps emend the line and make that clearer, though 'on' limits it to either a mountain or an island (an ambiguity which don't much matter at that point)." (SL, 180) The primary force of the image is not its reference to a literal event in time, but its expression of affinities between Eastern and Western "interpretations of nature"—as its recurrence in the present tense in Canto LXXXVIII forty years later lets us know: "Père Henri Jacques still / speaks with the sennin on Rokku." (C, 582)

As these examples demonstrate, the danger of mistaking deliberate diver-

---

20. Introduction to *Noh or Accomplishment*, reprinted in *Translations*, p. 222.

21. Unpublished letter to Harriet Monroe, dated January(?) 1917, in the *Poetry* Magazine Papers, 1912–1936, University of Chicago Library.

gences for errors and the impossibility of simulating Pound's eclecticism regarding corrections render a policy of correcting the authorial errors in *The Cantos* unsound. Further, they show that the "corrections" Pound's editors have tended to advocate and, in some cases, have actually made far exceed the limits of editorial authority as it is ordinarily conceived. Most important, they imply a misunderstanding on the part of the editors that involves much more than the errors in the text. The errors which the editors attempted to correct cannot be conceived apart from the authority that informs the poem as a whole, in all its complexities. The errors which Pound wished *not* to correct must be understood as a part of his "intentions" for his poem, in relation both to his aims for the poem at the outset and to the final achievement that the words on the page constitute. In both the above examples, while the editorial changes pay little heed to the author's intentions, it would be too much to say that they seriously hinder our reading. But the interest of the contradictory positions of author and editors, the contesting of authorial intention by editorial intention, is not limited to textual criticism. It is not merely the corrections in themselves but their motives that claim our attention, for the adventures of the letter in Pound's text unlock issues of the spirit that speak much louder than the literal words, whether accurate or inaccurate.

We might begin an inquiry into the ideology of the errors and their correction by asking what it is about Pound's poem that has caused scholars to value literal accuracy with respect to its sources so highly. Coleridge, inspired by Milton's Mount Amara, could imagine his Mount Abora in "Kubla Khan" without moving his editors to enforce fidelity to his source. Keats could even substitute Cortez for Balboa in "On Looking into Chapman's Homer," confusing the exterminator of the Aztecs with the first European to lay eyes on the Pacific, and still be excused by the editors of the *Norton Anthology*, who judge that this error "matters to history but not to poetry." What is acceptable in these texts, however, is unacceptable in Pound's. Indeed, the hundreds of "corrections" for the text of *The Cantos* proposed by scholars attests to the discomfiture which the errors in the poem cause some of its readers.[22] Eastman expresses something of this discomfort in her discussion of alternative stances toward authorial error in *The Cantos*:

> One might contend that we cannot judge *The Cantos* as we would a
> piece of scholarly research or a prose argument from historical or literary
> sources because *The Cantos* is poetry. Therefore, once the printer's mistakes are corrected, the poet's really don't matter. This is itself an ex-

22. Eastman reports that Eva Hesse's list of corrections numbers eight hundred, and that Achilles Fang proposed a proportionate number for the first thirty cantos (*Story*, 9).

traordinary assumption about aesthetics, equivalent to saying that the poetry is the "redeeming feature" of the work. Pound himself argued against such reasoning. . . . He did not ask any special dispensation for his poem on the basis that poets are not expected to get their facts straight when they are giving the reader the facts. Rather, Pound earnestly believed that poets were the only ones who could. *The Cantos* is his testimony in the case. To grant special pleading for poetry is to ignore Pound's claims for it and to devalue his actual achievement in the poem.

[*Story*, 9]

While much of the unpublished evidence of Pound's views on textual matters contradicts the position here attributed to him, Eastman's defense of the corrective stance expresses the special urgency with which Pound's editors press their remedies for deviance—exemplified in her attributing to Pound an earnest belief that only poets can get their facts straight. That the editorial judgment which, in Keats's case, finds that the poet's error matters to history but not to poetry should, in Pound's case, become an extraordinary assumption about aesthetics points to the fact that *The Cantos* is a *qualitatively* different kind of poem from Keats's or Coleridge's: an epic, not a lyric; a self-proclaimed poem including history, not a fantasy of poetic power or a literary rhapsody. It is a poem about public values which, as the early manuscripts show, began in an effort to find a poetic form adequate to modern history, and Eastman, though mistaken in thinking that Pound was committed to factual accuracy above all else, is entirely right to suppose that he would have rejected an aestheticist defense of his errors.

To resist accepting the errors on the grounds that they do not matter to poetry is not necessarily to embrace a policy of correction on the grounds that they matter to history, however. Indeed, the extraordinary assumption about aesthetics which, according to Eastman, informs a conservative stance toward authorial error is balanced by what seems upon reflection to be an extraordinary assumption about history implicit in the corrective stance. To suppose that correcting the errors would be equivalent to getting the facts straight, and that straight facts would ensure a consensus about history, implies belief that there is something called History which admits of perfection with respect both to its linguistic record and, by extension, to our understanding of it. It implies, in other words, that History has an absolute existence, independent of our experience and representation of it, which the poetic text can capture. A claim for the possibility of such a perfect correspondence is implicit in conventional poetic forms, however complexly the thematic ambiguities, counterplots, unfinishability and so forth of a particular poem may subvert or contradict it (*The Aeneid* is perhaps the preeminent example). The experiment of *The Cantos*, while it originated in the desire to discover and explore some fundamental structures in human history, continually met with surprises, uncertainties, and contradictions that pointed to the necessity— and, no less, to the difficulty—of learning to conceive history apart from the certainty of story and the closure of form. As the compositional history of Canto IV illustrates, the contingencies of history continually interrupted and overrode the designs of History—of the structuralist formal idea with which Pound replaced the story with its preordained ends, the "beautiful lie" of epic tradition. The epic task Pound undertook entailed creating a form and language which could register such incursions of history into History, of actual experience into ideas about the world; and for this reason, the historicity of *The Cantos* is not of a kind which precludes error. On the contrary, it is precisely the seriousness of the poem's engagement with the world that gives its errors a significance not found in Coleridge's divagation or Keats's mistake. Error, the root meaning of which is traveling or wandering, is integral to epic; Odysseus, Aeneas, Dante, Don Quixote, Spenser's Redcrosse, Milton's Adam and Eve all wander in and out of the errors, moral, tactical, and spiritual, that give their stories shape and meaning. In Pound's modern epic, in which the happening of history supersedes the closure of story and the author replaces the hero as exemplar of the self in the world, error remains the risk of trial and adventure. The difference between Pound's wanderings and those of the earlier epic heroes, however, is that theirs ultimately return them to a world of stable values. Odysseus's travels and travails end in his *nostos*, or homecoming. Aeneas's wanderings bring him from the timeless past of myth to the fiction of a historical origin invoked to endow with meaning all the events of human time to follow. Don Quixote's "sane" Christian recantation upon his deathbed reverses the effect of his parodistic wandering, in which begins the modern effort to wake from the dreams of authoritative stories to the uncertainties of history. Both Spenser's and Milton's epics endow wandering in history with meaning by imagining it as a progress toward a Christian paradise. All these epics are designed so that errantry ends in a paradisal home in which wandering ceases and all error is redeemed.

What makes Pound's epic both different and definitively modern is that its wandering is unclosed by any such redemption. The mutually mirroring salvations of aesthetic form and thematic paradise (conceived as the dream of a purpose which guides and justifies human history) are both ultimately renounced in *The Cantos*, because Pound had, as he said, "no Aquinas-map," no idea or philosophy from which to trace a governing design for his poem including history. His strategy, instead, was to record his own experience of that dialectic between desire and actuality that is the history of *The Cantos*, and simply to *wait* for the significance of that record to reveal itself. "When

I get to end, pattern *ought* to be discoverable," he wrote to John Lackay Brown. "Stage set à la Dante is *not* modern truth. It may be O.K. but *not* as modern man's." (SL, 293) The history which the poem includes does not fall away like a scaffolding as a transcendent meaning emerges from it. The kind of meaning after which Brown was inquiring never does emerge from Pound's epic, not because the poem is unfinished or a failure but because the history of which it is made never did, in fact, redeem itself into a conventional story, a form in which "it all coheres." But its failure to resolve into a story, paradoxically, *is* its story. The poem is the history and the history is the poem: a record of a world without epistemological certainty, which offers no rest from wandering—a world in which error is all.

The authorial errors in the text of *The Cantos*, then, may be viewed as the "foot-prints" of the unfinished and unfinishable wandering which Pound's epic discovers—against its author's initial hopes as well as its readers'—to be modern history, modern experience. The editorial stances which it is possible to take toward these errors reflect in significant if indirect ways correlative stances toward error as such, for it seems likely that our discomfort with the small errors has more than a casual relation to our discomfort with the inconclusive form of the poem as well as with Pound's real-life errors. In the unresolvability of error or wandering in its three fields in *The Cantos*—letter, form, and, in the widest sense, the history of its making—the history of epic takes a radically different turn.

The Cantos, indeed, appears in certain crucial ways to be the epic to end all epics. In *The Cantos*, the symbolic collision of the Western epic tradition—and the alphabetic writing that carries it—with the metaphorical East invoked by the Chinese ideograms scattered through the text marks the limits of the Western *epos*, grounded since the *Iliad* in a tradition of conquest by violence. There can be very few readers for whom the Chinese characters ever become translucent signs. Their most powerful import remains, even after one learns their significations, the unassimilable difference with which their obscure and silent presence confronts the Western reader. Their alien mode of representation betokens all that exists beyond the closed culture celebrated by the Western epic tradition; their mere presence, apart from particular meanings, frames and limits the humanistic traditions of the Western epic, throwing into relief its ethnocentric conditions. The association of epic culture with speech, tale, and song—the meaning of the Greek *epos*, linked to Latin *vox*—becomes literally and graphically evident in Pound's juxtaposition of Western and Eastern forms of writing. The struggle of *The Cantos* to "make Cosmos" (C, 795), to further a new "civilization" in the twentieth century, is imaged in this juxtaposition, in which the Western *epos* no longer appears as if circumscribing all universal, "human" value within the bounds of what Jacques Derrida has termed its "phonocentric" and transcendentalist traditions.[23] The Chinese writing in Pound's text obscurely signals its anti-epical dimension: a symbolic "going East" of the Western epic, an attempt to escape the correlated epistemological and symbolic models which have, since the *Iliad*, underwritten in the name of "humanity" the traditions of cultural conquest to which Pound opposed his modern epic. *The Cantos'* anthropological array of fragmented images and its open form mark the end of the celebration of the closed culture, with its "basis" in a single, coherent belief (see chapter 1, pp. 12–19), not with the nostalgia of which the poem is so often accused but in acknowledgment that this tradition founded in violence can no longer be imagined as reconcilable with "humane" values given the absolute destructive power which twentieth-century technology has achieved.

To analyze fully the anti-epical dimensions of Pound's epic would require many pages, but it suffices for the textual question to suggest its relevance to the diminishing value that Pound attached to the letter of his text, its "literal" accuracy. We recall his rejoinder to a scholar's query about standard transliteration of Chinese characters: "I refuse to accept ANY alphabetic display as final/ AND the sagetrieb/ different spellings used to indicate the stream wherethru and whereby our legend came." Pound's insistence on the historical aspects of orthography reflects his awareness that language is conventional, underwritten by historical and social factors and not by a transcendent and absolute authority. On the other hand, the kinds of changes Pound's editors made, against his own toleration of error in his text, reflect the view that language and culture have "absolute," static, and standard forms which the poem's mirroring preserves and which its deviations threaten. This assumption is implicitly countered by Pound's advocacy of sagetrieb, a true "philologer's" notion. Conceiving the forms of language and culture as historical and therefore relative, and their authority as social rather than transcendent, Pound's sagetrieb values the diachronic traces of thought and language, the historical directions of their metamorphic flowing and the paths of their dissemination, over standardized orthography. The sagetrieb principle opposes a commitment to the ideal of a static, homogeneous, dominant

23. Although the linguistic aspects of Pound's orientalism originate in a positivist interest in the concept of a natural language, his incorporation of Chinese in the text of *The Cantos* creates, as Derrida remarks, an "irreducibly graphic" poetics. In light of Derrida's argument about the ethnocentricity of Western concepts of language, speech, and writing in *Of Grammatology* (trans. Gayatri Chakravorty Spivak [Baltimore: Johns Hopkins University Press, 1977]; see especially pp. 3–26 and 74–87), Pound's Chinese interpolations gain powerful resonances. Derrida posits a historical conflict between linear and nonlinear forms of writing, a "war" of linear writing against the pluridimensional "mythogram," a primal form of writing which held "technics (particularly graphics), art, religion, economy" in unity. (pp. 85–86) See also Joseph Riddel,"'Neo-Nietzschean Clatter'—Speculation and the Modernist Poetic Image," *Boundary 2* 9–10 (1982): 209–39.

culture identified with "standard" forms, as befits a poem which, to fulfil its project of "including" modern history, must register not one closed culture but a polyphonic global interpenetration of cultures, languages, and histories.

We may observe the relation between Pound's sense of the historical basis of culture and significant authorial error in his text in the Chinese History/John Adams diptych—Cantos LII–LXXI, first published in 1940. His juxtaposition of Chinese history and Revolutionary American politics is a thematic rather than orthographical application of the sagetrieb principle, implying a line of descent from Confucian ethics through the French Enlightenment—via Jesuit sinologists such as Père Joseph-Anne-Marie de Moyriac de Mailla, whose *Histoire générale de la Chine, ou Annales de cet empire* (1777–83) is the principal source for the Chinese History Cantos—to Adams and Jefferson, heirs of the Encyclopedists.[24] Pound's giving over one hundred seventy pages of his poem to this complex exemplum, though unique in its particular form, participates in the heightened political urgency in American art of the thirties: his interest in China and in John Adams was for the sake of the present, not the past. And this context is reflected both in the poetics of the Adams Cantos, their hurried, fragmented, note-taking style, and in the many errors which scholars have identified in the text.[25]

Pound's didactic motive is, by critical consensus, all too obvious in these cantos, which offer very little to conventional poetic taste. Pound was attracted to Adams as a "canonist," a social thinker who helped to institute the values of the new nation, and his presentation of Adams urges the importance of remembering his ground-laying thought in a period of social and economic crisis. Yet both the tortuous poetics and the errors in these cantos qualify Pound's canonizing of the canonist: the sequence is not a shrine but an "instigation," an effort to recover whatever value for the present there might be in a rich American past that had been in effect forgotten. The note-taking style issues from the fact that Pound is composing these cantos as he reads Adams's complete works for the first time; even as he wrote, he complained of the fact that Adams's work was out of print, observing testily that he could see no "regeneration of American culture while Marx and Lenin are reprinted at 10 cents and 25 cents in editions of 100,000 and Adams's and Jefferson's thought is kept out of the plain man's reach." (SPr, 162) In a

24. See Donald Davie, *Ezra Pound: Poet as Sculptor* (New York: Oxford University Press, 1964), pp. 164–67.

25. William Vasse, for example, lists fifty errors in the Adams Cantos in his "American History and the Cantos," *Pound Newsletter*, no. 5 (January 1955), p. 19, and Frederick K. Sanders supplements these with a list of ninety-nine more in *John Adams Speaking: Pound's Sources for the Adams Cantos* (Orono: University of Maine Press, 1975). For a fuller discussion of authorial error and other editorial problems in the text of the Adams Cantos, see my "Pound's John Adams: A Textual Study of Canto LXII" in "Groundwork for an Edition," pp. 275–359.

sense, then, Pound's errors are in keeping with the Adams Cantos' documentary expression of the obscurity into which Adams's work had fallen. (Ironically enough, the first American edition of the Adams Cantos billed them on the dust jacket as the "John Quincy Adams Cantos.") The errors also reflect Pound's historical position with respect to his material, qualifying his own canonizing stance. As Davie shows, after his desperate political efforts of the thirties and early forties, Pound came to believe that the tradition of 1776 had failed for reasons inherent in its premises.[26] Yet what is interesting about the Adams Cantos, composed in 1938–39, is how far their documentary poetics already limits their didactic intention. Their fragmenting mode presents neither historical fact nor authorial judgment in absolute terms, but rather situates the author in history. In the first Adams Canto, Pound pillories Alexander Hamilton, who, as first secretary of the treasury, established the Bank of the United States, tying governmental administration tightly to moneyed interests. In so doing, he explicitly circumscribes his own authority by locating it in history, in a specific time and place:

> and as for Hamilton
> we may take it (my authority, ego scriptor cantilenae)
> that he was the Prime snot in ALL American history
> (11th Jan. 1938, from Rapallo)   [C, 350]

This limitation of authority occurs implicitly as well, in the fact that the fragmentary notes of which the text consists do not transmit Adams's history effectively but rather come into existence as a gesture which connotes curiosity about the past for the interests of the present. Pound himself distinguished his intentions from the historian's, writing to one reader, "Epos is not COLD history. . . . The historian can add footnotes/ in fact the philologers are busy already. Not there, the poem ain't, to explain the history, but to arouse curiosity."[27] The poetics of Cantos LII–LXXI registers the incongruity of epic culture, conceived as a closed world view representable by a single, coherent voice, and the wilderness of modern history. As the modern "epos" is qualified, so is the concept of poetic authority: no divine muse guarantees the modern poet's authority, which must present itself as grounded in history rather than in transcendent truth.

Pound's historical qualification of his own authority in the Adams Cantos makes explicit what was implicit in his poetic modes all along. As early as Canto IV, he had begun to employ poetic strategies, such as the "ideogrammic method," in which meaning is not conveyed directly by signifying

26. See Davie, *Ezra Pound: Poet as Sculptor*, pp. 165–66.
27. Unpublished letter to Lewis Maverick dated September 2, 1957, Beinecke Library.

language but constructed in collaboration with the reader. If this collaboration fails, so does that dimension of meaning, along with the poetics of metaphor designed to create it. The "authority" of the text is thus diffused between author and readers, reflecting, again, its historical and social rather
than transcendent ground. Pound in his modern epic replaces Odysseus as
epic protagonist, but this substitution is not one of hero for hero. The noble,
if fallible, hero of ancient Greek culture is replaced by a representative figure
making its way through the perils of modern history. Whereas Odysseus, as
king and captain, possessed for the Greeks a recognized social position and
authority, and Homer, the bard, had the mystified and mythified social authority of the Muse for his tale, Pound as poet-protagonist can claim for his
poem only the authority of experience. In this way, the "divine" authority of
the Muse is returned to history and to the social agreement—or lack of it—
that permits or refuses the reading of the poem.

Yet, though both thematically and through its poetics *The Cantos* subverts
the traditional concept of epic authority, redefining it as a collaboration between author and readers, critical and interpretive responses to the poem
have tended to assume precisely the models of history and authority which
the poem puts in question. Several critics have argued that Pound's history-
writing is biased. Both Ron Baar and Noel Stock, for example, analyze his
treatment of the Bank War and judge that it favors Jackson's point of view;
and Donald Davie, Harvey Gross, and others find his account of Confucian-
ism wanting in historical accuracy and balance.[28] On their own terms, these
judgments have point, but they mistake the terms of Pound's engagement
with history. As a writer of history, Pound was conscious that his own time
and place determined his perspective on the past. For him, history-writing,
like art, was always "local" (C, 678), and he did not employ the forms of
objectivity. More important, Pound's consciously polemical modes of history-
writing do not simply reject an objective perspective but rather call into
question the possibility of historical objectivity. As early as "Near Perigord,"
Hugh Selwyn Mauberley, and his brilliant rendering of the history of Sigismondo Malatesta in Cantos VIII–XI, Pound had designed poetic modes of
history-writing to render the dynamic flux and chaos of events and the sub-
jectivity of their narration. He had deliberately renounced the illusion of an
accurate representation of historical events from a distanced, objective perspective for an illusion of events represented at first hand in all their imme-
diacy, incompleteness, and doubtful meaning; as, for example, in the Malatesta Cantos, narrated by a composite voice which speaks at different moments

28. See Ron Baar, "Ezra Pound: Poet as Historian," *American Literature* 42 (1972): 531–43;
Noel Stock, *Poet in Exile: Ezra Pound* (New York: Barnes and Noble, 1964), pp. 194–209;
Davie, *Ezra Pound: Poet as Sculptor*, 160–61; Harvey Gross, "Pound's *Cantos* and the Idea of
History," *Bucknell Review* 9 (1968): 14–31.

from the vantage point of the chronicler Gaspare Broglio, of Sigismondo's brother Domenico, a soldier of his army, and of the poet confronting the traces of a past in its fragmentary documents.

Pound's history-writing, far from simply departing from an objective point of view, assumes the deeply problematic nature of the concept of historical objectivity, a fact which interpreters of his poetics have tended to overlook. Joseph Frank, for example, concludes his influential essay "Spatial Form and Modern Literature" with the observation that what occurs in modernist forms is "the transformation of the historical imagination into myth"; the modernists have abandoned "the objective historical imagination" and have created forms which strive to transcend history and temporality. Citing Mircea Eliade's view that modern literature is "saturated with nostalgia for the myth of eternal repetition, and, in the last analysis, for the abolition of time," Frank effectively silences the very considerable historical urgency of modern art and ignores its attempts to confront the *difficulty* of epistemological and communicative acts.[29] In fact, however, Pound's modes of history-writing are informed by an insight into the profound interdependence of history and language. The history cantos' experimental forms embody the idea that, as Hayden White puts it, historical thought "remains the captive of the linguistic mode in which it seeks to grasp the outline of objects inhabiting its field of perception."[30] This condition, analogous to the "Heisenberg microscopes" of quantum physics, encompasses objective or realistic literary modes no less than others. To identify historical objectivity with a temporally straightforward linguistic structure is to assume a model of history that is essentially linear and sequential, requiring for its representation a linear language capable of representing sequence and causality. But the modern physics that evolved alongside modern art has shown our assumptions about temporality to be precariously founded, suggesting that the forms of modern art do not imply an escape from history so much as they challenge the illusion that objectivity inheres in strictly linear and sequential forms of knowing. To complicate Frank's notion of "the objective historical imagination" with the awareness that language and representation are always moved by desire is to acknowledge that what has been said of Pound could be applied to all who write history: that he was the kind of historian who, loving his truth, was bound to distort his facts. To assert, then, as Baar does, that "Pound's *Cantos* lay claim to the validity of historical scholarship [and] claim to be truthful representations of historical events"[31] is to project upon Pound a historical idealism to which his poem does not subscribe. Indeed, it would be more ac-

29. Joseph Frank, "Spatial Form in Modern Literature," in *The Widening Gyre: Crisis and Mastery in Modern Literature* (Bloomington: Indiana University Press, 1963), p. 60.

30. White, *Metahistory*, p. xi.

31. Baar, "Poet as Historian," p. 531.

curate to say that he tailored his facts to abet his "truth." In the Malatesta Cantos, for example, Pope Paul II, in real life tall and so handsome that his conclave would not permit him to take the name "Formosus" for fear of his seeming vain, is nicknamed "fatty Barbo," "Little fat squab 'Formosus'" (C, 51). Again, in Canto XI the lines "And Vanni must give that peasant a decent price for his horses, / Say that I will refund" have their origins in a note which reads: "And don't let Giovanni get gypped in that horse deal." (PA) Neither of these distortions, however, makes Pound's portrait of Sigismondo any less accurate in its general import. In a more recent revisionary history, *The Malatestas of Rimini*, Philip J. Jones concurs with Pound's view that the pope's vilification of Sigismondo was politically inspired rather than founded in fact, and it is this revision of the record that Pound's portrait is designed to achieve.[32] Had his purpose been to present an accurate and straightforward account of the historical facts, he would certainly have failed in it but, as it is interpretation and polemic that inform his treatment of historical material, it is on a different plane that the poem asks to be engaged. "It does not matter a twopenny damn," Pound wrote in *Guide to Kulchur*,

> whether you load up your memory with the chronological sequence of what has happened, or the names of protagonists, or authors of books, or generals and leading political spouters, so long as you understand the process now going on, or the processes biological, social, economic now going on, enveloping you as an individual, in a social order. [51–52]

That it is historical "process" and not isolated facts which Pound aims to represent in *The Cantos*, his divagations from his sources dramatize by their very irrelevance. His concern was to make the reader aware through the act of reading of the historical currents and contexts in which thought, language, and poetic form are inextricably rooted. Norman Holmes Pearson advocated corrections in the text "for those who wish to get history, and to get it through Cantos,"[33] and Sanders recommends correcting "the documentary data of history" presumably for the same reason; but even with all the factual errors in the text corrected, no reader could "get history" from *The Cantos* in any sense that depends upon correctness in details. On the other hand, to attempt to read the poem is immediately to become imaginatively embroiled in the historical process to which Pound committed his poem from the beginning. Some of the manuscripts for the historical cantos make this point strikingly, giving evidence of Pound's concern to create the aura of historical process in *The Cantos* even, sometimes, at the expense of the facts surrounding the poem's

32. Philip J. Jones, *The Malatestas of Rimini* (Cambridge: Cambridge University Press, 1972). See also Michael F. Harper, "Truth and Calliope: Ezra Pound's Malatesta," *PMLA* 96 (1981): 86–103.

33. Unpublished letter to Pound (PA).

literal process. As early as the Malatesta Cantos, the documentary mode of
The Cantos was at moments just that—a *mode*, a technique, simulable pose
rather than literal position, like the "trick / Of the unfinished address" mentioned in "Three Cantos." (I, 114) Later, in the Adams Cantos, Pound placed
documentary tags in the text—

> 18th assistant whereof the said Thomas Adams
>   (abbreviated)   [C, 341]
>
> ten head 40 acres at 3/ (shillings) per acre   [C, 341]
>
> dash had already formed lucrative connections   [C, 368]

—which indicate characteristics not of Pound's source but of his own notebook: "(abbreviated)," "shillings," and "dash" all refer to Pound's first draft,
not to Charles Francis Adams's *The Works of John Adams*. By means of such
"tricks," Pound makes the act of composing the poem continuous with its
representation of history. Its artful self-representation makes the haste, the
urgency, and the partiality of this act, its own historical contingency, a part
of the record.

Elsewhere in *The Cantos*, Pound made it a point to leave "blanks in the
record" for the things he didn't know or wasn't sure of, laying no claim to
the absolute (or divine) authority bound up with straight declaration and
underwritten by an epic muse. In *The Pisan Cantos*, where epic and lyric
modes converge, his documentary technique becomes a poetic instrument of
remarkable sensitivity, able to render lyric consciousness in—and as—its
historical moment. In these cantos, written at a time and place where Pound
had no books, no record but his memory, he often marks the blanks or fuzzy
places with rhetorical brackets, as for example in remembering "the old Dynasty's music / as it might be at the Peach-blossom Fountain / where are smooth
lawns with the clear stream / between them, silver, dividing" or "the grass
on the roof of St What's his name / near 'Cane e Gatto'" or "somebody's
portrait of Rodenbach / with a background / as might be L'Ile St Louis for
serenity" or an anecdote of Swinburne: "When the french fishermen hauled
him out, he / recited 'em / might have been Aeschylus / till they got into Le
Portel, or wherever / in the original." (C, 538, 529, 512, 523)

The ease with which these lapses of memory are acknowledged could occur only in the exercise of a poetic authority antithetical to that claimed by
Homer, Dante, or Milton. Implicitly, what the reader knows, loves, and remembers is as much to be valued as what the poet is remembering. Meaning
resides not in the significations of his words but in their exemplary function;
his memories are representative rather than constitutive treasures. The name

of the port to which Swinburne was conveyed is of no importance; the particular memories only exemplify the comfort that their sustaining presence brings to the poet in the prison camp. In some sense, their "meaning" is that, as he puts it, "What thou lovest well remains / the rest is dross." (C, 520-21)

Pound's demarcation of the historical limits of his own authority within the poem goes a long way toward explaining his tolerance of error in his text—how, for example, he could regard a mistake as a saving sign of the author's ignorance and insist on preserving it. His stance toward the errors in the text reflects a radical transformation of our three-thousand-year-old Western tradition of epic authority, and it is this that accounts for the fact that we still tend to read the poem as though it claims, or ought to claim, the *kind* of authority on which our literary tradition is founded. The historical idealism that leads readers to value correct facts over grasp of historical process, to imagine anyone—the author or ourselves—as capable of taking up an objective vantage point outside history, is also what leads readers to expect from Pound a superior authority that the poem, in representing itself as a poem including history which is itself included in history, is at pains to reject.

It is possible, then, that our habitual assumptions about the intentions of *The Cantos* reveal less about the poem than about the unconscious expectations we bring to it. As a case in point, we may consider Ian F. A. Bell's recent remarks on Hugh Kenner's promotion of *The Cantos'* "curriculum" as a form of closure. Bell argues that

> Kenner's reading of "curriculum" as selection and concentration provides one of the clearest statements we have on the nature of authoritarian rhetoric: curricular concentration is inevitably a seeking after power, the power derived from a selective process designed to refine language for the purposes of manipulation and which always imposes "foreclosures" exactly in the disguise of "possibilities." The assumption of patterns of correspondence . . . becomes, for the modernist writer, a justification for omitting or denying the full range of discourse in favour of the stark solidity of objects which in effect stand on their own and merely signal silently towards the discourse of their hidden unity. This justification announces itself exactly as an ambition for the increased activity of the reader.[34].

Bell's point is an important one, and to a great extent it is justified by the

---

34. Ian F. A. Bell, *Critic as Scientist: The Modernist Poetics of Ezra Pound* (New York: Methuen, 1981), p. 236. Bell is commenting on Kenner's "Art in a Closed World," *Virginia Quarterly Review* 38 (Autumn 1966): 597–613, in which Kenner argues that "What happens in the 'Cantos,' in short, is the deliberate imposition of the closed field on material virtually infinite. . . . [T]he closed field becomes that point of concentration which in proportion as it grows smaller concentrates more intensely the radiant energies of all that we feel and know." (pp. 612–13)

arduous demands *The Cantos* poses for any reader. Even if we understand the project of Pound's ideogrammic poetics as that of producing constellations of images that are transparent in meaning, the failure of his structuralist ideogram to be readable in this way creates the necessity of precisely that kind of reading that Bell decries: the laborious reconstruction of a plausible whole from the broken fragments on the page. But, whether or not one agrees with Bell that to read in this way is to capitulate to an obscure and dangerous exercise of power over the reader by the poet, this activity evades the central difficulty of reading *The Cantos* and its major challenge: that of understanding its form in relation to the historical conditions to which it responds, without denying or repairing its fragmentariness and its failure to conclude, and without smoothing over the difficulties it presents by substituting a reconstituted paraphrase of its sources for the thing itself.

In this light, the proper object of Bell's critique appears to be not so much the poem as certain habits of reading, grounded in long-established but fundamentally problematic assumptions about literary forms in relation to history. These assumptions underlie the reader's attempt to construct a whole from the fragments on the page, to assume and strive to make explicit "the discourse of their hidden unity." Oddly, Bell's misgivings concerning modernist forms seem to imply that nonmodernist aesthetics *can* somehow admit "the full range of discourse," which is to say that they have privileged access to something like truth (although he qualifies this implication in judging modernist forms more pernicious only in degree than "a domesticated history, a version of the past flattened out into the comforting fiction that conventionally representational art promises" [p. 246]). The relative merits of conventional and modernist forms aside, however, I would suggest that Bell's view takes insufficient account of the problematizing of truth implicit in the compromised success/failure of *The Cantos'* collaborative poetics. Pound's poetics of the fragment, I have argued, evolved as an experimental search for forms of order adequate to modern experience, forms that could endow experience with meaning and order without denying the impossibility of conclusion and completion. It is the impossibility of capturing the unity of things finally and totally in any discourse that informs this poetics which, as it is realized in the poem, gestures not toward *the* discourse of the fragments' hidden unity but toward the partiality and contingency of every effort to write history.

I would argue, then, that Bell's point too easily reduces the poet's purposes—and, indeed, those of "the modernist writer"—to a particular critic's at a particular moment. It fails, just as an uncritical adoption of the poem's curricular authority fails, to read *The Cantos* as the historical "record of struggle" Pound said that it was, both explicitly (GK, 135) and implicitly, in the errors, "blanks," and other markers of historical contingency in its text.

For the purposes of this discussion, Kenner's and Bell's positions are not as far apart as they may seem: Kenner desires that the poem should be a locus of curricular authority so that he may affirm it as such, and Bell, that the poem should *claim* to be a locus of curricular authority so that he may reject it as such. Both, in other words, project upon the poem the authority of a sacred book, successful or failed.

In all fairness, both positions rest on aspects of Pound's poetics which appear to support them: Bell's on the structuralist ideology (exemplified in the composition of Canto IV) in which the "ideogrammic method" has its origin, and Kenner's, on the fact that Pound's historical qualification of his own authority was mixed with hopes that the poem would ultimately "co-here," still apparent in his late judgment of it as a "botch" and in "Canto CXX." Neither, however, takes into account the experimental character of Pound's early poetics and the historical context of that experiment, and nei-ther acknowledges the implications of its "failure." Kenner, perhaps, does not acknowledge the failure of the poem's original project at all, and Bell over-looks the fact that it is in the nature of the ideogrammic method to "self-destruct" if its premises are false: if, for example, a reader does not under-stand "red" in looking at a schematic juxtaposition of iron rust, a cherry, a sunset, and a flamingo, then the symbol's intended meaning fails.[35] The prac-tical difficulties presented by Pound's poetics are so great that it seems almost absurd to imagine it as arising from the desire to exert a limiting and con-straining power over the reader. To the contrary, I, for one, have found *The Cantos* the least teachable of books. Its poetics indeed demands collaboration, yet to conceive that collaboration as a mindless capitulation to a hidden agenda imagined to lie behind the apparent innocence of its fragments is to replace the historically grounded, *representative* authority which the poem implicitly and explicitly claims and enacts with the higher, or transcendent, authority attributed to all sacred books. As it is precisely such manipulability on the part of the reader that the ideogrammic method is designed to subvert, and as the power of so demanding a poetics to coerce the attention of a critical reader must be inconceivably small, the accusation that Pound's *Cantos* exert covert authority by linguistic manipulation appears less an accurate descrip-tion of the poem than a new variation on an old theme in Pound studies: the critic's disappointment at not having found, after much effort, the hoped for center, totality, or power that would redeem such energies. In fact, fifteen years ago critics could reject the poem, as Bell does, for precisely opposite reasons. At that time, the common assumption was that Pound *ought* to pre-sent himself as "master of the situation" and that his poem ought to be ana-

35. Pound makes the ideogram for "red" his archetypal example of the ideogrammic method in *ABC of Reading* (1934; New York: New Directions, 1960), p. 22.

lyzable as a structure of "sustained passages [joined] musically or any other way, into larger units, and thence into cantos, each one self-contained yet part of [a] whole" informed by "larger purpose"; and the common complaint—in this example, Noel Stock's—was that *The Cantos* fails to satisfy such expectations.[36] What these opposite descriptions of the poem have in common is a localization of power, or authority, in text and poet, whereas the poetics of *The Cantos* assumes an illimitable and indeterminate diffusion of power/authority through the historical process which envelops author and readers alike. Both descriptions deny that very critical power that Pound's poetics—the ideogrammic method no less than the documentary mode—sought not to coopt but to bring into play: "Properly, we shd. read for power. [One] reading shd. be [one] intensely alive. The book shd. be a ball of light in one's hand." (GK, 55) However fundamental our scholarly tracing of sources and their interrelations is to study of *The Cantos*, it is not in itself the act of reading Pound designed, and it is finally only groundwork and prelude to the actual challenge his poem including history presents and, I think, rewards. Yet Bell's critique has great value in illuminating the extent to which its authoritarian Pound only mirrors the expectations of authority, the desire to be told what to think, feel, and value, that we as readers bring to the poem. The bad faith implicit in the act of reading, the easy abdication of critical authority, is exactly what modernist form challenges in exposing the difficulty of linguistic acts of understanding, meaning, and communication.

Pound's stance toward the errors in his text, then, has a heuristic value in leading us to reevaluate not only the achievement of his *Cantos* but our understanding of its project and the assumptions by which we judge it. The presence of the errors gestures toward a more difficult idea of paradise than the one with which Pound began his modern epic in 1915. Even then, taking up the perennial epic theme of war, Pound set his poem against the violence with which the *Iliad* so ambivalently inaugurates the Western tradition, the tradition of heroic tragedy whose continuing conditions now threaten the destruction not merely of cities but of that very earth which Homer could describe as breeding generations of warriors like leaves. One of his earliest gropings toward *The Cantos* was an image of the great error of World War I, represented in the uncomprehending soldier's monologue of MS Ur1; that catastrophe instigated his search for constants of human experience which might unite diverse peoples at a level beyond their conflicting deities, as imaged in the Jesuit communing with Japanese sennin at the end of that early draft. Pound's ideogrammic method, his lifelong interest in the East, the historical relativism which transforms the concept of epic authority in

36. Noel Stock, *Reading the Cantos: The Study of Meaning in Ezra Pound* (New York: Minerva/Pantheon, 1966), pp. 116–17.

The Cantos, all branch from this root. This dream of a common language gave urgency to his lifework, his effort to imagine a new "civilization"— defined, as he wrote in "Provincialism the Enemy," as "the enrichment of life and the abolition of violence." (SPr, 199) Pound's effort in *The Cantos* to represent forms or patterns in history in the abstract was an attempt to discover a basis for truly universal human values in a world no longer served by its dominant traditions of war and conquest, a world which far exceeds the bounds of the Judeo-Christian theological imagination; and his hope was indeed, as he says in *Guide to Kulchur*, "totalitarian."[37] But if Pound's dream was of an ultimate order of human experience to which one could appeal in seeking an end to intercultural violence and economic exploitation, his poem's claim to greatness rests in its unretouched enactment of the failure of this dream. Although the failure of his early dream eventually led him to carry on a desperate campaign for an *instituted* order (evidenced in his interest in such figures as Confucius, Adams, and Coke) and brought him to make pernicious and disastrous political choices, in the poem in which he recorded his own struggle through modern history that dream of wholeness and order retains the form of desire. If Pound did not find what he was seeking, the "natural" language of transparent metaphor posited in Fenollosa's poetics, still his commitment to the unendingly diverse actualities of the world he lived in kept him from imposing a linguistic and formal order he did not find.

What is more, Pound's commitment to a poetics of history, to bringing words and the world together, issued in his inventing a poetics which permitted him to find what he was not looking for: that difficult idea of paradise that begins to emerge in *The Pisan Cantos*. There Pound records the anguish of giving up the old paradises, old ideas of redemption:

> I don't know how humanity stands it
> > with a painted paradise at the end of it
> > without a painted paradise at the end of it
> the dwarf morning-glory twines round the grass-blade   [C, 436]

But even as he suffers the "magna *NUX* animae" which his own errors have brought upon him, fragments of brightness intrude from the Pisan landscape; and with them the paradise gropingly designated by an aphorism of 1940—"The essence of religion is the *present* tense" (SPr, 70)—begins to emerge in his language. In saying this, I do not mean to sentimentalize the morning-glory or to deflect attention from the seriousness of the misjudg-

37. See Matthew Little's examination of the history of this word and of Pound's "peculiar" use of it in "Pound's Use of the Word *Totalitarian*," *Paideuma* 11 (1982): 147–56.

ments that brought about the poet's incarceration in the prison camp. Rather, I want to suggest that the wandering of attention from paradises lost to the grass-blade traces a more profound movement toward a quite literal understanding of paradise as "the present tense"; and of language, the trace of conscious being, as history, heaven, and hell. The Pisan refrain, "Le Paradise n'est pas artificiel / l'enfer non plus," resituates both paradise and hell in the here-and-now: "unexpected excellent sausage," "the smell of mint under the tent flaps," the minute observation of "an ant's forefoot," the recurring waves of remorse, as "Les larmes que j'ai créees m'inondent." The extreme simplicity of these images makes it easy to miss their import: the discovery of the *paradiso terrestre* that Pound had sought so long and so erringly, in the inferno of the prison camp: in the moment, the "present tense," and in the unending miracle of life observed attentively, with weeping ("Dakruon, dakruon"), in the ant, the wasp, the "green midge half an ant size," the mint that "springs up again in spite of Jones's rodents." Only so simple a paradise, existing at once in history and beyond cultural difference, could answer Pound's earlier motive. As the threat of death made him feel the profoundly simple miracle of the earth, glimpsed in the metamorphoses of Canto IV, so our lately developed technological power to destroy this earth, achieved only months before he wrote *The Pisan Cantos*, gives epic significance to what he would later remember from Washington as "the Pisan paradise."[38]

It is this paradise of the moment, this natural paradise, that Pound also evokes in what are now *The Cantos'* last lines in the American edition:

I have tried to write Paradise

Do not move
Let the wind speak
that is paradise.

The lines express the failure of the ("totalitarian") idea of paradise with which he began, the dream of an encompassing poetics, of a writing, an authority, adequate to "make Cosmos." Yet his refiguring of his former idea of the paradise of human desire in the natural paradise of the earth's unworded speech, even as it announces the failure of the dream that presided over *The Cantos'* beginnings, repeats an early moment in the poem's text and history, the words of the wind poem's king in Canto IV: "No wind is the king's." No longer, however, is the "wind's" power greater than the king's; what has changed in the fifty years separating these moments is precisely that relation of natural to human power that would, formerly, have rendered Pound's "Let the wind

---

38. Unpublished letter to "Somers" dated 1949, Beinecke Library.

speak" a merely rhetorical, or "poetic," idea. Having lived through his life
and his poem, Pound judged the failure of his dream harshly, asking forgive-
ness from "the gods" and from "those I love." But from a vantage point outside this epic autobiography, it is possible to see what Pound from within
could not: that the fragments, both the "spezzato" paradise and the "errors
and wrecks" that are the final poem, in their very partiality make cosmos
more truly than any dream of totality could do.

The fragmentary paradise that Pound wrote, then, was not the one he
intended at the outset to write; yet it seems in retrospect the only one possible to a modern poem including history. He began to write, as we usually
begin to read, in the expectation that his fragments would eventually constitute a coherent whole, and in the end he still believed in a cosmos that "coheres all right / even if my notes do not cohere." (C, 797) He never quite
grasped the paradoxical truth uncovered by his epic wandering, of the necessary, inevitable, and ultimate partiality of all human experience and knowledge, the actual incompleteness, formal implications to the contrary, of all
notes on cosmos. He judged the poem from the standpoint of a failed wish
"To make Cosmos" (C, 795) without realizing that he had done so, not *despite* the fact that, as he said, "my errors and wrecks lie about me" (C, 796)
but *because* his poem including history with its transformed and transforming language succeeds in representing the constitutive status of error, the
partiality of vision, the diversity of experience, and the diffusion of social
authority and power in modern experience. The poem that began as "drafts"
in the expectation of an eventual wholeness—*A Draft of XVI. Cantos*, *A
Draft of Cantos 17–27*, *A Draft of XXX Cantos*—concludes in the volume of
1968, titled simply and finally *Drafts and Fragments of Cantos CX–CXVII*.

The form of *The Cantos* thus challenges and defeats our fantasies of wholeness, completion, and authority, no less than it did its author's. If we are
drawn to this modern epic as to an encyclopedic representation of modern
culture, we discover not a sacred book but a "ragbag" full of errors, not
divagations from a center but an epic wandering that never reaches home.
The promise that lures us of an ordering force to constellate the bewildering
fragments of history, experience, and tradition into "the rose in the steel dust"
is not fulfilled. To read Pound's poem on these terms, which are in some
ways its own, is to judge it a failure. But the drama of its struggle to renounce
the "painted paradise," whether historicist or religious, and of its progress
toward the fragmentary and compromised but possible paradise of history
balances that failure with an unlooked for, and still hardly understood, success. I would, then, argue against the conclusion Michael André Bernstein
reaches at the end of his fine study of the modern verse epic, his interpretation of *The Cantos'* fragments as "splinters of a redemptory wholeness" and
as an "appeal, to a *potential* totality," which, as it were, patches back together

the shattered hopes of the poet.[39] The hope for "redemption" might attach itself instead to the "splinters" themselves, to the "spezzato" Pisan paradise that denies neither hell nor history and lays no claim to what Bernstein calls "a vision of an enlightened totality." (p. 275) The Pisan style, broken as it is and full of errors and "blanks," is yet an unsurpassed instrument for recording what it helps us to know as history. It is in essence a chronicler's style, not a historian's; a style which recalls Benjamin's remark that a "chronicler who recites events without distinguishing between major and minor ones acts in accordance with the following truth: nothing that has ever happened should be regarded as lost for history."[40] And it is this metonymic Pisan style, alive to every chance and contingency—and not the metaphoric style of Canto IV—that best fulfills and "redeems" Pound's desire, early and late, to write Paradise. In the midst of an essay on the idyl, Schiller writes, "All peoples who possess a history have a Paradise."[41] Insofar as the Pisan style delivers to us our own present, in the awareness that every act of consciousness makes history as it makes cosmos, it writes into literary history the different paradise Pound sought.

The authorial errors in *The Cantos*, then, and Pound's resistance to corrections ("'Fang-Pearson' text as accurate as the natr of the goddam author permits"), have a considerable heuristic value in precipitating the issue of authority in the modern epic. Indeed, given the exigencies of the modern epic, the errors, in their representative function, come to seem not a failure of poet and poem but rather an aesthetic and ideological necessity. Otto Rank has observed that in modern cultures, which lack a strongly unifying collective ideology such as Aquinas's and Dante's Christian cosmology, the struggle for the self-representation of the culture must be borne by the artist alone: "the great artist finally has to carry it personally, in artistic development and in human suffering"; "he does not practice his calling, but *is* it, himself, represents it ideologically."[42] It is not incidental to the claims one can make for Pound's experimental and revisionary deployment of epic authority that he risked, made, recorded, and paid dearly for errors which were not solely his own but the crucial errors of twentieth-century history; and further, that his poem records them not simply as events but as modes of thinking and of using language.

39. Bernstein, *The Tale of the Tribe*, p. 273.
40. Walter Benjamin, "Theses on the Philosophy of History," in *Illuminations*, p. 254.
41. Friedrich von Schiller, *Naive and Sentimental Poetry and On the Sublime*, ed., trans., and introduced by Julius A. Elias (New York: Frederick Ungar, 1966), p. 148; quoted by Bernstein, p. 271.
42. Otto Rank, "The Artist's Fight with Art," in *The Myth of the Birth of the Hero and Other Writings*, trans. F. Robbins and Smith Ely Jelliffe, ed. Philip Freund (New York: Vintage, 1964), pp. 187, 190. The first passage is also cited in my commentary on Pound's "Fragment, 1944," *Yale Review* 71 (Winter 1982): 163.

But perhaps the greatest interest of the errors rests in the fact that in undermining the traditional conception of authority, transforming the poet from privileged diviner to representative, erring consciousness, they also dismantle even as they draw into play the dynamics of the powerful political reflexes of hero worship and scapegoating that are so deeply and dangerously engrained in Western humanism.[43] This political psychology has played as striking a role in the reception of Pound's poem including history as in the history of poet and poem. In his hero worship of Mussolini and his scapegoating of Jews, which he was to judge his "worst mistake,"[44] Pound committed glaring, irrevocable, and consequential instances of the two most crucial errors of twentieth-century history. The two sides of this political coin recapitulate themselves, though in far weaker form, in the judging of Pound himself by readers and critics: not only in the relatively minor matter of stances toward error in the text (which correction idealistically denies and castigation scapegoats) but on the level of literary and social politics, almost as though to confirm the representative status of Pound's modern epic. If the dismantling of this dangerous political psychology is the final import of Pound's epic, his poem including history, if the "foot-prints" of this representative—and, so Rank would suggest, sacrificial—epic autobiography are followable to the end, where "worst mistakes" can be vicariously understood, then the errors might indeed be thought paradisal inscriptions, leading its readers as they led the poet to see the inevitable error of all ways, and so, perhaps, teaching us to limit the field—technological as well as verbal—in which our wandering takes its course.

43. See Sandor Goodhart's suggestive discussion of the operation of scapegoat psychology in reader response in his "Lestas Ephaske: Oedipus and Laius' Many Murderers," *Diacritics* 8 (1978): 55–71.
44. "A Conversation between Ezra Pound and Allen Ginsberg," p. 29.

CHAPTER 4

"How shall philologers?":
On the Editorial Project
for *The Cantos*

This is not a work of fiction
nor yet of one man
—Canto XCIX

As the preceding textual studies of *The Cantos* show, Pound's fifty-year effort to compose a modern epic resulted in the creation of a work that is inextricably rooted in its own history. In light of his turn away from stories, from beautiful lies and historicist paradises, to drafts and fragments of the modern world, the phenomenon of error emerges as a constitutive event in *The Cantos* rather than an aberration from a preordained plan. Authorial errors in the text disrupt idealizing conceptions of the relation between literary form and the happening of history in ways that are consistent with Pound's poetics as well as with his ambivalence toward the correction of his text. Both the errors in the poem and Pound's attitude toward them as documented in letters and other supporting evidence call into question not only the desirability but the possibility of that ideally corrected text which the New Directions editorial committee implicitly assumed as its goal.

The argument for retaining substantive authorial errors in the text, however, leaves many questions concerning the editorial task for *The Cantos* unresolved. The current text contains several kinds of error not considered in my earlier discussion of Pound's substantive mistakes: authorial errors of spelling and punctuation; variations in lineation and spacing; printer's errors and authorial errors of transmission. In addition, Pound revised his text at several points in the long history of its publication, introducing changes into one or another of the British, American, or Italian editions which were never incorporated in the others. Finally, the corrections attempted by the New Directions editorial committee themselves become problematic in light of the argument for retaining Pound's substantive errors.

Thus the current text of *The Cantos* could be regarded as adequate only by taking to its last extreme the argument for the historical authenticity of error in Pound's epic; that is, by assuming that the ideal text of *The Cantos* is simply the existing text, the unretouched result of the poem's long and eventful history of production, transmission, and attempted editorial correction. Even for this idea of the text, however, a variorum edition documenting that history would be required to realize fully the historical principle that informs it. It is also possible to conceive of a text of *The Cantos* edited according to principles other than those which inform the extremes of a radically corrected text on the one hand and the text in the last state it attained in the author's lifetime on the other. Pound's own ideas about the editing of his text also ranged between these two positions. "Git the ideaHHHH   Canto text as printed," he wrote to his New Directions editors during the fifties,[1] apparently meaning to deflect attention from small details of the text to the substance of his poem. But this remark may indicate not so much approval of the text "as printed" as dissatisfaction with the editorial proceedings at hand. So, at any rate, suggests a countervailing remark that Pound made to Donald Hall in a 1960 interview: "Of course there ought to be a corrected edition because of errors that have crept in."[2] While the evidence documenting the textual history of *The Cantos* calls into question certain assumptions that its editors have tended to make, it also shows that *The Cantos* presents one of the most challenging editorial problems in twentieth-century literature. If this textual history indicates that we must reevaluate the aims and procedures of the editorial project for *The Cantos*, it also exposes the problems in the text now current and the importance of articulating their implications.

This chapter will offer a preliminary discussion of the editorial project for *The Cantos*, exploring some alternative ways of conceiving its aims and procedures. My purpose is not to argue for any particular position—it is too early in the discussion for that—but to cast some light upon the operations of editorial authority and to suggest something of the range of choices which editorial judgment must address. I will begin by discussing the problem of defining the task of editing *The Cantos* in general terms and conclude with an editorial model of Canto IV designed, on the one hand, to exemplify one possible editorial method; and on the other, to complete the documentation for the text of the Fourth Canto, and in doing so, that cross section of *The Cantos'* compositional and publication history begun in chapter 2.

THE CONCEPT OF AUTHORITY AND THE EDITORIAL PROCESS

The problem of conceiving the editorial task for *The Cantos* begins with defining the nature of authority in the poem. The editorial task has generally

---

1. Quoted by Eastman, *Ezra Pound's* Cantos, p. 9.
2. "Ezra Pound" in *Writers at Work: The Paris Review Interviews: Second Series*, ed. George Plimpton (New York: Viking, 1965), p. 58.

been conceived as aiming to produce a definitive edition consisting of accurate and complete historical documentation and a text which realizes as faithfully as possible the author's intentions for the work. James Thorpe, for example, writes, "The ideal of textual criticism is to present the text which the author intended," identifying and eliminating any changes that have taken place without the knowledge and consent of the author.[3] Whatever the practical difficulties which might prevent this ideal from being realized in actual cases, the author's intention itself is presumed to possess a clear and definite outline; it consists in "those intentions which are the author's, together with those others" of which the author approves or in which the author acquiesces.[4] Thorpe's formulation and discussion of authorical intention allows for considerable complexity, but Pound's case exhibits more dramatic complications than most. His decision to write a poem including history committed him to a historical poetics of process, collaboration, and accident. The question for present purposes concerns the ways in which these aspects of Pound's "intention" imply divergences from conventional editorial aims and procedures.

Pound's construction of epic authority as historical and social rather than transcendent and absolute assumes the collaborative authority toward which, as Thorpe observes, works of art always tend. Pound not only acknowledged but appreciated and occasionally even delighted in the participation of editors, printers, and calligraphers in determining the physical form of his text. An idiosyncratic speller and an impressionistic scholar, he was often grateful for correction. He expected his printers to use their own experience and judgment in the spacing of his free verse on the page, though he too gave special attention to lineation and spacing in making corrections in the proofs.[5] As for the efforts of his editors, as chapter 3 shows, Pound agreed or disagreed depending upon the particular case and according to no discernible principle; and this eclectic response to randomly offered corrections makes the distinction that Thorpe invokes between changes authorized or acquiesced in by the author and unauthorized changes difficult to apply.

The ambiguities of intention created by editorial collaboration in *The Cantos* are illustrated by Eva Hesse's bilingual edition of *The Pisan Cantos*, published in 1956. This text contains a large number of editorial corrections in the English text, some of which certainly have Pound's authority and others of which do not. Pound also mentioned to Pearson that Hesse had in her

3. James Thorpe, *Principles of Textual Criticism* (San Marino, Ca.: The Huntington Library, 1972), pp. 50–51, 79.
4. Ibid., p. 31. G. Thomas Tanselle, however, points out the importance of distinguishing between authorial intention and acquiescence (or expectation); see "Recent Editorial Discussion and the Central Questions of Editing," *Studies in Bibliography* 34 (1981): 52, 62f.
5. For documentation, see my "Groundwork for an Edition," chap. 1. See also C. G. Petter, "Pound's *Personae*: From Manuscript to Print," *Studies in Bibliography* 35 (1982): 111–32.

translation "improved one line of Pisans . . . also some bullseyes."[6] Hesse's collaboration immediately "entered" the authorized English text in an oblique and surprising way: although no change was made in *The Pisan Cantos'* text, Pound memorialized Hesse's intervention in Canto CII of *Thrones*, that part of the text he was then in the process of composing: "Eva has improved that line about Freiheit." (C, 729) The authority for Pound's text thus appears, at times, to extend *The Cantos* beyond its own edges, which bend out with "ragbag" elasticity to incorporate readings of itself—much as part 2 of *Don Quixote* finds the characters criticizing the inadequacies of their own representation in part 1. The Hesse improvement is a material example of the collaborative authority implied in the intricate network of sources and text in *The Cantos* and of the lines of force that connect its words to the world.

Although the collaborative nature of authority in *The Cantos* is evident in Pound's response to Hesse's text, the case only complicates the editorial issue, for the Hesse edition also shows two changes expressly disallowed by Pound on his marked copy of the galleys for the New Directions edition (now in Columbia University Library): "heures" for "heurs" and "memoria" for "memora" in Canto LXXIV and Canto LXXVI, respectively. The problem that arises here is not merely that of distinguishing between readings Pound approved and those he did not but of whether such a principle of selection is appropriate to *The Cantos* at all. Given the conditions of Pound's *Cantos*, is it only the felicitous collaborations of editors which are to be incorporated into the text, or does the nature of authority in the poem open it to less agreeable effects as well? Logical consistency would seem to suggest that no distinction can be made between desirable and undesirable effects of collaboration, but logical consistency is not the only criterion relevant to the form of a poem including history. Common sense, at any rate, counters by observing that the incursions of accident upon the text must be limited if the text that Pound wrote is to be preserved at all.

The importance of this question of how far, for editorial purposes, *The Cantos* is to be understood as not the work of one man is illuminated by the most striking example of collaborative authority in the poem: "Canto CXX," the concluding canto of the current American text and the one from which the title and epigraph of this book are taken.[7] The text of *The Cantos* as Pound left it at his death ended with the "Notes for CANTO CXVII et seq." Only in the 1972 printing of the New Directions text did the six lines now

6. Unpublished letter of January 31, 1955, in the Norman Holmes Pearson Papers, Beinecke Library.

7. I would like to emphasize that the use of "Canto CXX" in my title and epigraph is not intended to affirm that these lines are Pound's intended ending for *The Cantos*; but neither would I wish to deny their many-dimensioned appropriateness as its last lines. Rather, I draw upon them because they strikingly embody the ambiguities of history, form, and intention in the poem and suggestively connect these issues with editorial ones.

titled "CXX" appear at the end of the poem. These lines have a curious history, which Donald Gallup has documented in his *Bibliography*. They first appeared as lines 23, 16–18, and 24–25 of the "Fragment from Canto 115" published in *Threshold* in Belfast, Ireland, in 1962. They were omitted from "From CXV" in the volume publication of *Drafts and Fragments of Cantos CX–CXVII* in 1969. That same year, however, the lines were rearranged and reprinted as "Canto 120" under the by-line "The Fox" in *Anonym*, a little magazine published at Buffalo, New York. The Library of Congress lists no registration of copyright for either *Anonym* or "Canto 120." "Canto 120" next appeared in a New Directions memorial advertisement in *The New York Times Book Review* published shortly after Pound's death on November 1, 1972, which noted that the lines were "copyright 1969 by Ezra Pound";[8] and it appeared as "CXX" at the end of *The Cantos* in the next New Directions printing, issued on December 22, 1972, at which time it was copyrighted as new material in *The Cantos* by the Estate of Ezra Pound.

According to Mary de Rachewiltz, the primary reason for this radical alteration of *The Cantos'* ending was to protect the copyright of the six lines (although this purpose could have been accomplished equally well by registering the *New York Times Book Review* text). The current (since 1975) Faber text of *The Cantos*, which consists of sheets printed by New Directions, omits "Canto CXX" because, as Peter du Sautoy explained in a letter to the *Times Literary Supplement*, "we did not feel certain that these lines were what Pound intended to come at the end of the long poem."[9] Mary de Rachewiltz concurs in the opinion that their placement at the end of *The Cantos* was not authorized by Pound. Any attempt to establish with certainty the status of these lines must of course await whatever evidence concerning the Buffalo publication may eventually come to light. But the evidence as it stands demonstrates that not only small and relatively inconsequential readings but the very shape of Pound's poem, the paradoxical closure of its unfinished and unfinishable text, are at stake in the editorial treatment of its collaborative authority.

The Hesse example and "Canto CXX," while they do not point to any practical solutions to the editorial problem of collaborative authority, represent that authority in such a way as to undermine any notion of final authorial intention in *The Cantos*. They show that the authority that informs *The Cantos* is not monolithic, and that its finality is as contingent as death. (Pound wrote to Pearson, "Cantos won't be finished until my demise, shd always reserve possibility of death-bed swan.")[10] Like many literary works that their

8. *New York Times Book Review*, November 26, 1972, p. 42.

9. Peter du Sautoy, "Pound's 'Cantos,'" Letter to the Editor, *Times Literary Supplement*, August 20, 1976, p. 1032.

10. Unpublished letter of December 5, 1958, in the Norman Holmes Pearson Papers.

authors much revised, it possesses an irreducible temporal depth which any attempt to edit the poem must register.[11] The historical and collaborative authority of *The Cantos* suggests that we must reconceive the text not as an object which the editorial process aims to perfect but as the trace of a temporal process which, as Eva Hesse's improvement and the ambiguities of "Canto CXX" testify, is neither contained and bounded by the author during his life nor concluded and closed off by his death. The authorial intention of *The Cantos* is perhaps best conceived as the written record of a theoretically illimitable linguistic process which the editor aims to trace, through a form of representation complex enough to separate and analyze its many temporal states. Under this description of authorial intention, *the* text of *The Cantos* is conceived not as a flat and final "reading text" but as the fully and accurately documented text in all its historical changes. The editorial representation of this four-dimensional entity would be a variorum text which documents as fully as possible the circumstances of the poem's publication history as well as the variants that that history produced.

One important advantage of such a conception of the editorial project is that its emphasis upon the historical dimensions of the text provides a method for treating editorial corrections of questionable authority, such as those produced by the New Directions editorial committee. Whether or not an editor decides to retain those corrections in the reading text—a problem I will shortly consider—they, like "Canto CXX," hold an authentic and significant place in the poem's textual history and must be fully documented in the apparatus. Such a procedure would register their place in the poem's history without necessarily accepting the text they produce as the best text. It would also resolve the contradiction presented by the New Directions corrections, an instance of collaborative authority in which author and editors appear to have held radically different views of the ideal text. Once the collaborative dimension is acknowledged as intrinsic to the poem (which does not mean that collaborators' effects are not to be distinguished from the author's own), all grounds for the idea that, say, a return to the text as it stood prior to the editorial committee's work on it would more closely approximate Pound's intentions than does the current text disappear. By conceiving the text as its fully documented history, the editor could give priority to Pound's significant toleration of error without erasing the dimension of collaborative authority. In this way, the editor could avoid the peculiar position of attempting to "de-correct" Pound's text, to undo the idealizing efforts of earlier editors in def-

11. The temporal dimension of authority in *The Cantos* exists in relation to Pound's own intentions as well as to those of his collaborators, as the matter of his own revisions during the publication history of his text shows. See the discussion of authorial revisions in Canto IV below.

erence to a new ideal; for a text conceived as its complete history and represented in a fully documented variorum edition would "correct" past errors by historicizing those efforts, not by eradicating them.

The historical and collaborative nature of authority in *The Cantos*, then, renders the concept of a final authorial intention for the words on the page highly problematic, an ideal that is not only impossible to apply to the textual evidence but incompatible with the consequences of Pound's artistic intention of writing a poem including history. Indeed, Pound's documented ambivalence toward the major efforts to correct his texts can be construed as a refusal to *have* a final intention; a refusal to indicate a single preferred state for the text of a poem that he considered drastically unfinished with respect to that fullness toward which he had once imagined his "drafts" to be tending. In retrospect, however, the unfinished end of *The Cantos* appears inherent in its epic project. As no absolute spatial or temporal limits circumscribe the authority of *The Cantos*, only accidental ones, so the broken fragments of the words on the page gesture toward that larger text of the world, toward "Cosmos." If the palimpsest of *The Cantos* consists literally in the record of Pound's changing intentions, its *potential* field is the intertextual web, the sources—not only books but the actual and figurative voices of experience—that determined the words on the page. Thus the collaborative and historical authority constructed in *The Cantos* is theoretically limitable only by the history of written and spoken language which informed Pound's linguistic activity. This idea of *The Cantos'* authority is obviously impossible to represent by any editorial means; but it points to the inadequacy of any attempt to orient the editorial project for *The Cantos* toward producing a critical text which claims to realize the final authorial intention.

The text of *The Cantos* may at first appear to involve highly idiosyncratic aberrations from the "normal" conditions of texts, and its implications for the conception and aims of the editorial project might be judged to be of merely local interest. It is illuminating, then, to place it in the context of some current theoretical debates in the field of textual criticism. In Jerome J. Mc-Gann's view, at present "Textual criticism is in the process of reconceiving its discipline."[12] McGann argues that a crisis in the theory and methodology of textual criticism has arisen in recent years in reaction against a post-Enlightenment tradition of "ideas about the nature of literary production and textual authority which so emphasize the autonomy of the isolated author as

12. Jerome J. McGann, *A Critique of Modern Textual Criticism* (Chicago: University of Chicago Press, 1983), p. 2.

to distort our theoretical grasp of the 'mode of existence of a literary work of art.'" (p. 8) Against this assumption of the autonomy of literary authority, McGann proposes "a socialized concept of authorship and textual authority" (p. 8) which puts in question certain assumptions about the nature of the editorial project that have evolved from the idea of the "author" as an isolated person possessing all legitimate power over the text—particularly the concept of the definitive edition producing a critical text which claims to realize the author's final intentions for the work.

McGann relates what he sees as the current crisis in editorial theory to the "hermeneutics of *textualité*" developed over the past decade and argues that the concept of a final authorial intention which informs the ideal of a definitive edition is deeply problematic from both the historical and the philosophical points of view. (p. 68) The rule of final authorial intentions assumes, McGann observes, that the sole location for the "authority" of literary texts is the author, whereas in fact the production of literary works in modern culture depends upon a complex system involving not only the publication process—in which author, amanuensis, publisher, editor, and printer participate—but the wider "social nexus" within which subjects and issues, linguistic possibilities and the reception of literary works, are defined. The extravagant number of exceptional cases which "elud[e] in various ways . . . the basic working premises of the discipline" (p. 2) suggests the necessity of rethinking the concept of authority and its consequences for the way in which the editorial task is conceived. The methodology evolved to produce a definitive edition must be revised, McGann writes, through "a complex structure of analysis which considers the history of the text in relation to the related histories of its production, reproduction, and reception. We are asked as well to distinguish clearly between a history of transmission and a history of production. Finally, these special historical studies must be embedded in the broad cultural contexts which alone can explain and elucidate them." (pp. 122–23)

The problems currently being addressed by textual critics as McGann outlines them place the problematic nature of literary authority discovered in the case of Pound's *Cantos* in a new perspective. No longer does it appear to be a peculiar exception to the rule; rather, the conditions that make it seem exceptional are perceived as belonging to all literary works, however thoroughly dominated and obscured by myths of transcendent imagination. In its special character as a poem including history, *The Cantos* can perhaps be regarded as a paragon of exceptions, an *epic* embodiment of the social, historical, and collaborative conditions which attend the production of all texts. Pound's question, "how shall philologers?" in Canto XCIII, arising in the midst of the act of composing his modern epic, anticipates some of the issues involved in restoring to the modern discipline of textual criticism a broader and more complex sense of historical context.[13]

One of the most important consequences of the redefinition of authority for the editorial project is that it points to the active and participatory nature of editorial authority. If authority in *The Cantos* is collaborative, to edit the poem is to exercise an authority that has played a part in the intentions that govern it from its beginnings and that the editorial project continues by virtue of its very existence. Indeed, it could be argued that such authority operates, in a sense, even in the absence of an editorial project: if to edit the poem at all is to intervene in its textual history, not to edit it affects its history equally, since it stops that history at an arbitrary point. Whatever text the editor decides to produce will be in an important sense a product of the *editor's* authority. The decisions and choices that determine the treatment of textual error will reflect her or his sympathies and judgments as well as a reading of the poem and its history. The authority exercised by editors upon the text of *The Cantos*, then, might best be conceived not as attempting to realize the author's final intentions, though all evidence of Pound's intentions is crucially relevant to the project, but as attempting to document a more complex structure of intentionality which is not limited by the traditional concept of the author. That structure would itself "include history" in taking account not only of the author's intentions but, insofar as possible, of both the broader determinants and the possible interpretations of those intentions.

Granted the desirability of a variorum text and the importance of regarding this historical text rather than any critical (or eclectic) text as the object of the editorial project, some practical questions as to how to conceive the aims and procedures of the editorial project remain. While it is too early to attempt to define those aims and procedures, it is possible to consider some alternative approaches to the practical problems it presents. One point which it is useful to make at the outset concerns the relation of the various text to the extensive manuscripts accumulated during Pound's composition of *The Cantos*. As is evident from chapter 2, the volume of manuscript material for *The Cantos* is very large, particularly with respect to the first thirty cantos. The present study handles the problem of what would otherwise be an unman-

13. For a different approach to the problem of relating modern textual criticism to the discipline's historical development, see G. Thomas Tanselle, "Classical, Biblical, and Medieval Textual Criticism and Modern Editing," *Studies in Bibliography* 36 (1983): 21–68. Whereas McGann's argument is designed to deepen modern editors' recognition of the exercise of their own authority and to broaden the range of historical evidence to be considered in the editorial process, Tanselle emphasizes continuities between early and modern editorial practice in order to illuminate fundamentals of the discipline as at once unchanging and adaptable to the exigencies of both particular historical moments and specific cases.

ageable quantity of material by separating genetic concerns from textual issues, producing one text that documents the history of Canto IV from its inception to its first publication in volume form and another documenting the poem's publication history from the setting copy for that first edition forward. A complete edition of the textual history of *The Cantos* could also follow this model. It would present the manuscripts for *The Cantos* in a facsimile edition alongside annotated transcriptions, perhaps collating later manuscripts with the setting copy manuscripts or with the texts of the first editions; and it would present the publication history in a variorum text that collates all texts from the setting copy forward. Separating the two stages of the poem's textual history would permit both stages to be approached through methods attending to their differing interests and uses for scholars.[14]

Another question that arises in relation to the conception of the variorum text concerns the "copy-text" chosen as the basis for the collation. I have suggested that the editorial process must aim to produce not a critical text but a historical text, the documented record of the poem's multilayered and multiperspectival intentions. But the choice of copy-text remains an important decision: it will inevitably be taken as privileged over other forms of the text—as in a sense it must be—and it is of course likely that it will serve as the basis for other editions of the poem. The questions, then, are how to choose the text which will serve as the basis for the collation; and whether to edit it once chosen, and if so, how.

We can approach this question through considering two alternative conceptions of the text: a critical or eclectic text, that is, a text constructed on the presumption that it is possible to distinguish what McGann calls "true errors and deteriorations" from "legitimately produced variants"; and a "best text" chosen from the various editions and presented without editorial intervention. Neither of these possible texts would claim definitive or ideal status; both assume the historicity of the editorial endeavor. And neither can lay sole claim to Pound's approval, given his advocacy in the fifties of "Canto text as printed" and in 1960 of "a corrected edition because of errors that have crept in." Both alternatives must be considered, then, on their own merits.

The editorial model of the Fourth Canto which concludes this chapter exemplifies an eclectic text, and a discussion of the procedures of this method may be found there. The arguments in favor of an eclectic text mainly con-

---

14. I am elaborating here on a suggestion made by Louis L. Martz in discussion with the Committee on the Center for Ezra Pound Studies, Beinecke Library, that an eventual facsimile edition of the manuscripts for *The Cantos* must properly be conceived and executed as part of the definitive edition of *The Cantos*—"definitive" being understood to apply to the scholarship and apparatus, not to a critical or reading text, following G. Thomas Tanselle's important clarification of this term in "Greg's Theory of Copy-Text and the Editing of American Literature," *Studies in Bibliography* 28 (1975): 197.

cern its power to construct a "reading text" in which both accidentals—including the ephemeral lineation and spacing of Pound's free verse lines—and revisions may be registered while ascertainable errors of transmission and any effects of editorial interference to which Pound voiced objection may be eliminated. The strongest objections to an eclectic approach are, first, that it involves a more active intervention of editorial authority, with more room for editorial misjudgment and error, than does the best text approach; and second, that it produces a new text, one that never before in the poem's history existed. The former objection is mitigated somewhat by the recognition that any new edition, whether or not it produces a new text, constitutes an exercise of editorial authority; and the latter by the fact that the composite construction of authority in an eclectic text allows for the production of a text in which the author's express intentions can be accorded first importance.

The advantage of the best text approach, on the other hand, is that it reproduces an actual state of the text and so has claims to historical authenticity that a critical text cannot make. An editor could choose, for example, to produce the "Canto text as printed" which Pound commended to the New Directions editors. Not only can this text claim Pound's express authorization (though it is not the only idea of the text he approved); it also precedes the ambiguous corrections made by the New Directions editors. Alternatively, an editor might decide that the best text of *The Cantos* is simply the text as history left it at the time of Pound's death—or even after the addition of "Canto CXX"—on the grounds that this text, though corrupted with many kinds of error from trivial and irritating ones to substantial and highly significant ones, exhibits graphically and literally the integral place of error in the poem and the collaborative nature of its authority. Such a choice would value a text which, for all its errors, contains a record which is an education in the workings of authority in history, a theme no less relevant to the critical approaches that have evolved in the wake of *The Cantos* than to the history of the poem's making. Or again: close study of the text suggests that the Faber and Faber editions of individual sections of *The Cantos* sometimes followed Pound's explicit wishes for the form of his text more closely than did the New Directions texts,[15] and the best text could be judged to be a composite text made up of the best text for each section of *The Cantos*.

While the best text approach would produce a text that had an actual place in the poem's history, it might be objected that, given the importance of the historical dimension of Pound's text, one state of the text cannot be judged "better" than another. Another advantage of the best text approach, however, is that the technology for optical scanning which will make it possible to

15. For evidence, see my "Groundwork for an Edition," chap. 1.

collate printed texts by computer is already on the horizon. Collation by computer would bring a historical text of *The Cantos,* which would otherwise seem an almost impracticably awesome task, into the realm of feasibility; and a historical text based on the best text approach would be much easier and much less expensive to produce than a critical text. On the other hand, computer technology would also greatly facilitate the production of a critical text.

At present, it is too early in the discussion of the problem of editing *The Cantos* to choose between these two alternative approaches—the best of the text's many incarnations or an eclectic text produced according to clearly stated principles; and an argument which definitively elevates one choice over the other may never be possible. It appears that any editorial policy for *The Cantos* will have to justify itself by local rather than timeless criteria, and no choice will be possible until further discussion from other critical and scholarly perspectives has enlarged our understanding of the issues involved. I shall conclude this discussion, then, not by arguing for the merits of one of these alternative conceptions of the editorial project for *The Cantos* but by presenting an example of the more complicated of the two alternatives, a critical text of Canto IV which documents its publishing history from 1924, when Pound completed the setting copy for *A Draft of XVI. Cantos*, through 1970, when the last changes were made in the text. I follow the eclectic method not to recommend it but because, of the two, it is most in need of exemplification, since its procedures are more complicated (and, perhaps, controversial) and its results harder to imagine. Its interest is in providing a text which does not claim definitive status but rather attempts to clear the reading text of effects which bear only accidental relation to Pound's aesthetic intentions while documenting as fully as possible the poem's publication history.

AN EDITED TEXT OF THE FOURTH CANTO

A Historical Overview, 1924–75

Pound completed the setting copy for the Three Mountains Press deluxe edition of *A Draft of XVI. Cantos*, hand printed by William Bird, on January 6, 1924. As Pound was planning to spend several months of that year in Italy, Bird suggested that they meet to go over the setting copy together "'to get it as near as possible letter perfect.'"[16] Bird's printing proceeded at a leisurely pace, however, and as Pound was in Paris during part of the period of its production, he may have had a hand in the proofreading. His letters of 1923–25 show that he remained in close contact with Bird about the prog-

16. Noel Stock, *The Life of Ezra Pound* (New York: Random House/Pantheon, 1970), pp. 332–33.

ress of the book throughout its production. Pound was delighted with the finished product, writing to Bird, "COMPLIMENTI. . . . Vurry noble work. And up to date *no* misprint of any importance—only an *i* for an *o* at the end of Piccinini, where it don't matter a cuss. Mos' remarkable. . . . Placuit oculis." (SL, 195)

Despite Bird's care in editing Pound's setting copy and printing the text, the Three Mountains edition is not quite letter-perfect. It contains a number of printer's errors. In addition, Bird apparently had to make some editorial decisions without consulting Pound, for the text of Canto IV contains some dubious, if minor, departures from Pound's typescript as well as one change which Pound later rejected, restoring his own reading in the setting copy for *A Draft of XXX Cantos*. In the setting copy for Canto IV, Pound's "mirrours" and "blurrs," which agree with all previous texts, are changed to "mirrors" and "blurs," and his "a'top" becomes "a-top" in the printed text. Since Pound never altered any of these words in later texts, these changes may have been made with his approval. The alteration of "slivver" to "sliver," however, seems to have been made by Bird without consulting Pound, who restored the archaic spelling in the setting copy for the Hours edition.

The text of Canto IV was not reprinted for five years, during which Pound was at work on Cantos XVII–XXX. In 1930, it appeared in the new deluxe edition, *A Draft of XXX Cantos*, published by Nancy Cunard's Hours Press. The setting copy for the first sixteen cantos was a set of revised and corrected page proofs of the Bird text. Except for Canto VI, Pound did not take the opportunity to alter any of the early cantos significantly. In Canto IV, he refined the wordplay on Itys's name ("'Tis. 'Tis. Ytis!") and made a number of other, more minor changes. The printing of the volume was too large a project for Cunard's press, and Pound chose François Bernouard, "maître-imprimeur," to print the text. Pound was in Italy during the printing of this volume, and Nancy Cunard supervised the production. Their correspondence suggests that both read proof for the Hours edition, but the finished text contains a number of misprints. Pound appears to have made no revisions in the proof stages of the text.

Three years after the publication of the Hours edition of *A Draft of XXX Cantos*, the collection was reprinted by Farrar and Rinehart in the United States and by Faber and Faber in England. The American edition was set from the Hours text and contains few variations from it. The British edition was probably set from a copy of the Farrar and Rinehart proofs and contains many small corrections and revisions; in Canto IV, for example, "bark" in line 107 is altered to "barge." The 1933 publication thus resulted in two different texts which thereafter descended independently of one another. Pound revised the Faber text only once, in 1950. The Farrar and Rinehart text was reissued by New Directions in 1940 and has since been reprinted in all the

New Directions collected editions. The New Directions text of Canto IV was also revised only once, in 1970, incorporating changes suggested by the New Directions editorial committee.

The 1961 publication of Mary de Rachewiltz's Italian translation of the first thirty cantos, with an edited English text on facing pages, resulted in a third text of Canto IV. The setting copy for the English text was an edited version of the Faber text of 1950, and the Lerici text shows that at some points where the British and American texts differ as a result of independent typesettings and revisions, the Faber text was compared with the New Directions text and the New Dirctions variants were inserted. It contains editorial corrections (although, according to Mary de Rachewiltz, her editorial work was highly unsystematic) and authorial revisions and was approved by Pound himself. There are, then, four authoritative texts of the first thirty cantos: the French, the British, the American, and the Italian.

The first thirty-two lines of the text of Canto IV were reprinted in the three editions of the *Selected Poems* in 1949, 1957, and 1975. These texts contain no variants from the New Directions text of 1948 other than one compositor's error in spacing and its correction. Canto IV was reprinted in both the Faber (1967) and the New Directions (1970) editions of the *Selected Cantos*, each of which underwent independent revision. It is uncertain whether or not Pound was consulted about the alterations in these texts. The replacement of the Greek in lines 86–87 of the Faber text, an authorial revision of 1950, with the earlier New Directions reading may indicate that Pound came to prefer the earlier reading (erasing the link of Catullus with Sappho implicit in the use of Greek), or may simply reflect an editor's attempt to make the British text correspond to the American text. As the New Directions text contains an erroneous correction of the punctuation in lines 19–23, and as Pound's interest in correcting his text faded after the early sixties, the second possibility seems likelier. For this reason, these texts are not treated as authoritative in this editorial model.

Textual Problems

Apart from Pound's own substantive errors and the secondary errors made by editors trying to correct them, the most important textual problem in *The Cantos* concerns the variants in the American, British, and Italian texts which resulted from their independent revision by the author. The New Directions text prior to 1970, when the editorial committee began making their changes, had been continually reprinted, unrevised, from the plates of the first American edition of 1933 (FR33). The Faber text was revised twice, once for the 1933 British edition (FF33, typeset from a revised set of proofs for the American edition), and again in 1950 for *Seventy Cantos* (FF50), the first

British collected edition of *The Cantos*; and it contains many variants from the New Directions text. The Lerici edition of 1961 (L61), which took the Faber text of 1950 as its copy-text, also contains new authorial corrections and revisions. Canto IV contains several examples of variants in the three texts resulting from these several independent revisions:

line 17	FR33:	Ityn, Ityn!
	FF50, L61:	Itys, Ityn!
86–87	FR33:	. . . Hymenaeus Io!
		Hymen, Io Hymenaee! Aurunculeia!
	FF50:	. . . Ὑμην,
		Ὑμεναι ὦ, Aurunculeia! Ὑμην, Ὑμεναι ὦ,
	L61:	. . . Ὑμήν,
		Ὑμέναι ὦ, Aurunculeia! Ὑμήν, Ὑμέναι ὦ,
88	FR33:	The scarlet flower . . .
	FF50:	A scarlet flower . . .
	L61:	One scarlet flower . . .
89	FR33:	And So-Gioku, saying:
	FF50, L61:	So-Gioku, saying:
90	FR33, L61:	"This wind, sire, is the king's wind,"
	FF50:	"This wind is the king's wind,"
93	FR33	And Ran-ti, opening his collar:
	FF50:	That Ran-ti opened his collar:
	L61:	And Ran-ti opened his collar:
107	FR33:	The bark scrapes at the ford,
	FF50, L61:	The barge scrapes at the ford,

The editorial procedure for this problem may seem obvious: simply to incorporate all revisions into the edited text, choosing the most recent revisions in cases where the line received more than one. The matter is not quite so simple, however. As these examples show, Mary de Rachewiltz's Italian text, which takes the Faber edition of 1950 for copy-text, incorporated some of the readings from the New Directions text where the two differ due to the Faber revisions. These readings presumably represent Pound's own preferences and show that he had second thoughts about some of his earlier revisions. But according to Mary de Rachewiltz, the Lerici text was not edited systematically, so that we cannot be sure whether the Faber and Faber variants which the Lerici text contains were actively chosen or simply overlooked in the copy-text. Only three of the seven revised lines in Canto IV, then, may with certainty be said to represent the author's latest preference: the New Directions reading in line 90 and the two new revisions in lines 88–89. The other readings which were already present in the copy-text may or may not have been brought to Pound's attention as variants, and he may or may not have chosen them in preference to the New Directions readings. In cases in which no evidence of Pound's preferences exists, the editorial policy with regard to revisions might be to incorporate the latest authorial revision in the edited text except where there is evidence that Pound preferred an earlier reading to a later revision.

Because this editorial model is intended as an exploration of textual problems in *The Cantos*, the collations annotate the accidental variants in the texts, with the exception of obvious misspellings and typographical errors which Pound himself corrected immediately or in a later draft; the number of dots indicating pauses and elisions; and variations in lineation and spacing which do not affect the disposition of words within a line. A more practical policy for a variorum text of *The Cantos* would be, of course, to annotate only those accidental variants judged to be important to the sense or sound of the poem. The collations bring to light a number of textual matters which require editorial consideration: punctuation and spelling, printer's errors, and errors made by Pound as he recopied his own drafts. Further, Pound's free verse poses a special problem in accidental variants: the determination of the shape of the poem on the page.

The New Directions alteration of the wind-poem passage, discussed in chapter 3, is a good example of a case in which punctuation changes significantly alter the meaning of the lines. Pound was quite careful about punctuation. He treated it experimentally in the early stages of composition, making many changes from one draft to the next, and he also made many corrections and revisions in his printed texts. His minute attention to details of punctuation is illustrated by his restoration of the second dash in line 121, omitted by the printer from the Three Mountains text, on the setting copy for the Hours edition: "Procession,—'Et sa'ave, sa'ave, sa'ave Regina!'—." In many of the accidental variants in Canto IV, we find nothing which markedly affects the sense of the poem: Pound's exchanges of periods, semicolons, and commas have negligible effect on both the flow of the lines and their meaning. Hyphens in words and variations in the number of dots used to indicate pauses and elisions are similarly unremarkable in their effect on the poem's sound and sense.

In many cases, however, Pound uses accidentals to augment or enhance effects of meaning. His revisions in these cases have an interest which justifies their annotation in the apparatus of the edited text. An example of such a case occurs in line 110, which originally read "By Angouleme, gray stone-posts leading nowhither." (See chapter 2, collation, MS C.) After a progression through semicolon, comma, and full stop in the subsequent texts, Pound revised the line to read "Gray stone-posts leading . . ." in the setting copy for the 1925 edition, the dots trailing off to suggest possibilities that the earlier reading had cut off. Canto IV also contains many examples showing replacement of declarative punctuation with exclamation points, tracing the progressive escalation of tone which occurred as Pound worked on the canto. Thus, "Troy but a heap of smouldering boundary stones." (line 1); "ANAXIFORMINGES," (line 2); "'Ityn," (line 16); "Ityn," (line 20); and "Danaë," (line 102) in MS C all become exclamations in MS D or MS E. The same change occurs in "Cadmus of Golden Prows!" (line 4) and "Aurunculeia!" (line 87) in *Poems 1918–21*. And line 77, which read "Behold the tree of the visages," in early drafts, gains first a momentous heightening of tone by means of capitalization and quotation marks in MS E; and later, the exclamation point in the setting copy for the 1925 edition: "'Behold the Tree of the Visages!'" Such a change illustrates on a minute level the romance of Pound's text, for, as chapter 1 shows, the image has no referent outside the poem (the early manuscripts show its origin in "Ecce arbor vitae" [Behold the tree of life]).

In addition to employing punctuation for special effects, Pound also uses it to indicate how the poem should sound when read aloud. In Canto IV, for example, he alters the usual spelling of "Ise" (line 75) to "Isé" to direct its pronunciation. He slows the cadence of line 66: "'Pergusa. . . .pool. . . .pool . . . .Gargaphia." And he experiments with indicating the pronunciation of "regina" in line 122 in several ways in the early texts: "réginá" (MS E); "regínā" (P); "REGinà" (019b).

These examples illustrate the importance of documenting punctuation variants in editorial models of *The Cantos*. An editor would incorporate punctuation revisions in an edited text in the same manner as substantive revisions, identifying and correcting those which are printer's errors. In Canto IV, as it happens, punctuation variants are readily distinguished from printer's errors. For example, the two punctuation variants in the Lerici text— "stone:" for "stone;" in line 27 and "dark." for "dark," in line 46—are compositor's errors owing to the fact that both marks are broken in the Faber copy-text. The omitted punctuation after lines 14 and 76 in the Hours text is also most likely a printer's error, for both appear on the setting copy, and Pound's characteristic treatment of punctuation in revising was to alter or augment it rather than to delete it. The capitalization of "Sennin" in the Hours text (line 111) resulted from an ambiguous-sized, handwritten "s" in the setting copy; becuse all earlier texts read "sennin" and because the word again appears as "sennin" in Canto LXXXVIII forty years later, the original orthography is restored.

Pound himself in his function as copyist also made occasional typographical errors as he retyped his drafts. In Canto IV, he appears to have made three such errors in the setting copy for the Three Mountains edition: he omitted the commas after line 69 and in line 114; and, in deleting the outer set of quotation marks enclosing lines 16–32, he forgot to remove the opening quotation mark from line 19. Whether to restore the earlier readings in the first two instances is a matter of judgment, since one cannot be certain that they were oversights rather than intentional revisions. Given Pound's tendency to change or add to (rather than delete) punctuation in successive drafts, however, and the loss of clarity which these changes effect, the likelihood is that the omissions were accidental and the restorations are desirable.

A second textual problem affecting accidentals is unorthodox spelling. Pound had trouble with spelling and relied on his editors' corrections. When he first began publishing in *Poetry*, he wrote to Harriet Monroe, "And for godsake correct my spelling!"[17] On the other hand, as he soon came to recognize, he made this task rather difficult for his editors by intentionally employing a variety of deviant spellings—for example, the punning "Ityn." Canto IV contains several examples of Pound's deviations from standard spelling: "Rhodez" in line 29; "a-top" in line 36; "*soleils*" in line 69; "So-Gioku" in line 89; and "Terreus" in line 115. The last was corrected to "Tereus" in the Lerici text; the correct spelling also occurs in MS C, which further justifies the change. The correction of the other errors is problematic, however. William Bird, who, it appears, changed "mirrours" to "mirrors" and "blurrs" to "blurs" (lines 5, 7) in the setting copy for the Three Mountains text, also altered Pound's spelling of "slivver," only to have Pound restore his preferred archaic spelling in the setting copy for the Hours edition. The New Directions editors corrected "*soleils*" to "*soleills*" in 1970; it is likely that this change would have been a matter of indifference to Pound, who remarked to one of the scholars working on the text that there was "no standard spelling before 1500 anyhow."[18] "So-Gioku," altered to the standard transliteration "Sō-Gyoku" in 1970, is best left uncorrected, as Pound rejected the standardization of transliterations of oriental words in *The Cantos* in favor of the readings of his sources—in this case, the Fenollosa notebooks. "A-top" is Pound's characteristic spelling, used in all the early texts of Canto IV after MS A (which has the usual spelling, "atop") except the setting copy for the Three

---

17. Letter to Harriet Monroe, undated, in the *Poetry* Magazine Papers, 1912–1936.
18. Ezra Pound to Norman Holmes Pearson on a list of changes which Pearson suggested for *The Cantos*, Yale Collection of American Literature.

Mountains edition, which has "a'top." Since it reappears in the Three Mountains printed text, it may indicate an authorial change in proof, and for that reason it is retained in the edited text. Finally, "Rhodez" is an error for "Rodez," a town in Provence. Boutière and Schutz's variorum edition of the troubadour lives does not list "Rhodez" as a variant spelling,[19] but as Pound is using an old word, as with "*soleils*," perhaps the criterion of orthodoxy weighs lighter than that of historic and aesthetic authenticity. "Rhodez" is the word Pound wrote and retained through many years of opportunities to revise it— perhaps because the "h" heightens the airiness of the word's sound and hence that of the whole line: "and the wind out of Rhodez / Caught in the full of her sleeve." Many of Pound's deviant spellings, then, will be found to have their reasons, or to be validated by his remark on variable "spelling before 1500." For others the same arguments advanced for preserving his departures from factual accuracy may apply: the history of the poem as reflected in its errors has more significance than literal accuracy would achieve. In this example, the imaginary scene called "Rhodez" is arguably a more appropriate setting for the overlay of myths in the passage than the "correct" "Rodez" would be. In any case, as the above examples show, an editor must proceed with caution in making corrections.

One last editorial problem not found in more conventional verse is posed by Pound's free verse, with its irregular indentations, half-lines, lines run over, and spatial separations between sections. The lineation and spacing of *The Cantos* is far more liable to compositor's errors than are sonnets and villanelles, and such errors when made are more likely to pass unnoticed. A page break coinciding with a line break between two sections, for example, may easily result in the two sections being run together in the next printing. The look of the cantos in their final printed state was very important to Pound, and an essential part of the editor's task is to determine lineation and spacing. The later manuscripts for Canto IV show a remarkable consistency of shape. Pound expected the printer to maintain the shape of the setting copy, but he also expected some regularizing of his erratic indentations in the typescript; and, as he put it on the setting copy for *Cantos LII–LXXI*, he wished the printer "to use own skill in getting a good page." (PA)

In the case of Canto IV, Pound had three fine hand printers, all chosen by him personally, for the first printing of the poem in 1919 and the first two collected editions of 1925 and 1930. The three texts vary in lineation and spacing. The Rodker text is set on a line of fewer characters than are the other editions, resulting in several turnover lines, and it places half-lines flush right, giving variable indentations. Bird's Three Mountains Press edition preserves the arrangement of Pound's last manuscript and regularizes the

19. Boutière and Schutz, *Biographies des Troubadours*.

sizes of the indentations from the left margin. Bird may well have consulted Pound about this matter when they met to go over the setting copy; in any case, Pound was delighted with the final product. The Hours edition, set by François Bernouard from page proofs of Bird's text, maintains Bird's lineation and spacing with some exceptions—for example, line 74, broken in the Three Mountains edition, is run on in the Hours edition, a change Pound marked in the Hours setting copy.

Pound's desire that the printer use his own skill in composing the page makes an eclectic treatment of lineation and spacing undesirable. The best editorial procedure might be, then, to select the text which conforms most closely to the verse arrangement of the manuscripts and to adopt this text as copy-text or as copy-text for lineation and spacing if other factors require a different copy-text. The chosen text must be checked against the manuscripts; any obvious errors in following Pound's typescripts would be corrected, and any authoritative changes in the spacing in later editions would be incorporated in the edited text.

Copy-text and Emendation

Because the text of Canto IV is so well documented, the choice of copy-text for a critical text is not crucial, for the authority of variants can usually be determined without much doubt. The editor can thus afford to choose the copy-text on the ground of its fidelity to the free-verse arrangement indicated by the setting copy manuscript. (The manuscript itself is not a good choice for copy-text because of the peculiarities of Pound's typing style and because Pound expected the printer to make some adjustments in lineation and spacing.) Canto IV offers two possibilities for copy-text: the first two editions of the final version of the canto, Bird's Three Mountains Press edition of 1925 and the Hours Press edition of 1930. Both are deluxe editions done by hand printers, but Bird's is the better choice because it is closer to Pound's manuscript and because Bernouard's contains variations which seem to be printer's errors—for example, the closing of the line spaces around line 126, not marked in the setting copy.

The ornamental "P" at the left margin of the opening page of the Bird text necessitates some adjustments of the indentations in the text on that page; these have been made to correspond with the indentation sizes of the other pages. The four marginal tags at lines 16, 33, 82, and 102 occur only in the copy-text. I have numbered the lines at the left margin.

The copy-text has been collated with all the texts listed in the Sigla and emended as follows:

1. Pound's errors and divergences from his sources, both of fact and of orthography, are maintained and the source readings given in the textual notes.

2. Authorial revisions made in the Hours setting copy, the 1933 and 1950 Faber and Faber editions, and the Lerici text are all incorporated in the text. The New Directions revisions of 1970 are not assumed to be authorial. The rationale of each New Directions revision is given in the Textual Notes.

3. Printer's errors are corrected, as are those apparent errors which Pound made in transcribing and transmitting his own text (lines 49, 69, and 114). References to earlier texts not included in the collation are given in the Textual Notes.

4. The lineation and spacing are those of the copy-text except where emended by Pound in later texts.

5. Other emendations and decisions not to emend are explained in the Textual Notes.

6. A list of the emendations in the copy-text follows the Textual Notes.

Transcription of Variants

Only the final readings of the collated texts are given. The deletions in the Three Mountains setting copy may be found in the genetic collation, and those in the setting copy for the Hours edition may be inferred.

All variants are recorded except for differences in lineation and spacing which do not affect the disposition of words within a line, and variants in the number of dots used to indicate a pause or elision. These features are those of the copy-text.

The collation employs the standard form for the listing of variants: line number, lemma, right square bracket, variant(s), and siglum or sigla. Textual readings are given in roman type and editorial commentary is italicized. Editions not specified are understood to agree with the lemma. Where no lemma appears, the reading given is understood to replace the entire line in the texts noted.

When the reading of the lemma results from an authoritative correction or revision, the point of correction or revision is specified: for example, "*corr. L61*" or "*rev. FF33.*" When the revision or correction does not occur in all subsequent texts, those in which it does appear are specified.

A dash between two sigla in the leftmost line of descent in the stemma indicates that the reading is that of all texts between the sigla, inclusive. Thus *ScXVI–ND70* indicates that ScXVI, TM25, ScXXX, H30, FR33, ND48, and ND70 all contain the reading. It says nothing of the Faber texts, the Lerici text, or the New Directions *Selected Cantos*, all of which are individually specified.

Two signs record punctuation variants: a wavy dash (~) replaces a word when the variant occurs in an attached punctuation mark, and a caret (ʌ) notes deletions of punctuation marks. Thus, "mouth.]~ʌ" *H30* indicates that the period after "mouth" is not found in the Hours text.

Sigla

The list and description of texts in the Sigla are based largely on Donald Gallup's *Ezra Pound: A Bibliography*. For further reference, the numbers assigned the texts in the *Bibliography* are given following the publication date. Sigla enclosed in brackets indicate texts which do not differ from those from which they descend for the purposes of the Collation; these sigla do not appear in the Collation. Variants in the texts they identify are the same as those listed for the earlier selected editions from which they descend.

ScXVI   Setting copy for Three Mountains Press edition, dated January 6, 1924. Author's typescript, 6 numbered pages with revisions in ink and pencil by author and editor. (PA)

TM25   *A Draft of XVI. Cantos* (Paris: Three Mountains Press, January 1925). A26.

ScXXX   Page proofs of the Three Mountains edition with author's corrections and revisions, used as setting copy for the Hours Press edition. (PA)

H30   *A Draft of XXX Cantos* (Paris: Hours Press, August 1930). A31a–b.

FR33   *A Draft of XXX Cantos* (New York: Farrar and Rinehart, March 15, 1933). A31c.

FF33   *A Draft of XXX Cantos* (London: Faber and Faber, September 14, 1933). A31d.

ND48   *The Cantos of Ezra Pound* (New York: New Directions, July
[=ND65]   30, 1948). A61a. The text of Canto IV remained unchanged throughout the five additional printings of this edition and the two printings of the second edition (A61e) of 1965.

N49S   *Selected Poems* (New York: New Directions, October 7, 1949).
[=N57S]   A62a. Lines 1–32. This text was reprinted in a new edition
[=F75S]   of *Selected Poems* published by New Directions in 1957 (A62b) without change except for the closing of the line space between lines 12 and 13. In *Selected Poems 1908–1959* (London: Faber and Faber, October 27, 1975; A97) the text is again reprinted unchanged except that the line space is restored.

FF50   *Seventy Cantos* (London: Faber and Faber, September 1, 1950).
[=FF54]   A61b. This text is reprinted unchanged in the 1954 and 1964

[=FF64]   Faber and Faber editions of *The Cantos of Ezra Pound* (A61c and A61d).

L61   The edited English text of Mary de Rachewiltz's bilingual edition of Cantos I–XXX, *I Cantos, di Ezra Pound* (Milan: Lerici—Scheiwiller, [October 1961]). D81.

F67S   *Selected Cantos* (London: Faber and Faber, December 7, 1967). A89a. Printed by offset from the Faber text of *The Cantos* with some revisions based on the New Directions text.

N70S   *Selected Cantos* (New York: New Directions, October 21, 1970). A89b. The *Selected Cantos* text was reset for the American edition and numerous alterations were made. The text differs from ND48, F67S, and ND70.

ND70   *The Cantos of Ezra Pound* (New York: New Directions, No-
[=ND75]   vember 11, 1970). A61f. The New Directions plates were
[=FF75]   revised for this edition, and a number of alterations were made in the text of Canto IV. Canto IV has remained unchanged since this revision in the five New Directions printings to 1975, and in the Faber and Faber edition, which consists of sheets printed from the New Directions plates.

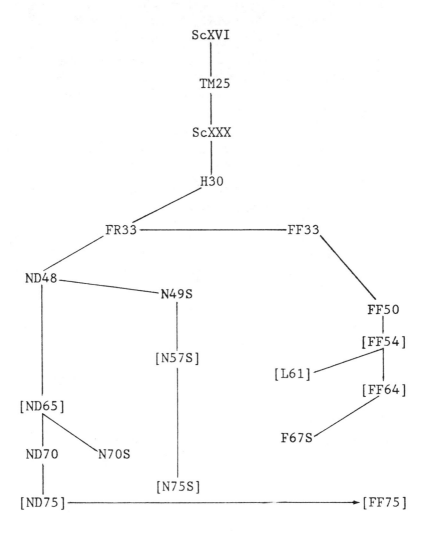

Figure 2. Stemma for Canto IV: Schematic representation of the relationships among the texts of Canto IV from 1924 to 1975.

THE FOURTH CANTO

Palace in smoky light,
Troy but a heap of smouldering boundary stones,
ANAXIFORMINGES! Aurunculeia!
Hear me. Cadmus of Golden Prows!
5   The silver mirrors catch the bright stones and flare,
Dawn, to our waking, drifts in the green cool light;
Dew-haze blurs, in the grass, pale ankles moving.
Beat, beat, whirr, thud, in the soft turf
           under the apple trees,
10   Choros nympharum, goat-foot, with the pale foot alternate;
Crescent of blue-shot waters, green-gold in the shallows,
A black cock crows in the sea-foam;

And by the curved, carved foot of the couch,
       claw-foot and lion head, an old man seated,
15   Speaking in the low drone . . .:
               Ityn!   Itys
Et ter flebiliter, Itys, Ityn!
And she went toward the window and cast her down,
      All the while, the while, swallows crying:
20   Ityn!
        "It is Cabestan's heart in the dish."
        "It is Cabestan's heart in the dish?
        "No other taste shall change this."
And she went toward the window,
25   the slim white stone bar
Making a double arch;
Firm even fingers held to the firm pale stone;

Note: The marginal tags at lines 16, 33, 82, and 102 are found only in the copy-text.

Title: IV *ScXVI, H30–ND70, FF33, FF50, F67S from* Canto IV *N49S* Canto IV *L61, N70S*
    5 mirrors] mirro[u]rs *ScXVI*
    7 blurs] blur[r]s *ScXVI*
  14 seated,] ~ˌ *H30 and all later texts*
  17 Itys] Ityn *ScXVI–ND70, N49S, N70S, FF33; revised FF50, L61*
  19 All] "~ *all texts*
  21 "It] ˌ~ *N70S*
  23 "No] ˌ~ *N70S*
  27 stone;] ~: *L61*

Swung for a moment,
                and the wind out of Rhodez
30 Caught in the full of her sleeve.
                . . . the swallows crying:
'Tis. 'Tis. Ytis!
      Actaeon . . . . .   Actæon
        and a valley,
35 The valley is thick with leaves, with leaves, the trees,
The sunlight glitters, glitters a-top,
Like a fish-scale roof,
        Like the church roof in Poictiers
If it were gold.
40   Beneath it, beneath it
Not a ray, not a slivver, not a spare disc of sunlight
Flaking the black, soft water;
Bathing the body of nymphs, of nymphs, and Diana,
Nymphs, white-gathered about her, and the air, air,
45 Shaking, air alight with the goddess,
        fanning their hair in the dark,
Lifting, lifting and waffing:
Ivory dipping in silver,
        Shadow'd, o'ershadow'd,
50 Ivory dipping in silver,
Not a splotch, not a lost shatter of sunlight.
Then Actaeon: Vidal,
Vidal. It is old Vidal speaking,
        stumbling along in the wood,
55 Not a patch, not a lost shimmer of sunlight,
        the pale hair of the goddess.

The dogs leap on Actaeon,
        "Hither, hither, Actaeon,"
Spotted stag of the wood;
60 Gold, gold, a sheaf of hair,
        Thick like a wheat swath,
Blaze, blaze in the sun,
        The dogs leap on Actaeon.

---

32 Ityn, Ityn! *ScXVI, TM25; revised ScXXX*
36 a-top] a'top *ScXVI*
41 slivver] sliv[v]er *ScXVI*   sliver *TM25, N70S; corrected to* slivver *in ScXXX*
44 air, air,] ∼, ∼. *N70S*
46 dark,] ∼. *L61*
49 o'ershadow'd,] ∼ʌ *all texts*

Stumbling, stumbling along in the wood,
65 Muttering, muttering Ovid:
   "Pergusa. . . .pool. . . .pool. . . .Gargaphia,
"Pool. . . .pool of Salmacis."
   The empty armour shakes as the cygnet moves.

Thus the light rains, thus pours, *e lo soleils plovil*,
70 The liquid and rushing crystal
   beneath the knees of the gods.
Ply over ply, thin glitter of water;
Brook film bearing white petals.
The pines at Takasago
75   grow with the pines of Isé!
The water whirls up the bright pale sand in the spring's mouth.
"Behold the Tree of the Visages!"
Forked branch-tips, flaming as if with lotus.
   Ply over ply
80 The shallow eddying fluid,
   beneath the knees of the gods.

Torches melt in the glare   Hymenæus
   set flame of the corner cook-stall,
Blue agate casing the sky (as at Gourdon that time)
85   the sputter of resin,
Saffron sandal so petals the narrow foot: Ὑμὴν,
 Ὑμέναι᾽ ὦ, Aurunculeia! Ὑμὴν, Ὑμέναι᾽ ὦ,
One scarlet flower is cast on the blanch-white stone.

   So-Gioku, saying:
90 "This wind, sire, is the king's wind,
   This wind is wind of the palace,
Shaking imperial water-jets."

---

 69 *soleils*] *soleills ND70, N70S*   plovil,] ~ ‸ *all texts*
 74–75 at Takasago *dropped one line in ScXVI, TM25; revised ScXXX*   pines . . . grow . . .
pines] pine . . . grows . . . pine *ND70, N70S*
 76 mouth.] ~ ‸ *H30 and all later texts*
 83 set] Set *ScXVI, TM25; revised ScXXX*
 86 Ὑμὴν,] Hymenaeus Io! *ScXVI–ND70, N70S, F67S*   Ὑμην, *FF50*   Ὑμήν, *L61*
 87 Hymen, Io Hymenaee! Aurunculeia! *ScXVI–ND70, N70S, F67S*   Ὑμέναι ὦ, Aurunculeia! Ὑμην, Ὑμέναι ὦ, *FF50;*   Ὑμέναι ὦ, Aurunculeia! Ὑμήν, Ὑμέναι ὦ, *L61*
 88 One] A *ScXVI–ND48, FF33*   The *FF50, F67S; revised L61, ND70, N70S*
 89 So-Gioku] And So-Gioku *ScXVI–ND48*   And Sō-Gyoku *ND70, N70S; revised FF50,*
L61, F67S
 90 wind, sire, is] wind is *FF50, F67S; original reading restored L61*

And Ran-ti opened his collar:
"This wind roars in the earth's bag,
95   it lays the water with rushes;
No wind is the king's wind.
      Let every cow keep her calf."
"This wind is held in gauze curtains . . . . ."
  "No wind is the king's . . . ."

100 The camel drivers sit in the turn of the stairs,
      Look down on Ecbatan of plotted streets,
"Danaë! Danaë!   Danaë
      What wind is the king's?"
Smoke hangs on the stream,
105 The peach-trees shed bright leaves in the water,
Sound drifts in the evening haze,
      The barge scrapes at the ford,
Gilt rafters above black water,
      Three steps in an open field,
110 Gray stone-posts leading . . . . .

Père Henri Jacques would speak with the sennin, on Rokku,
Mount Rokku between the rock and the cedars,
Polhonac,
As Gyges on Thracian platter, set the feast,
115 Cabestan, Tereus,
      It is Cabestan's heart in the dish,
Vidal, or Ecbatan, upon the gilded tower in Ecbatan
Lay the god's bride, lay ever, waiting the golden rain.

By Garonne. "Saave!"
120 The Garonne is thick like paint,
      Procession,—"Et sa'ave, sa'ave, sa'ave Regina!"—

---

93 And Ran-ti opened] And Ran-ti, opening *ScXVI–ND48*   That Ran-ti opened *FF50*
And Ran-ti opening *F67S*   And Hsiang, opening *ND70, N70S; revised L61*
    95 rushes;] ~." *ND70, N70S*
    97 calf."] ~., *ND70, N70S*
    99 "No] ,~   king's . . . ."] ~ . . . , *ND70, N70S*
    107 barge] bark *ScXVI–ND70, F67S, N70S; revised FF33, FF50, L61*
    111 Père Henri Jacques, *ScXVI, TM25; revised ScXXX*   sennin] Sennin *H30 and all later*
texts
    112 Mount] On Mount *ScXVI, TM25; revised ScXXX*
    114 platter,] ~, *ScXVI and all later texts*
    115 Tereus] Terreus *ScXVI–ND48, FF33, FF50, F67S; corrected L61, ND70, N70S*

Moves like a worm, in the crowd,
Adige, thin film of images,
Across the Adige, by Stefano, Madonna in hortulo,
125 As Cavalcanti had seen her.

    The Centaur's heel plants in the earth loam.

And we sit here . . . .
        there in the arena . . . .

121 Regina!"—] ~!"ˌ *TM25; corrected ScXXX*
122 crowd.] ~, *ScXVI, TM25; revised ScXXX*
123 thin] this *TM25; corrected ScXXX*
125 her.] ~, *ScXVI, TM25; revised ScXXX*
127 . . . .] ---- *ScXVI*

Textual Notes

19 All] Lines 16–32 were originally enclosed in quotation marks; lines 21–23 were a quotation within a quotation, enclosed in two sets of quotation marks. In retyping the poem for ScXVI, Pound removed the outer set of quotation marks but forgot to remove the one in line 19. The editors of N70S noticed the error, but, not having the earlier texts to refer to, corrected it incorrectly by removing the opening quotation mark from line 21.

27 stone;] The punctuation change in L61 (~:) resulted from a broken letter in the setting copy (FF50) and is not an authoritative revision.

29 Rhodez] The correct spelling is *Rodez*.

36 a-top] Though the setting copy reads "a'top," "a-top" is Pound's preferred spelling, occurring in all the manuscripts after MS A.

41 slivver] Pound changed the standard spelling of TM25 back to the archaic spelling in ScXXX.

44 Nymphs,] The comma was deleted in O19b, the final state of the Rodker text, but Pound retained it in the last manuscript, ScXVI, so it is retained in the text.

46 dark,] The punctuation change in L61 (~.) resulted from a broken letter in the setting copy (FF50) and is not an authoritative revision.

49 o'ershadow'd,] The comma was added in O19b, the final state of the Rodker text, and omitted from later texts, which descended from the first state.

69 *soleils*] Pound's spelling is retained here, as in L61. The motive of the ND70 revision seems to have been conformity with the spelling of the word in Arnaut Daniel's "Lancan son passat li giure" in Pound's *Translations*.

74–75 pines . . . grow . . . pines] The ND70 revisions attempt conformity with the Noh play *Takasago*.

86–87 The accents in the Greek have been corrected, following Liddell and Scott.

89 So-Gioku] The ND70 revision is the standard transliteration of the Japanese name. Pound's transliteration, taken from Fenollosa, is retained, as it indicates his source for the material.

93 Ran-ti] The ND70 reading, "Hsiang," is the name of the king in the original Chinese poem; Ran-ti (or Ran-tai) is the name of the palace (Orchid Terrace).

95–99 The punctuation changes in these lines in ND70 represent the editors' attempt to make the structure of Pound's text conform to that of the original Chinese poem.

111 sennin] The capitalization of "sennin" in H30 appears to be an error due to an ambiguous holograph initial letter in ScXXX. It is corrected on the basis of previous texts and its recurrence as "sennin" in Canto LXXXVIII.

111–12 Rokku] Achilles Fang points out that "Rokku is not a mountain" (*The Analyst*, no. 2 [September 1953]: 9).

113 Polhonac] The early manuscripts (AA.10–17, A.72–74, B.100, C.112–16) indicate that "Polhonac" is an error for Raimon of Castel-Roussillon, Cabestan's murderer and Soremonda's husband.

114 plattcr,] Pound omitted this punctuation mark in typing ScXVI, probably by accident. All previous texts read "platter,". Gyges] Possibly an error for Astyages in Herodotus's *Histories*, book 1.

List of Emendations in the Copy-text

17 Itys] *FF50;* Ityn
19 All] *editorial;* "All

32 'Tis. 'Tis. Ytis!] *ScXXX;* Ityn, Ityn!

41 slivver] *ScXXX;* sliver

69 plovil,] *editorial;* plovil

74 *lineation, as in ScXXX;* the pines

at Takasago

83 set] *ScXXX;* Set

86 Ὑμὴν,] *FF50, corrections L61 and editorial;* Hymenæus Io!

87 Ὑμέναι' ὦ, Aurunculeia! Ὑμὴν, Ὑμέναι' ὦ,] *FF50, corrections L61 and editorial;* Hymen, Io Hymenæe! Aurunculeia!

88 One] *L61;* A

89 So-Gioku, saying:] *FF50;* And So-Gioku, saying:

93 And Ran-ti opened] *L61;* And Ran-ti, opening

107 barge] *FF33;* bark

111 Père Henri Jacques would speak with the sennin, on Rokku,] *ScXXX;* Père Henri Jacques,

112 Mount] *ScXXX;* On Mount

114 platter,] *editorial;* platter

115 Tereus] *L61;* Terreus

121 Regina!"—] *ScXXX;* Regina!"

122 crowd.] *ScXXX;* crowd,

123 thin] *ScXXX;* this

125 her.] *ScXXX;* her,

Index